THE BLAKE ESCAPE

HOW WE FREED GEORGE BLAKE– AND WHY

●

**MICHAEL RANDLE
& PAT POTTLE**

3/378183

HARRAP
London

To Anne and Sue

First published in Great Britain 1989
by HARRAP BOOKS Ltd
19–23 Ludgate Hill London EC4M 7PD

© Michael Randle and Pat Pottle 1989

ISBN 0 245–54781–9

Typeset by
Poole Typesetting (Wessex) Ltd

Printed in Great Britain by
Mackays of Chatham Limited

Contents

Acknowledgements

Our warm thanks to the staff at Harrap for their assistance, and to the directors for their courage in publishing this book. Special thanks are due to Susanne McDadd, whose advice and suggestions were invaluable.

We acknowledge also with thanks permission from the following to reproduce published material: Macmillan & Co and Stein and Day, New York, for the extracts from *Life* by Zeno; Macmillan Inc., New York, for the extracts from *The Springing of George Blake* by Seán Bourke; to Don Taylor and Methuen for extracts from *Sophocles: The Theban Plays; The Times* for extracts from reports and editorials. We apologize to anyone else whose copyright has inadvertently been infringed.

We want to also thank Anne and all those who gave unselfish help in 1966, sometimes at considerable personal risk, and to those after we were publicly named in 1987 who wrote to us expressing sympathy and support, or offering us asylum.

The book relies in part on an account written by us in 1967 (but destroyed in 1987), and on our shared recollections. The dialogue is of necessity reconstructed, but is as close in spirit and detail to our recollection of what occurred as we could make it. Our presentation of the people involved is also bound to reflect our personal outlook and judgement; we apologize to those involved for any shortcomings or injustices. A few minor details have been altered to protect third parties, but that aside, the account is as full and honest as we could make it.

March 1989

Michael Randle
Pat Pottle

CHAPTER ONE

The Road to
Wormwood Scrubs

Narrated by Michael Randle

'Even at this late hour', the judge, Mr Justice Havers, said, 'it would affect my mind in considering what is the appropriate sentence if these accused were to tell me that they now realized that, however honest and sincere their convictions are, they were completely misguided and assure me they will give up this campaign of civil disobedience and will not commit any more criminal offences.'[1]

It was 20 February 1962. Six members of the Committee of 100 – the radical anti-nuclear organization founded and led by Bertrand Russell – stood in the dock at the Central Criminal Court, the Old Bailey. They had been convicted on two counts of conspiracy under Section One of the Official Secrets Act for their part in planning an occupation and sit-down the previous December at the United States Air Force base at Wethersfield, in Essex. Pat Pottle and myself were among them. The other defendants were Terry Chandler, Ian Dixon, Trevor Hatton and Helen Allegranza.

Each of us was asked in turn if we would give the undertaking that the judge required. Each in turn refused. Mr Havers then made a final speech before passing sentence:

> You stand in the dock convicted of serious criminal offences against the safety of this country. It was not for want of trying on your part that your plan did not succeed. It did not succeed because the majority of people of this country, many of whom you tried to incite, have far too much common sense and are law-abiding people and also because the authorities massed a sufficient number of police officers and other people to prevent your entering upon the aerodrome . . . .
>
> I gave each and every one of you a chance to tell me whether, even at this late hour, you now appreciated that your actions were misguided and that you were prepared to abandon this plan of civil disobedience and were prepared to give me an assurance that you would not do any further criminal acts in pursuance of this campaign; but none of you

have been willing to tell me that or to give me that assurance. I can only therefore deal with you on that footing, and I have to pass a sentence which is adequate to the offences you have committed and which will deter others from committing similar offences.[2]

I was the first to be sentenced, followed by Trevor and Ian. We were given eighteen months imprisonment on each count, to run concurrently. Helen was next, and received a twelve-month sentence.

'With respect, my Lord,' she interrupted him, 'I wish to be considered equally guilty with my friends.'

'You will do as you are told,' the judge replied.

That's how Pat and I remember the incident. The transcript, which often rounds off the rough edges, reports him as giving a more measured response – 'I fully appreciate what you say, but your sentence will be one of twelve months.'[3]

Finally Terry Chandler and Pat were each sent down for eighteen months.

As our names were called the warders standing immediately behind seized us firmly by the arms to prevent any last-minute fracas or attempt to escape. Then, when all the sentences had been passed, we were led – still held firmly by the arms – from the dock to the maze of corridors lined with prison cells underneath the Central Criminal Court.

Despite the guilty verdict and the long sentence, our mood was buoyant. We had not been overawed by the solemnity of the court or intimidated by the threat of a long prison sentence into backing down. And we had dramatically made our central point – that nuclear weapons were synonymous with preparing for genocide. Air Commodore Magill, director of operations at the Air Ministry, had gone into the witness box and acknowledged that 'if the circumstances demanded it' he would press the button that would kill millions of people. His statement was widely reported; some people were later to argue that it was perhaps the most important statement ever to have been made in an English court of law. We were confident too that the trial would mark an upturn in the fortunes of the Committee and of the nuclear disarmament movement in general.

But now came the hard part. No sooner had we reached the bottom of the steps leading from the dock than the wardress with Helen told her she would have to leave us to be taken to Holloway gaol.

'Good-bye, lads,' Helen said, as she was led away. 'See you at the Appeal Court. Keep your spirits up.'

She was putting a brave face on it, but for her it was a particularly lonely moment. Her sentence might be shorter than ours, but she faced by far the toughest ordeal, separated from her friends in Holloway.

Then came another – unexpected – blow.

'Chandler, Dixon, and Randle!' one of the warders called out, 'Right, you three, come with me; you're for Wandsworth.'

'Sod it!' Pat said as we parted, 'I thought at least we'd all be together.'

I would miss him – and Trevor too. Trevor, the Committee of 100 Treasurer, cut a oddly respectable figure in the suit and collar and tie which he always wore, but he had a mischievous sense of humour which revealed another side of his character. Ten days before he had been the best man at my wedding to Anne.

Terry, Ian and I were banged up in a cell together to await the transport to Wandsworth. I had known Ian since the early 1950s, when we were both active in the pacifist and non-violent action groups of that period, and later in the Direct Action Committee against nuclear war. Terry I had got to know more recently. At twenty-one he was the youngest of the group, but already a prison veteran. He had done time before in the young offenders wing at Wormwood Scrubs and in Wandsworth. The latter, he assured us, was a far better nick to be in. Nobody bothered you there.

The mood became sombre. I thought of Anne, whom I had caught a glimpse of in tears as we were led away from the dock. We had spent one precious weekend together since our wedding, plus a few evenings when the trial was going on and we prisoners were still on bail. Now we had only one half-hour visit a month to look forward to.

I don't remember how long we remained locked up but it was dark when the cell was reopened and we were led out to an awaiting coach. Terry and I were handcuffed together; Ian to another prisoner. The handcuffs were hard and cold against the bare flesh of my wrists, and were locked so tightly that they pinched my skin. But as the coach pulled out of the yard by the side of the Central Criminal Court we were heartened to see a knot of demonstrators with placards, who had waited patiently to wave us support.

As it transpired, Terry, Ian and I spent only one night in

Wandsworth. Next day the authorities decided that we should be 're-starred' – i.e., treated as though we were first offenders; presumably they decided that as all our previous offences had been in connection with non-violent demonstrations, we were not 'old lags' in the usual sense of the term. Terry, I think, was a little disappointed. But had it not been for that decision I would probably never have met George Blake or the man who was chiefly responsible for organizing his escape, Seán Bourke.

The four or five years preceding our trial at the Old Bailey in February 1962 had been a stirring period. From small beginnings, a movement of mass protest and civil disobedience had emerged to challenge the Government's nuclear and foreign policy. The gravity of the charges against us, and the length of the sentences handed down, were a measure of the seriousness with which the authorities viewed the new movement.

1956 had been the watershed. Eden's imperialist adventure at Suez broke the deadening post-war consensus on British foreign and military policy. You could almost say that the 1960s began with the demonstration against Suez in Trafalgar Square addressed by Aneurin Bevan, and the near-riot which followed it.

The Soviet invasion of Hungary was no less crucial. It disillusioned many on the Left and precipitated an exodus of intellectual and organizational talent from the Communist Party that went over to the nascent radical movement. In 1957 the New Left movement emerging in Britain centred on the universities and on two publications: *The New Reasoner*, edited by two former members of the Communist Party, Edward Thompson and John Saville, and the *Universities and Left Review* – these were to merge in 1960 to become the *New Left Review*.

The second half of the 1950s saw a flowering of critical and creative talent in Britain, with a younger generation of writers, producers, actors, directors, and musicians challenging the ideas and conventions that had dominated the British cultural scene in the post-war era. Prominent among these were John Osborne, Arnold Wesker, Shelagh Delaney, Robert Bolt, Bernard Kops, and John Arden in the new wave of younger playwrights; John Braine, the novelist; William Gaskell, director of the Royal Court Theatre which first staged the works of many of these playwrights; Lindsay Anderson, the theatre and film director; Christopher Logue, poet and playwright; George Melly, art critic and jazz musician; John

Berger, critic and novelist; Vanessa Redgrave, the actress; and others. All those – and many more besides – were to become involved in the anti-nuclear campaigns of the late 1950s and early 1960s.

It was in this changing situation that a small group of non-violent activists who had worked since the early 1950s found a new receptivity to their ideas and style of action. In the summer of 1957 a Quaker, Harold Steele, attempted to sail to Britain's H-Bomb testing site at Christmas Island in the Pacific. He failed to get farther than Japan, but after his return in November 1957 supporters and other volunteers met and formed the Direct Action Committee against Nuclear War. Its first organizing secretary was that redoubtable peace campaigner Pat Arrowsmith. It was this body which adopted the now famous nuclear disarmament symbol and organized the first Aldermaston March over the Easter weekend of 1958.

The Campaign for Nuclear Disarmament had meanwhile been launched at a large meeting in Central Hall, Westminster, in February 1958. Conceived initially as a pressure group that would exert influence within government and decision-making circles, it quickly got caught up in the enthusiasm generated by the Aldermaston march, and within a few months of its launching had become a mass movement of popular protest.

The Direct Action Committee remained a relatively small pioneering group. Its best-known demonstrations are probably the first Aldermaston march – now almost universally, though mistakenly, attributed to CND – and two rocket-base demonstrations near Swaffham in Norfolk in December 1958. Its final – and in some ways most successful – project after Aldermaston was a six-week march (from Easter to Whitsun 1961) – from London to the US Polaris base at Holy Loch in Scotland. There a spectacular seaborne 'direct action' took place, involving attempts to board the Polaris-carrying submarines based in the loch.

My own involvement in the peace movement was with this direct-action wing. I had been active in groups in the early 1950s after I had registered as a conscientious objector to military service in 1951, and was on the organizing committee of the first Aldermaston march. I was first arrested at one of the Swaffham demonstrations in December 1958, and in October of the following year travelled to Ghana to take part in the Sahara Protest Expedition (a protest against the French atomic testing site at Reggan in the Algerian Sahara).

It was while I was still living in Ghana that moves were made to set up a new committee for direct action on a mass scale – the Committee of 100. Launched in October 1960 with a call to resistance entitled *Act or Perish* by Bertrand Russell and the Rev. Michael Scott, it recruited many of the younger people from the world of arts and letters mentioned earlier, as well as an older generation such as the poet and critic Sir Herbert Read, the Scottish poet Hugh MacDiarmid, and the 82-year-old artist Augustus John.

The Committee of 100 was the brainchild of a radical American student, Ralph Schoenman, who argued that a new approach was needed to involve large numbers in non-violent civil disobedience. He proposed firstly that the committee should be large enough, and should include a sufficient number of very well-known people, in order to make it difficult for the authorities to arrest them all – as they had the members of the Direct Action Committee resident in Britain in December 1959. Secondly, he proposed a system of pledges prior to a demonstration. Unless a minimum number of people had pledged themselves in advance to participate, the demonstration would be cancelled. Thus participants could be reasonably confident that they were part of a *large* action, not of a small group risking heavy sentences. I returned from Ghana in October 1960 just prior to the Committee's inaugural meeting, and was elected its first secretary.

1961, the first full year of the Committee's existence, was also the high point of its activities. Five thousand people participated in its first action on 18 February, a sit-down outside the Ministry of Defence timed to coincide with, or shortly precede, the arrival of the US submarine *Proteus* (armed with Polaris missiles) at Holy Loch in Scotland. Despite police warnings that anyone taking part in the demonstration would be risking arrest, no action was taken. Bertrand Russell (aged eighty-nine) and the Rev. Michael Scott posted up a declaration on the main door of the Ministry warning that people were ready to rise up against a government engaged in preparations for nuclear genocide, and after three hours Russell led a triumphal procession back up Whitehall. This was followed by other successful actions which ensured massive media coverage for the movement.

During this period there was sharp deterioration in East–West relations, with Laos and Berlin providing the flash-points in a mounting crisis. In South–East Asia a build-up of US forces looked as though it might be the prelude to massive intervention. In West Berlin in July President Kennedy, in his famous *'Ich bin ein Berliner'* address, pledged that America would go to war if necessary to uphold the freedom of the city. Amid mounting rumours that the East German authorities were planning to seal off East Berlin, thousands fled to the Western sector. In July alone an estimated 30,000 people fled from East to West. On 13 August a barbed-wire barrier was erected, to be replaced five days later by the permanent Berlin Wall itself.

In late August the Soviet Union resumed nuclear-weapons testing. The Committee of 100 condemned this move and organized a lightning sit-down demonstration in front of the Soviet Embassy at which 116 people were arrested, myself among them. On 17 October 1961 four members of a five-person delegation, including Pat Pottle, staged a sit-in inside the Soviet Embassy over its nuclear-testing activities. Four days later over five hundred people were arrested at a sit-down outside the Embassy organized by the Committee. Pat Pottle was again one of the participants. Another was my future wife Anne.

Public concern in the summer of 1961 at the mounting East–West tension certainly swelled the numbers of the people taking part in the weekend of major demonstrations planned by the Committee for 16–17 September. The first part of the action, on 16 September, was to be at the Holy Loch base; the second part was to be in London the following day. There the demonstration was to follow the pattern set by a 29 April action – a traditional public meeting in Trafalgar Square, followed by a march down Whitehall and a 'Public Assembly' in Parliament Square.

Heavy-handed intervention by the authorities increased still further the numbers prepared to take part. On 12 September Russell and thirty-seven other members of the Committee answered summonses to appear at Bow Street Magistrates court. Thirty-two of them, including Russell and his wife Edith, were sent to prison – in most cases for one month. Those imprisoned included well-known literary figures. Then, a few days before the demonstration was due to take place, the authorities banned the meeting in Trafalgar Square, using the Public Order Act which had been introduced in the 1930s to combat fascism.

But the movement had been well prepared and as soon as the arrests of Committee members took place a shadow committee took over. As I was among those in prison, a shadow organizing secretary was also appointed – this new secretary was Pat Pottle.

After the arrests and the banning of the Trafalgar Square rally, messages of support began to come in from all over the world, including one from Albert Schweitzer at his mission in Central Africa. Many people in Britain who had reservations about the Committee's strategies were shocked by the ban and resolved to defy it. In the event some 12,000 people took part in one of the most highly publicized demonstrations in the history of the anti-nuclear campaign. 1,314 people were arrested. ITV cancelled all its regular afternoon programmes to provide live coverage of the demonstration. The previous day, despite appalling weather, five hundred people had taken part in the Holy Loch sit-down which resulted in 350 arrests.

After this success the Committee decided to shift the emphasis of its demonstrations away from city centres to the bases where nuclear weapons were located. It set itself the goal of mobilizing 50,000 people for a day of simultaneous demonstrations in early December, some in city centres, others at bases. Ideally one or more bases would be immobilized, if only temporarily.

The date was eventually fixed for Sunday 9 December, and Wethersfield USAF base was one of the venues. The authorities responded with vigour. On 27 November Chief Inspector Stratton of Scotland Yard called at the Committee office in Goodwin Street in north London and questioned me about the general leaflet, and legal briefing document, we had prepared for Wethersfield. Nine days later the lodgings of Terry Chandler, Trevor Hatton, Pat Pottle and myself were simultaneously raided by Special Branch officers with search warrants issued under the Official Secrets Act.

In the Commons, the Minister of State at the Home Office, Mr Renton, warned on 7 December that Committee of 100 demonstrators at the USAF bases could face charges under the Official Secrets Act. On the same day troops erected miles of barbed-wire entanglements round the perimeter of the Wethersfield base. All police leave in the area for the day of the demonstration was cancelled, and several thousand troops were brought in to protect the base.

On 8 December Helen Allegranza, Terry Chandler, Ian Dixon, Trevor Hatton and I were arrested and charged with conspiracy under the Act. A warrant had also been issued for the arrest of Pat Pottle, but he managed to evade the police and went on the run for almost two months before deciding finally to come out of hiding so that we could all be together for the Old Bailey trial.

The turnout at the day of demonstrations, however, was disappointing. In all 7,500 people took part in the various actions, and there were 848 arrests. Compared with the DAC days, these were respectable figures. But they fell far short of the 50,000 people that the Committee had aimed for.

The turnout at Wethersfield was particularly poor. Some 600 people took part, as against the minimum of 1,500 that the Committee had reckoned were needed for an effective blockade of the base. Circling above the demonstrators in an RAF helicopter was the Secretary of State for Air – later Minister of Aviation – Mr Julian Amery. He declared in a much-publicized statement that the demonstration had been a flop.

Russell at once issued a rejoinder – which, however, received far less coverage. It pointed out that the 'victory' on which the political Establishment was congratulating itself amounted to no more than a public demonstration of the fact that the police, the RAF and the Army were *physically* stronger than several thousand unarmed demonstrators. However, the fact that thousands had shown themselves willing to risk prison, loss of livelihood, and possible physical injury provided grounds for hope of an ultimate victory for reason and humanity.

Despite these brave words, the sense of anticlimax within the Committee was strong. Our mood was subdued as we travelled back by train to London from Wethersfield. I remember a friend remarking that one consequence of the low turnout was that the authorities would probably not now proceed with the charges under the Official Secrets Act against myself and the other organizers. On this point, however, he was wrong.

When the Working Group of the Committee next met a resolution to stage an immediate return to Wethersfield was defeated. We decided that our best hope at this point was to turn the forthcoming trial into an indictment of government policy.

On 10 January 1962 all the defendants charged under the Official Secrets Act except Pat were remanded on bail at a hearing at Marlborough Street Magistrates Court. Pat made a highly publicized reappearance on 6 February on his way to attend a press conference to say why he had taken the decision to stand trial. The trial itself began at the Old Bailey on Monday 12 February.

We had been charged on two counts of conspiracy under Section 1 of the Official Secrets Act 1911. The first count was that we had conspired together to enter a prohibited place, Wethersfield Air Base, for a purpose prejudicial to the safety and interest of the State. The second count was that we had conspired to incite others to enter the base for such a purpose.

It was the clause 'for a purpose prejudicial to the safety and interest of the State' on which we intended to base our defence. We did not deny planning to enter the base or encouraging others to do so. Indeed, we had said quite openly that this was our intention, and had even sent copies of our mailings to the police. But we challenged the contention that preventing planes being loaded with nuclear weapons was prejudicial to the safety and interest of the State, taking this term to mean the public interest – the interest of the community as a whole.

There was, however, another more general issue at the heart of the trial. Regardless of whether or not we were technically guilty of the particular charge under the Official Secrets Act, was it justifiable in some circumstances (as the DAC and Committee of 100 contended) to refuse to co-operate with the law, even to defy it and to use non-violent direct action to obstruct policies sanctioned by a government with a reasonable claim to legitimacy? This was not, of course, a legal issue, but a moral and political one.

The Attorney General himself, Sir Reginald Manningham-Buller – later Lord Dilhorne – led for the prosecution, an indication of the importance the authorities attached to the case. He was seconded by Mr Mervyn Griffith Jones (best remembered for his question to the jury in the *Lady Chatterley's Lover* prosecution – 'Frankly, is this a book you'd want your wife and servants to read?')

Five of the six of us were defended by an eminent QC, Jeremy Hutchinson; Pat Pottle defended himself.

Nine months previously Manningham-Buller and Jeremy Hutchinson had led respectively for the prosecution and defence in another much-publicized prosecution under the Official Secrets Act at the Old Bailey – the prosecution of George Blake. No one on the Committee would, I imagine, have been sympathetic to espionage. But many of us were shocked by the savage 42-year sentence imposed by the court, and strongly agreed with the sentiment expressed by Hutchinson at Blake's appeal: 'This sentence is so inhuman that it is alien to all the principles on which a civilized country would treat its subjects.' It was Hutchinson's conduct of the Blake case, and especially these words of his, that influenced our decision to choose him as our counsel when we in turn were facing charges under the Official Secrets Act.

The trial started more than an hour later than scheduled because the murder case that preceded it overran its allotted time. It opened with the Attorney General rising to declare that there had been a very serious development. A leaflet entitled 'Regina versus The Committee of 100' was being distributed in the vicinity of the court.

I still have a copy of the leaflet. The key paragraphs in it run as follows:

> Every member of the Committee of 100 is responsible for the Committee's actions. But the Government is not prepared to apply the law impartially and has preferred to prosecute six individuals. We on the Committee are all responsible for the Wethersfield demonstration. We do not apologize for the demonstration which challenged the right of the Government to prepare to kill millions of people.
>
> We are proud of it and are determined that this kind of resistance shall continue on a still greater scale. It is the Government which is on trial charged with preparing to commit mass murder.

The names of all Committee members are then listed, starting with that of Earl Russell, OM, FRS. The leaflet also contains a map of the Wethersfield base, and on the back page advertises a public meeting in Trafalgar Square on 25 February entitled 'We Accuse' at which Russell would be the main speaker.

The judge agreed that this was prima facie evidence of a very serious criminal contempt. All the members of the jury would be asked if they had seen the leaflet before being sworn in. In the event, none had, and the case was able to start. But the judge made the granting of bail for the duration of the trial conditional upon an undertaking by us that we would not participate in or encourage any demonstrations or distribution of literature in the precincts of the court. With some misgivings we agreed to this.

The crucial legal issue in the first few days of the trial was whether or not we would be allowed to argue that our purpose in trying to immobilize the base was not prejudicial to the safety and interest of the State. On the second day the jury were allowed to absent themselves when Hutchinson and Manningham-Buller put their submissions on this matter. After a full day of debate the trial judge, Mr Justice Havers, ruled in the prosecution's favour. The defence would *not* be allowed to call evidence that it would be beneficial to the country to give up nuclear armament, or to cross-examine the witnesses on this point. The honest convictions of the defendants that it would be beneficial to the country to give up nuclear weapons were likewise ruled inadmissible.

Despite this ruling, the wider issues were aired – even if the jury were under instruction to ignore them. First, the prosecution read extracts from Committee publications which put the case for civil disobedience. Thus Manningham-Buller quoted from a policy memorandum:

> Civil disobedience is an unusual and extreme measure to take, especially in a more or less democratic society. It is made necessary because the situation we face is perilous in the extreme and because fundamental human rights are being violated. Even in a democracy civil disobedience may be called for in a situation of great urgency when the constitutional machinery is too cumbersome or too slow to meet the crisis or to safeguard human rights.[4]

Second, the Attorney General made a serious blunder by insisting when he was cross-examining me that I should answer a question about my personal beliefs – namely, whether or not I was a pacifist. Once he had done so, Hutchinson in his re-examination could not be prevented from questioning me about the basis of my belief that nuclear weapons were genocidal.

Hutchinson: As regards your personal views about this question which the jury have got to decide, about the purpose of going on to this aerodrome, what were your personal views as to why you went on to the aerodrome?

Randle: I went on to Wethersfield, and helped organize it to prevent the murder of millions of people.

Hutchinson: On what was that opinion based?

Randle: Based on the fact that atomic weapons, megaton bombs, can kill millions of people. They can knock out a whole city.

Hutchinson: Was it on the official figures in relation to the effect of that [Hiroshima] bomb that you based, among other considerations, your personal views?

Randle: It was indeed, yes.[5]

Third, and most importantly, Pat brilliantly exploited the leeway the judge felt obliged to grant him as an amateur among professionals to put forward arguments and to question witnesses in a way that was not open to Hutchinson. Thus the high point of the trial was the following exchange between Pat and the chief prosecution witness, Air Commodore Magill, director of operations at the Air Ministry:

Pottle: Air Commodore, is there any official order you cannot accept?

Mr Justice Havers: Is there what?

Pottle: Is there any official order from the government where the Air Commodore would say to himself: 'I accept orders, I am a servant of the government, but on this particular occasion I cannot accept this order?

Havers: He is an officer in the Forces of Her Majesty.

Pottle: So actually there is no order you would not accept?

Air Commodore Magill: It is my duty to carry out any order given to me.

Pottle: Would you press the button that you know is going to annihilate millions of people?

(I held my breath at that point, willing the judge not to intervene. I think most of the people in the public gallery of the court were holding their breath too.)

Magill: If the circumstances so demanded it, I would.[6]

After that exchange, Mr Justice Havers was quicker off the mark. Still, even the disallowed questions made their point:

Pottle: Air Commodore, do you agree with this statement: 'We must not forget that by creating atomic bases in East Anglia we have made ourselves the target and perhaps the bullseye of a Soviet attack'?

Havers: Don't answer that. I rule it out.

Pottle: That was a statement of Sir Winston Churchill.

Havers: You must not tell us whose statement it was.

And soon afterwards:

Pottle: Do you agree with the statement made by Mr Duncan Sandys in 1957, when he was Minister of Defence, when he said bases cannot defend people?

Havers: You cannot ask that.

Pottle: You have said, Air Commodore, you would accept any order from the State; any order that was given to you it would be your duty to carry this out. Adolf Eichmann's defence . . .

Havers: It is no good reverting to the Eichmann trial. You cannot mention him in this case.

Pottle: Would you consider a Soviet attack on Britain in the interests of the Soviet state?

Havers: Don't answer that. You know, Pottle, I have tried to give you a broad indication of the things you ought not to do. You do not seem to me to be paying the slightest attention to what I have said. You are going on asking these questions as if I had not said it.

Pat nevertheless persisted:

Pottle: In 1945, Air Commodore, men were put on trial at Nuremberg . . .

Havers: Where are you going to now? You are at Nuremberg now, are you?

Pottle: Yes.

Havers: You will have to leave Nuremberg.

Finally an exasperated Manningham-Buller intervened:

Attorney General: This is really deliberate disobedience of your Lordship's ruling.

Havers: I have given every latitude. He is quite right in saying he is there on a serious charge. It has never been concealed and it has always been present in my mind. [To Pat] I have given you every latitude, but there is a limit to what I shall allow you to do. I shall ask you to sit down in a moment.[7]

That effectively brought Pat's cross-questioning of the Air Commodore to an end. He had some success, none the less, in getting some further questions past the judge when examining other defence witnesses – notably the former Catholic Archbishop of Bombay, Archbishop Roberts, whom he questioned on the issue of whether civil disobedience could be morally justified against policies approved by the majority:

Pottle: This is exhibit 45, my Lord. [A copy of the Committee of 100 founding document, *Act or Perish*.] I wonder if the Archbishop could be given a copy of this?

Havers: Yes.

Pottle: If we could look under 'Constitutional Action Not Enough', it reads – Christian martyrs broke the law and there can be no doubt that majority opinion at that time condemned them for doing so.' Would you agree with this, Archbishop Roberts?

Archbishop Roberts: Entirely.

Pottle: Archbishop Roberts, in your opinion were they justified in their actions?

Roberts: Not merely justified but bound.

Pottle: They were bound to do this?

Roberts: Yes. If, for example, they were asked to worship a man, an Emperor, not a Christ whom they believed to be God, they were not merely allowed but strictly bound.

Pottle: So actually they committed civil disobedience?

Roberts: Strictly, yes.

Pottle: Thank you. 'We, in our day, are asked to acquiesce passively if not actively in actions leading to tyrannical brutalities compared with which all former horrors sink into insignificance.' Do you agree with that?

Roberts: Entirely, yes.

Pottle: Do you feel that the world today is in this position?

Roberts: I do.

Pottle: Do you feel, Archbishop Roberts, that there is justification for some more Christian martyrs?

Attorney General: My Lord . . .

Havers: No, I can't. I have given you very wide latitude and allowed you to put in a good deal more than you ought to have done already. Now you must stop. On that line you must stop. The only reason I have done it is because you have not got the advantage of being represented by counsel and I cannot allow you to do much more than you would be able to do if you had counsel.[8]

Pat also called Bertrand Russell and Vanessa Redgrave to the witness box, both of whom testified that they were equally responsible with those on trial for the Wethersfield demonstration.

Pottle: Did you, Miss Redgrave, conspire with others to incite people to go on to the Wethersfield base?

Miss Redgrave: Yes, I did.

Havers: Before you answer that, it is my duty to warn you that you are not bound to answer any questions which you think may tend to incriminate you.

Pat then repeated the question and Vanessa gave the same reply.

Pottle: And was the purpose in your view in the interests of the State?

Attorney General: We cannot have that.

Havers: No, we cannot have that.

Pottle: Was it your intention, Miss Redgrave, to incite these people to go there to block and immobilize Wethersfield base?

Miss Redgrave: Yes.

Pottle: And so you actually went there to try and stop planes from taking off, planes which you believed had nuclear weapons in them, and which you believed would lead to the deaths of millions of people?

Havers: She cannot answer that. You must not throw in a little tag at the end like that. Put it separately or else you will sit down.[9]

Among other witnesses were the physicist and double Nobel prizewinner Dr Linus Pauling, and the inventor of radar, Sir Robert Watson-Watt. All the witnesses, however, were severely restricted in the questions they could answer because of the ruling of the judge.

By Monday 19 February all the evidence had been heard and the summing-up speeches began. Pat spoke for twenty-five minutes in a powerful restatement of the Committee's case for civil disobedience in general and for opposing nuclear weapons in particular.

The vast majority of the social advantages obtained over the past century, he argued, had been brought about through civil disobedience, including the right of women to vote, and of men to join a trade union. Could any of us condemn *that* civil disobedience, or the civil disobedience that was currently taking place by Negroes in the United States?

The Committee, he continued, had organized demonstrations against nuclear weapons and nuclear war. The real object was to try to make the ordinary man and woman in this country aware of the danger of war. But, he said:

I could not call witness as to fact; I could not call witness as to opinion; I could not call witness as to views; I could not call witness as to the justification for committing civil disobedience; and I could not call witness as to the moral implications of possessing nuclear weapons.

You may ask: 'Well, what defence was left to him as to the purpose of his actions?' If you feel that we were not allowed to bring in evidence as to our purpose, then there is only one verdict you can possibly bring in, and that is 'Not Guilty'.[10]

The Attorney General summed up as follows:

> They seek, do they not, to put themselves above the law, and I ask you to consider for one moment what would happen if other bodies or persons, perhaps with very different views, adopted the same course. If that happened, if many other bodies did this, if they succeeded in their efforts, it would be an end to the rule of law. It would lead to the end of democracy, to anarchy, and possibly to dictatorship.[11]

The Attorney General was of course raising a crucial issue. We would have welcomed the opportunity for a serious discussion during the trial of the implications of civil disobedience in a democracy. But that was precisely one of the topics that the judge, urged on by the Attorney General, had systematically excluded.

Jeremy Hutchinson in his closing address was quick to seize upon this contradiction in the Attorney General's position:

> Why ask the question about civil disobedience? What has it got to do with the case if the only question for you to decide here is did they stop the planes, or mean to, and was it prejudicial . . .
>
> What has civil disobedience got to do with it? It has a vast amount to do with it, of course, if their intentions and motives and aims are relevant; of course it has, because the Attorney General said to you over and over again that they set out to break the law, and if that is said, then surely to goodness, they are permitted to tell you why. How on earth in all common sense – and for goodness sake let us apply some to this case – can you consider the purpose of anybody without looking at the views on which the purpose is founded? . . . In my submission, it is entering the clouds of cuckoo land, you know, to try and decide this case on the basis that these beliefs, intentions or views or aims are utterly irrelevant in that you are not to consider them in any shape or form.[12]

The judge in his summing up all but directed the jury to convict us. Despite this, and despite the fact that the whole basis of our defence had been ruled out of order, it took the jury just over four hours –

from 12.39 till 4.45 – to reach a verdict. They found us guilty, but added a plea for leniency.

In the Queen's birthday honours list the following June, Air Commodore Magill was awarded an OBE. On the very day he received his award, Eichmann, who also pleaded that he was only obeying orders, was executed in Ramleh Prison, Israel, and his ashes scattered in international waters over the Mediterranean.

CHAPTER TWO

Greetings from Louise

Narrated by Pat Pottle

After the judge passed sentence I turned to look up at the public gallery. My father gave a clenched-fist salute. My mother shouted out:

'But he's only twenty-three!'

As a member of a family with a long history of involvement in radical politics, I received the support of my parents, as indeed of my whole family. Their strength and warmth had been a great encouragement to me throughout the trial – despite the fact that my father had some reservations about the Committee of 100, which he considered too anti-Soviet.

The screws took us down to the cells beneath the court. I had been suffering from a cold for a few days and coughed when we reached the bottom of the staircase. A screw asked me in a sympathetic voice:

'Oh, dear, have you got a cold?'

'Yes,' I said, 'I've had it a few days.'

'Well you've got eighteen fucking months to get over it!' he replied, grabbing my arm and putting handcuffs on me.

This was my first encounter with Prison Officer Hawkins. He had slashed the peak of his cap so that it came down over his forehead, and it gave him a robot-like and sinister appearance. Not too long before I had been doing my National Service in the RAF and had met a lot of people like him. They were usually corporals, and with their slashed peaks, razor-sharp creases to their uniforms, they strutted around like peacocks, bullying new recruits. He was clearly someone to be avoided.

However, it was a relief to all of us to know what our fate was to be. We had thought we would get three years, and were in good spirits. But our morale would be quickly put to the test. I had always taken it for granted we would be convicted and imprisoned, but had never really considered the effects that separation from family and friends, and now from some of my fellow defendants, would have. We were all shocked when Helen was separated from us straight away to be taken to Holloway. We hugged and kissed her, and our hearts went out to her as she was led away on her own.

Michael, Terry and Ian had all been in prison before, so their destination was to be Wandsworth. As Trevor and I were 'first offenders', we were sent off to Wormwood Scrubs. We were all saddened at being split up – there was safety in numbers, especially for Trevor and me who were entering the unknown.

Two other prisoners accompanied us to the Scrubs; they were ex-policemen of the Flying Squad, sentenced for robbery. After a medical examination and a hot bath, we were taken to the cell block which, apart from the odd screw, seemed completely deserted. We were each given a blanket, potty, razor with one blade, and washing utensils. Trevor and I were allocated a cell on the top floor with a prisoner who was in for thieving at Heathrow Airport. It seemed every other prisoner was an ex-Heathrow employee! The whole cell block was like one enormous broilerhouse. Behind each of the hundreds of locked doors were three prisoners.

Lying in bed that first night, I thought that all my fears of what prison would be like underestimated the grim reality of it. No amount of floor scrubbing and polish could get rid of the smell that hundreds of men confined in close proximity produces.

The whole experience so far was reminiscent of my first few days square-bashing in the RAF. There was clearly a deliberate attempt to humiliate prisoners at the outset in the hope that this would crush any rebellious feelings. Being forced to take all one's clothes off and stand around while they were entered on our 'prisoners' possessions' sheet; waiting to have a quick bath, and then queueing up for ill-fitting prison uniforms were all part of this process. It was followed by a medical examination where in full view of other prisoners you bent over and 'spread your cheeks' while the doctor looked up your bum. To this day I can't imagine what he was looking for – but whatever it was he didn't find it on me. Finally there was the potty. The very idea of three grown men in a tiny cell being expected to perform their bodily functions in a potty within one or two feet of the others was a calculated humiliation.

But at least I was sharing a cell with Trevor, and knew we would boost each other's morale. We settled down to study the Home Office Prison Rules printed on a card that hung on the back of the door, where you would expect to find the tariff card in any good hotel. In bold type at the top it began, 'It is an offence against prison discipline to:' – and then listed a series of offences, ending with – 'or in any other way to offend against good order and discipline.' Trevor and I laughed. Such a catch-all rule made all the others superfluous.

We sorted out who would sleep where, and tried to settle down to a night's sleep. I had the lower bunk bed, Trevor the single bed opposite; while the other prisoner sharing the cell with us had the top bunk. We must have all decided individually not to use the potty but hold on until the door was opened again. At six in the morning a key turned in the lock and a voice shouted:

'Slop out!'

After breakfast, we were taken for exercise – this meant walking in a circle round the exercise yard for half an hour. As Trevor and I walked round together we saw the two ex-policemen from the previous day. We greeted one another and carried on. Another prisoner walked past the policemen and spat at them. Then a few more prisoners did the same. In no time at all the two were covered from head to toe in spittle. Hawkins was the screw on duty in the exercise yard that morning. He did nothing to protect the ex-policemen, who by now were beginning to be physically abused as well. It was only when other prisoners started picking up bits of brick from the place where workmen were doing alterations to the laundry block that Hawkins stepped in and took them away. The two policemen were never seen on the exercise yard again. Next morning they were moved to an open prison. We had had our first taste of prisoners' justice.

This was our first morning in prison. It seemed like Hell.

Prisoners on their first day inside are taken before either the Governor or Deputy Governor for a briefing on prison rules and routine. The Governor tells them precisely what offence they have been convicted of, the sentence the court has passed and the earliest date they can expect to be released if they earn maximum remission for good behaviour.

Thus, later that morning we were taken to the Governor's office for our introductory interview. I think it must have been the Deputy Governor on duty – the same Colonel Higham whom Terry, Ian and Michael were to clash with the following day. He told me he ran a tidy ship, and that if I kept my nose clean I would find him a fair man.

'But I'm warning you. If you cause disruption or get into trouble in any way, you'll find out I can be very hard indeed.'

His whole attitude and bearing was hostile and he finished the interview by inquiring sarcastically:

'Why is it that so many of your people have long hair and beards?'

'I really have no idea,' I replied. Then, looking at the prison chaplain who sat next to him, I added:

'Perhaps for some it has a religious significance, sir.'

Each morning all prisoners were assembled in the exercise yards outside the various wings before being marched off to various places of work. We were in C Hall – or C Wing – which was for 'short-term' prisoners – i.e. those serving sentences of four years or less, many of them awaiting transfer to open prisons or to closed local prisons. It also had some long-termers awaiting transfer to D Hall.

The head count would always take much longer for C Hall than for the others because the number of prisoners could change drastically from one day to the next because of the influx of new inmates and the departure of others.

A buzz would go around C Hall exercise yard as the long-term D Hall men were marched past on their way to work. They included murderers and other notorious prisoners.

We were soon to discover that in the eyes of the D Hall inmates we short-term prisoners were only playing at being in prison. When you told them you were doing eighteen months they would say:

'You're only here for Bed and Breakfast, then!'

Or:

'Eighteen months! That's just long enough for a shit and a shave!'

It was when the D Hall prisoners were being marched off to work, after I had been in prison two or three days, that another prisoner nudged me and said:

'That's George Blake.'

I looked over to see a group of about forty prisoners. I was struck immediately by their incredibly pale complexions, tinged, when you looked more closely, with a sickly yellow as though they were suffering from jaundice. It was the well-known 'prison pallor' which inmates acquire after several years inside.

Blake appeared deep in conversation with another inmate, occasionally nodding and smiling. He was quite small in stature, and his hairline was starting to recede. Another prisoner standing near me said:

'Fuck me, he's smiling! With forty-two years to do I'd top myself.'

Prison was run very much along military lines. Many of the staff

22

had been recruited from the armed forces – the screws from the ranks, and the governors and their deputies from the officer classes. They had managed to retain the Forces' knack of creating work where none really existed. The theory seemed to be that as long as people were occupied they couldn't get up to mischief. Senseless and boring work was better than no work at all!

I had been assigned to the mailbag shop, where by coincidence, Blake also worked. It was a large prefabricated building with an iron girder roof covered with corrugated sheeting. The right-hand side of the room was taken up by rows of sewing-machines, and on the left there were rows of chairs. In front of the sewing-machines was a slightly raised platform with a few chairs on it and a high stool from where the screw in charge would sit and survey his flock. He had two others to help him who either sat beside him or paced up and down the workshop, inspecting the quality of the work.

There were perhaps a hundred prisoners in the room. New arrivals in the workshop had to go through a period of sewing mailbags by hand. Those with long sentences, and shorter-term prisoners who were not being transferred from the Scrubs, would eventually progress to the sewing-machines. George, who had been in prison the best part of a year, had already made this progression. Although I saw him daily, we made no contact with each other apart from the occasional nod or greeting. All conversation between prisoners was carried out in a whisper. Anything louder and you were shouted at by the screws.

The material for making mailbags was hard and coarse – sewing it was not easy. You were given a large needle and thick twine which you pressed through the material with a leather thumb pad. Stitches had to be of a uniform size and distance apart. Wages were two shillings (10p) a week, which was just enough to buy a half-ounce of tobacco, a packet of cigarette papers and a box of matches. The needles were always in demand for splitting matches into four so that one's supply could last a week. After you had nicked a needle for yourself you could sell additional ones for a cigarette or two to prisoners working in other workshops.

Wages could be slightly improved if you exceeded your mailbag quota. However, this also gave the screws a bit more power over you. If they did not like you, or if you talked too much, then a mailbag could be rejected on the grounds that there weren't enough stitches to the inch or that they were uneven. Then you had to unpick the whole bag and start again.

23

During a prisoner's first two months he is not allowed 'association' – i.e. you could not go to evening classes or to the weekly film-
show. So it was with relief – enthusiasm even – that, when this
period was up, I signed up for Music Appreciation and Current
Affairs. Michael, Ian, Trevor and Terry had all joined the Music
Appreciation class, and this gave us an opportunity to be together
and to talk amongst ourselves. I was impressed by the range and
quality of the classes on offer, which varied from informal discussion groups to University Diploma courses. The Tutor in charge of
organizing the classes was an energetic Irishman called Pat Sloan.

At our first music appreciation class there were the five of us,
George Blake and a few others. It was run by an extremely pleasant
man who was not strict. It was here that we first had an opportunity
to talk to George.

I shall never forget Trevor's first question to him.

'How did you feel when the judge said "forty-two years" '?

George explained that it did not sink in immediately because
Lord Justice Parker, the judge, had given him fourteen years on
three counts to run consecutively. Only later did the enormity of the
sentence strike him. Trevor, who had a nice sense of humour,
responded:

'Well, never mind. With good behaviour you'll be out in twenty-
eight years!'

We all laughed. But though Blake seemed to take Trevor's remark
in good part, I was highly embarrassed.

We had a number of things in common with Blake, and I for one
felt an immediate rapport with him. Like him, we considered
ourselves political prisoners; we had been charged under the same
Act, defended by the same QC, and prosecuted by the same
Attorney General.

He told us he had followed our case with great interest and
wondered what effect our imprisonment might have on the peace
movement. Once, shortly before his trial, he said, he had been in a
police car and was excited to see hundreds of people taking part in a
demonstration against nuclear weapons. This could possibly have
been the Committee of 100 sit-down demonstration in Whitehall on
29 April 1961.

I had a number of such conversations with him over the next few
weeks. He told me how his wife and family were standing by him,
and what a great comfort this was. However, he found it terribly
inhibiting that during the half-hour visits from his wife once a

month a screw was stationed beside them the whole time, monitoring everything they said to each other. He had complained about it to the prison Governor, who had said he was merely following Home Office instructions.

I asked him how he was coping with such a long sentence. He replied that when the severity of the sentence had dawned on him he had gone through a period of deep depression. But now he had come through that although he was still unable to understand why he had received such a long sentence; he had co-operated with the authorities after his arrest, he said, and stressed that there was absolutely no truth in the press rumours that he had been responsible for sending British agents to their deaths.

The reaction of other prisoners to George was mixed. For some he was simply a traitor – a man who 'should have been topped'. But most prisoners had a great deal of sympathy for him, not because of what he had done but because of the vicious sentence given to him. This was demonstrated by the jubilation in Wormwood Scrubs when he escaped some four years later.

In general the screws were also sympathetic to George's position, and many admired him for the way he was facing up to his sentence. I heard one or two of them on several occasions citing George as an example to new prisoners who were shattered by the sentences they had received.

'You think you've got problems – just think of what's going through that poor sod's mind!'

I remember one screw expressing his sympathy with George in a bizarre way.

'That man', he said, 'should never have been given a sentence like that. What has he got to look forward to? – year after year in prison until he drops dead.'

I said I agreed completely, and he went on:

'I'm against capital punishment but in his case he should have been given the option of being hanged. I'm sure,' he added, 'if you put it to him and gave him a choice, he would prefer to be topped.'

By this time I had settled into the prison routine, and the days were beginning to pass more quickly. Life inside was not nearly as bad as my first impressions had led me to believe. We 'Ban the Bombers' were generally treated well by both prisoners and screws who were all convinced we would be writing about our prison experiences when we were released. Sometimes they would finish off a conversation with – 'That's another bit for your book!'

I had lost Trevor as a cellmate soon after we arrived in the Scrubs, since he was working in the kitchens and shared a cell with Michael. Fortunately, I got on reasonably well with the two other prisoners in my cell – it can make all the difference in prison when you're banged up in such a confined space.

At night, after lights out, I would spend hours thinking about life outside, about family and friends, about the forthcoming appeal. Most often, however, my mind would go back to the trial – to the things I'd said and missed saying, to the mistakes I'd made, to all those clever remarks you think of after the event.

I relived and relished the moment when the Attorney General asked Michael about his pacifist convictions, and thereby gave us an opening to talk about things the judge had earlier ruled out of order. We'd nicknamed the Attorney General Bullying-Manner at the end of the first day, and the name stuck until he became a peer as Lord Dilhorne – when *Private Eye* rather unkindly renamed him Lord Stillborn.

Sometimes when I was starting to feel sorry for myself, and the end of the sentence seemed a long way off, I thought of George Blake and the situation he faced. What would he be thinking about lying alone in his cell? The future – there was no future. His family? – he had destroyed his family. His friends? – he had betrayed them.

George's earliest date of release – i.e. if he earned the maximum remission for good behaviour, and if he survived that long – would be 1989: twenty-seven years away. By then he would be sixty-seven. If he served his full sentence without remission he would not be released until 2003, an old man of eighty-one. In reality it was a death sentence he had been given.

What options did he have? He could 'do his bird', as the prison jargon has it, fixing his mind on his release in 1989. But 1989 was so far off it could drive you mad even thinking about it. He could commit suicide – as every year some prisoners succeeded in doing. That was a solution of a sort, but a pretty drastic one. Or, finally, he could try to escape.

I set to thinking how he might achieve this – and indeed whether there was any way I might help him to do so. It was not that I was in the least sympathetic to the whole business of espionage. But I felt it was the British government who had trained and employed Blake in the first place to work as a spy and to look out for nationals from the Soviet bloc who might be persuaded, enticed or entrapped into passing information to the West or naming agents working for the other side.

George was reported to have betrayed the names of British agents to the Russians, some of whom, according to rumours and press reports, had been executed. I had no means of ascertaining whether this was true, or whether for that matter the British Intelligence Service and the CIA operated according to different rules from the KGB. The latter seemed unlikely; how many of those agents named by Soviet defectors had been quietly eliminated? But even if this were not the case, even if the Soviet side that George had chosen to work for out of political conviction were far more ruthless than the West in dealing with enemy agents who had been exposed, I would still have been totally against the sentence passed on George. As Jeremy Hutchinson had said at his trial, it was a sentence which no civilized state would pass on one of its subjects.

The 42-year sentence (based on three separate counts to run consecutively) also struck me as a manipulation of the Official Secrets Act, where the maximum penalty was set by Parliament at fourteen years. If spies could be charged separately for every individual item of information they passed to a foreign power, there was clearly no limit to the sentences that could be imposed.

The more I thought about it the more my gut response of wanting to help George was strengthened. I do not claim, however, that at this early stage I carefully weighed up all the political pros and cons. My motive was purely humanitarian. Out of common humanity I was willing, if I could, to help him.

My opportunity to broach the matter came when I was sitting next to George during the music appreciation class. We were at the back of the classroom and out of earshot of anyone else. I recall clearly the short conversation we had.

'Have you ever thought of escaping?'

'Many times.'

'Well,' I said in a more serious vein, 'if you can think of any way I can help you get out, let me know.'

It was late May. Early the previous month our appeal had been turned down by Lord Parker at the Court of Criminal Appeal, but with permission granted to appeal to the House of Lords on an issue of public importance. That hearing would begin within a few days. We were due to be sent to an open prison, but would remain in Wormwood Scrubs until after the hearing.

A few days after my conversation with George I was busily sewing mailbags when I saw George get up from his sewing-machine and motion to the screw that he wanted to use the lavatory. The screw nodded to say that it was all right for him to do so, and as George passed me he signalled with his eyes for me to follow him. I waited for about a minute and then went out after him.

The lavatories were at the back end of the workshop behind a partitioned wall. The bottom two to three feet of the partition was made of wood; the rest was glass-panelled so that the screws could see you at all times.

George and I stood peeing into the bowls. We were both aware that the screws could be watching us, so we said nothing. But as he finished and turned to leave he brushed past me and pushed something into my hand. Without looking down, I put it into my pocket.

As I returned to my work one of the prisoners near me said:

'Been talking to the traitor, have you?'

Reactions to George, as I said before, were mixed; many were sympathetic to him because of the length of his sentence, but others felt that no punishment could be too severe. I thought at the time – and this was certainly confirmed the longer I spent in prison – that no one need fear that 'patriotism', in its most narrow and jingoistic sense, is dead. It is alive and well and living in H M Prisons.

I had no idea what this man was in for; murder perhaps, rape, robbery? Whatever it was, he felt the need to have someone on whom he could pass a moral judgment, someone he could look down on.

Back in my cell at lunchtime I felt in my pocket and drew out half a bar of chocolate. Given the wages we were paid, this was like gold dust. Hidden between the wrapper and the chocolate was a note. It read:

> If you feel you can help me on your release, go to the Russian Embassy, introduce yourself and say 'I bring you greetings from Louise'.
>
> Between 10 and 11 o'clock we exercise in the yard outside D Hall. If a rope ladder is thrown over the wall at the spot I have marked X as near to 10.30 as possible, I will be ready.

The rough sketch underneath is shown opposite.

The note then continued:

> If this is acceptable to them, put the following ad in the personal column of *The Sunday Times*:

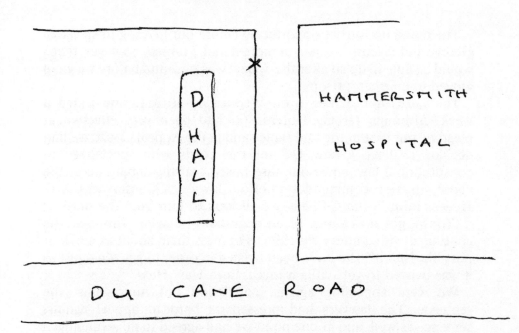

'LOUISE LONGING TO SEE YOU'

If this ad appears, the break will be the following Sunday. If they cannot help, place this ad:

'LOUISE SORRY CAN'T KEEP APPOINTMENT'

Thank you for your help. Memorise this note, then destroy it. – G

After reading the note several times, I burnt it. My immediate thoughts were not on the content of the note, but on the half-bar of chocolate. Did George mean me to eat it? Or was he only using it to conceal the note and expecting it back? After thinking about it for a few minutes, I ate it.

Back at work after lunch, I nodded to George to indicate everything was all right.

George's note had taken me by surprise. It was not the swiftness of his response that threw me but his suggestion of contacting the Russian Embassy and the revelation of his Russian codename. I at once ruled out any idea of going to the Embassy. I had no intention of getting mixed up with anyone's secret services, and certainly not with the KGB. In any case, George's plan of escape was pretty basic, and if I could get some help it could just as easily be carried out without any Soviet involvement. The main problem, it seemed to me, would be what to do with him once he was over the wall, and how to get him out of the country.

There was no further opportunity before our hearing to speak to George and discuss his plan in more detail. I hoped, however, that I would be able to do so after the appeal was over and before we were moved to an open prison.

The Lords appeal began on Wednesday 30 May and lasted a week. Although Jeremy Hutchinson had been very effective in pleading our case at the Old Bailey and at the Appeal Court, we had decided to have a new QC for the Lords who specialized in constitutional law, since our case raised constitutional issues. We chose, on the recommendation of our lawyer, a Conservative MP! He was John Foster QC, and we all took to him from the start.

'You've got no chance of an acquittal,' he said. 'The idea', he continued with a merry chuckle, 'is to mess them about as much as possible, isn't it? The law's been twisted in order to get you – just as it was twisted to get William Joyce, Lord Haw Haw.'

We were appealing against conviction but not against the sentence. The lawyers had pressed us hard to appeal against sentence as well, and at one point we had agreed to do so and even filled in the necessary forms. But none of us was happy about it. We had set out to break the law in particular ways and asked others to join us, and we had always maintained that if you set out to do something, having considered the consequences, you should not complain when things began to get uncomfortable. If others complained on your behalf, that was another matter; but for us the issue was one of principle. (Terry, however, observed: 'Had they decided to top us, we might have had to reconsider our principles!') Thus, before the Appeal Court hearing (on 2 April) we dropped the appeal against sentence.

We were granted permission to attend our appeal, and this gave us a welcome daily change from the drab prison routine. Each morning we were given our civilian clothes to wear before boarding a large coach to take us the few miles across London to Westminster. We were handcuffed in pairs, the odd-one-out being handcuffed to a screw. Prison Officer Hawkins was a member of the escort.

When we arrived at the Lords we were reunited with Helen, who had been brought from Holloway Prison. As always she was now immaculately dressed. And although she was not normally permitted any make-up in Holloway, she had been allowed some lipstick for her appearance at the Lords. She had used some of the lipstick as rouge and black boot polish as mascara, and she looked stunning.

Helen and I were the only smokers. I had managed to arrange for some tobacco to be left behind the cistern in the men's lavatory at the Lords, and I was able to share this with her.

Prison was a harsh ordeal for Helen. The rest of us were at least together, able to communicate with each other and boost one another's morale. She was entirely on her own. Sadly, we were never to see her again for she committed suicide shortly after her release. My memory of her will always be of those days in the House of Lords when she had made such an effort to show 'the boys' how well she was coping.

We arrived back at the prison each night too late for the normal prison meal, so the screws erected a large table for us to eat together. Whether this was out of kindness or necessity, I don't know. Whatever the reason, I have fond memories of those meals when we were sat together talking over the events of the day, laughing and joking.

The appeal, as expected, was turned down; the reasons were to be given later. Inevitably when we were back in the antechamber adjoining the sumptuous room where the hearing had taken place, the mood was somewhat flat.

'Oh, well,' I said with a sigh, 'that's the way the cookie crumbles.'

We were silent for a minute or two. The sun was shining on the river outside, and a red double-decker bus moved silently over the bridge. Then Helen repeated my phrase:

'Yes, that's the way the cookie crumbles.'

Suddenly Hawkins pounced on Terry, grabbed his wrist dramatically and pretended to be clamping on the handcuffs:

'Yes, I'm sorry,' he said – 'but that's the way it is!'

It broke the mood, and we all laughed. I could almost forgive him the slashed peak.

Unfortunately, my hopes of seeing George one last time before being moved were disappointed. We were not sent to work the day after the Lords had turned down the appeal but were instead assessed fit for removal to open prison. Trevor and Ian were to go to Spring Hill; Terry and myself to Ford. Michael was considered a far too disruptive influence to be moved to an open prison and was to remain in the Scrubs.

Before leaving I was able to talk briefly with Michael. I met him half-way up the iron staircase at one end of the wing and told him in a hurried conversation about my discussion with George. He pleaded caution. He was worried about the effects of such an action

31

on the peace movement if one was caught. I agreed that this was a serious consideration, and we left it at that.

It was to be more than four years from the time of my first talks with George before I would see and speak to him again. By then he would be out of gaol and in hiding – the most wanted man in Britain.

CHAPTER THREE

The Class of '62

Narrated by Michael Randle

When Pat first told me, in an exchange on one of the D Hall stairways, that he had talked to George Blake about an escape, my reaction was cautious.

'I don't know,' I said hesitantly. 'Wouldn't the press use it as a stick to beat the peace movement with?'

That had been my first thought. But at the same time the idea itself was appealing. I'd never had time for spies, but Blake's 42-year sentence had always struck me as iniquitous. And by then I had begun to know him a little.

However, for the time being there was nothing any of us could do. The House of Lords had just turned down our appeal and even with full remission, we still had over eight months to serve. Besides, Pat and the others were about to be whisked off to open prisons.

'Let's think about it,' I said, not wanting to turn the idea down flat, or to make any commitment.

It was early June. I had already lost seven days' remission and had a number of run-ins with the prison authorities. The first was when Terry, Ian and I had politely declined to call the Deputy Governor 'Sir' the day after we arrived at the Scrubs. He didn't take kindly to this. We all lost four days' remission and spent four days on 'non-associated labour' – the prison euphemism for solitary confinement.

A few months later, in May, I was again unfortunate enough to appear before the same Deputy Governor for hammering on the cell door one evening demanding that a fellow cell-mate with diarrhoea be allowed to use the landing recess.

'Use your pot!' the screw had called out, while the poor man sat on his bed holding his stomach, too embarrassed to do so in front of Trevor Hatton and myself. When I continued banging on the door, the screw eventually opened up but put me 'on report'. The following morning, after a farce of a hearing, the irascible colonel lopped another three days off my remission and docked me three days' pay.

However, the final straw for the authorities was a letter I smuggled out to the pacifist paper *Peace News* proposing a renewed campaign of civil disobedience aimed at ending nuclear tests. The item was picked up by the national press, and the incident caused embarrassment to the Home Office by reflecting badly on prison security. This, I think, was the main reason I had not accompanied the others to open prison.

But in many ways the decision suited me. I wanted to use my year in prison to take some 'O' and 'A' levels and qualify for university, and I knew from experience it was difficult, if not impossible, to study in the noisy dormitories of an open prison. The only thing I regretted was that Pat, Trevor, Ian and Terry were not staying behind with me.

The classes at the prison were generally excellent, a tribute to the energetic Tutor Organizer, Pat Sloan. I signed on initially for three of them: French, English Literature and Music; later I dropped the French but joined a Diploma Course in English Literature set up by the Extra-Mural Department of London University. It was through these classes that I became friends with George Blake.

I first met him at the music class which all five of us on the Wethersfield case attended.

'That's George Blake,' Trevor whispered to me, nodding in his direction. I looked over and saw a man of slight build and thoughtful brown eyes listening attentively to the music. What struck me – as it struck many who met him in prison – was his apparent composure in face of such a dreadful sentence. Here is the reaction of another long-term prisoner upon first meeting George in the prison library:

A man comes round the corner. He is wearing the patched uniform of the 'escapee', and he is closely followed by a screw . . . He stands quietly, looking across the counter, and as I pick up fresh cards to make out for him I am conscious of a serenity in his face that is completely at variance with the normal look of the newly convicted.

I pick up a pen, pull the card towards me, smile up at him and say: 'Number and name?'

I have written the number he has given me, and my pen has made the first, downward stroke of his name before the impact of what he has said strikes me.

He said, 'Blake'. It is George Blake, sentenced a week ago to forty-two years imprisonment. I complete the card and hand it over to him, and for a second our eyes meet. I turn away and point out to him where he will find fiction, and where biographies, and where travel books, and I am wondering what he is thinking as the oft repeated words fall parrot-like from my lips.

He turns away with the smile to which I am to grow accustomed, and moves over to the shelves. I watch him.

I see now that what I took to be serenity is taut control, for his smooth, unlined cheeks just miss the complete relaxation of acceptance. He is a dapper figure, smart in his new suit, and he moves swiftly and surely, yet without hurry from shelf to shelf . . .

Forty-two years' imprisonment. I am wondering what sort of a man the judge was who imposed this sentence, what sort of man it was who could sit, look straight at another, and sentence him to forty-two years' imprisonment, who could decide that another man was to be locked away for three quarters of a lifetime.[1]

The man who wrote those words was a ex-army officer serving a life sentence for murder. He developed his writing skills while in prison and became a full-time author upon his release in 1969, using the pen-name Zeno. He was the blue-band 'trusty' in the library while I was in the Scrubs and one of the most articulate and forceful contributors in the two other classes I attended – the English Literature course run by a tutor called Peter Bowering, and the English Diploma course which I joined in mid-July.

When Bowering heard that I was studying for 'A' level English Literature he obtained the permission of the class to take us through some of my set books, including Jane Austen's *Emma*, and E.M. Forster's *A Passage to India*. He also read and commented on all the essays I wrote for the correspondence course I had started.

The class attracted a particularly committed and talented group of people of widely differing backgrounds and views. Besides Blake and Zeno, there was an Austrian, Kurt, working on a novel which was to win the Koestler award. (This is an award instituted and financed by the author Arthur Koestler under which prisoners may write literary or musical compositions, or produce works of art which can be sold on the prisoner's behalf.) Zeno too had started work on a book about his experiences at Arnhem which won the Koestler award and was published under the title *The Cauldron*.[2] Later in the summer the class was joined by three young American radicals convicted of dealing in cannabis. They were particularly

35

valuable allies in some of the political debates that developed.

Zeno represented one pole of political opinion within the class, where sympathies generally lay to the left, or at least left of centre. He wore a moustache, held himself very erect, and always managed to get his prison uniform smartly pressed in the laundry workshop. He was contemptuous of working-class culture and politics generally and of the Labour Party in particular, and contended that art and literature were always products of the middle or upper classes. But he was a bit like Enoch Powell in that he didn't fit the stereotype of the right-winger, and on some issues held quite radical views; he was, for instance, totally opposed to capital punishment.

Zeno was not of course the name we knew him by in prison, though it came as no surprise to learn that he had chosen as a pseudonym the name of the Stoic philosopher. He used to argue that pain was not a problem. When it went beyond a certain intensity, you passed out; if you were still conscious it was by definition bearable. I remember he expounded this thesis once in the literature class. Bowering nodded as if in assent, but looked sceptical. None of the rest of us cared to take him up on the point.

Sometimes the debates in the class became heated. Once Peter Bowering read a parody of Rupert Brooke's piece. I remember only two lines:

> And stands the church clock at ten to bloody three,
> And is there bloody honey still for bloody tea?

At this point Zeno exploded. The parody was a cheap jibe, he said, his moustache fairly bristling. Bowering was apologetic but it was as much as he could do to mollify him. The reading of *A Passage to India* also occasioned some lively arguments. Zeno defended Britain's imperial role. So what if the British took their customs, outlook and eating habits to India – people from whatever country did the same when they settled abroad. And if Britain's role in India could be criticized, one had to remember that if she had not stepped in, some other European power would have taken her place. I remember discussing this point with the three young Americans one day on the exercise yard.

'There is no question,' one of them said, 'but that if Britain had not colonized India, one or more of the other European colonial powers would have done so. But one simply has to rule out that kind of justification for colonial expansion.'

I do not recall George becoming involved in any of the more

heated arguments. He tended to keep his counsel and to contribute only occasionally. Thus at this stage I still felt I knew him only slightly.

During the first three months of the sentence, while we were still on appeal, I worked in the bakehouse. It was one of the better places to be because you were part of a small team with a job to do, and the screws had an interest in keeping the team happy. All the bread for the prison was baked there, plus the odd rockcake. My job, with one other prisoner, was to slice the bread in a small anteroom off the bakehouse proper. It was a boring job, but if the work got done no one bothered you.

One of the perks of the job was the unofficial mid-morning tea break. Another, if you fancied it, was the occasional helping of home brew. This was made in co-operation with the kitchens next door who supplied the base of stewed figs and prunes while we provided the yeast. It came out as a black, evil-looking brew and I didn't care to try it myself, especially as it was made up in one of the pails used for scrubbing floors. But people did drink it, and got drunk on it just the same – sometimes prisoners would turn up in the morning complaining of hangovers! Eventually one prisoner was caught carrying a whole pailful up to his cell, having covered it with a dirty floorcloth to give the impression that he was going to scrub the cell floor. That curtailed the brewing activities, at least for a time.

The only problem with the bakehouse lay in the hours you had to work. You started early in the morning to prepare the breakfasts, you had a shortened lunch break and usually missed the exercise period in the afternoons, and you worked weekends. I decided I needed this time for study, so with some reluctance I applied for a transfer. The day after Pat and the others were sent to open prisons I was moved to the tailor's shop. That's how I came to meet Seán Bourke, the man chiefly responsible for organizing George Blake's escape from Wormwood Scrubs.

At the beginning I didn't have much to do with him. As assistant to the chief cutter, he was part of an elite within the workforce along with four or five other prisoners with minor administrative responsibilities such as handing out the scissors and needles. One of their jobs was to brew the morning and afternoon tea for the PO (Principal Officer), a dour man called Ted, and for the other screws. This meant that twice a day they disappeared into the office area and had a cup for themselves.

The majority of the prisoners worked on the sewing machines which occupied most of the floorspace, making overalls. I sat with a group of half a dozen on a wooden bench sewing on buttons by hand. Next to me was a man who had blown up his father-in-law's car. He delighted in telling and re-telling the story, describing with glee the blue flash that had accompanied the explosion and the look of bewilderment on his father-in-law's face. The latter, fortunately, was standing far enough away to avoid injury.

After a few weeks I graduated to a machine which PO Ted had adapted to sew on buttons. I was now facing Seán, and only a few feet away from him, and we soon found a rapport.

Seán had been sentenced in December 1961 to seven years in prison for sending 'an infernal device' in the post to the home of Detective Constable Michael Sheldon, in Crawley, Sussex. He had borne Sheldon a grudge, and had packed a biscuit tin with explosive and shot that would blow up in the face of whoever opened it. But Sheldon had been suspicious and held it well away from himself. When the device went off the shot impacted harmlessly into the ceiling. Inside the lid of the tin was the inscription: Requiescat in Pace.

Seán explained that Sheldon had spread rumours that he was a homosexual which caused him to lose his job at a youth centre. He said he had even taken out a High Court injunction against Sheldon but was too angry and impatient to await the court hearing.

However, Montgomery Hyde, who wrote a book about Blake, states that Seán was actually convicted – chiefly on Sheldon's evidence – of sexually interfering with boys and sentenced to a short term of imprisonment.[3] We have not checked this independently, but assume that Hyde's information is correct.

At all events, Seán appeared genuinely to regret what he had done. On several occasions he said to me:

'Christ, Michael, suppose that man's wife had opened that parcel. Suppose it had killed one of his children. It was a mad and wicked thing I did.'

Seán told me of an experience he had in one of the 'hanging gaols' – I forget whether it was Wandsworth or Pentonville – after his conviction on the parcel bomb charge. The screws took him on a conducted tour of the execution block: the condemned cell and the execution area itself. They had even opened the trap-door to show where the condemned man would drop. There but for the caution of Detective Constable Sheldon he would have ended his days.

'If I wasn't cured already,' he said, 'the sight of that trapdoor would have done it.'Twas terrifying.'

Gradually I learned more about Seán's background. He had been born and raised in Limerick, attending a local school run by the Christian Brothers, a lay religious order renowned for their strict discipline. Seán began to play truant from school, hanging out with a group of other lads doing the same thing. At the age of twelve and a half he was caught stealing a bunch of bananas and sentenced in the juvenile court to spend three years in the reformatory in Daingean in Co. Offaly, run by the Oblates of Mary Immaculate. Seán subsequently recorded a talk for Radio Telefis Eireann (RIE) about some of his experiences there. He described the conditions of the regime there as harsh.[4]

After leaving the reformatory he had travelled to England where not long after his arrival he was convicted of receiving a stolen wireless set and sentenced to fifteen months in Borstal. However, it was his experiences at the reformatory that probably affected most profoundly his outlook and subsequent behaviour.

Seán and I got on well. He had a lot of charm, a sense of fun and a sharp, sceptical mind. I remember once expressing to him my puzzlement about another prisoner serving a long sentence for robbery with violence since he seemed on the face of it to be the gentlest of persons.

'What could possibly have made him do a thing like that?' I asked.

Seán shot me a quizzical look.

'He was short of money,' he answered dryly.

Once we cut out together a small cloth figure depicting a screw dangling from a rope, and glued it to the glass panel of the workshop toilet. It would help, we thought, to keep people's spirits up. PO Ted called us both into his office:

'I know what that's meant to be,' he said to me. 'It's me being topped, isn't it? It was you and Paddy who did it. It's a good job I have a sense of humour, otherwise I'd nick you both.'

On another occasion we accidentally burnt the bottom clean out of a PO's kettle by turning on the gas under it when it was empty. He was not amused. By then I had been demoted from button machine operator to workshop cleaner. I had refused to work on overalls destined for the Admiralty. Cleaning was regarded as a punishment job as you spent your time sweeping up and scrubbing floors. But I found it less boring than sewing on buttons, whether by hand or machine. It also meant I shared the perk of the morning and afternoon cups of tea.

There was another Irishman in the workshop, Pat M, with whom Seán and I were both friendly. He worked in the office area and was in charge of handing out the scissors and making sure they were accounted for at the end of the day. He was a small, self-contained man, who usually didn't say too much, but was capable of expressing his opinions with great conviction and without minding whom they annoyed. He had no time for prisoners trying to make light of their offences – if people had done wrong they should face up to it. I never learnt what he had been convicted for and the closest he ever came to telling me was one day when he shook his head sadly and said that it was the drink that had been his downfall.

During the Cuban missile crisis he and I got into a fierce argument which ended with us yelling abuse at each other.

'Bomb the bastards! Bomb the bastards!' Pat shouted, raising his voice more and more as his anger got the better of him.

'Bloody American imperialists!' I yelled back at him, equally incensed.

'What's going on? What's going on? Do you think this is Hyde Park Corner? Shut up at once, both of you, or I'll have you nicked.'

Seán reacted differently to the Cuban missile crisis. He was singularly impressed when Khrushchev indicated his willingness to climb down over the dispute by means of a telegram to Bertrand Russell – who had earlier cabled him to draw back from the brink and to act through the United Nations. The exchange was on the front pages of most newspapers on Friday 26 October, with many of the popular papers carrying pictures side by side of Khrushchev and Russell. I recorded Seán's comments in a prison journal which I kept and later smuggled out of prison:

> If your movement had achieved nothing in the past, and achieves nothing more in the future, what has happened on this occasion justifies, and more than justifies, its existence and all the sacrifices that have been made.

Despite the row over Cuba, Pat and I got on well. There was one particular incident by which I will always remember him. Towards the end of my time at the Scrubs the Committee of 100 started to run into problems with some of its prominent figures. Early in 1963, the press reported that Bertrand Russell had resigned as the Committee's president. Not long afterwards came the news that Vanessa Redgrave had also resigned. When I came in the morning Vanessa's resignation was reported Pat had an impish grin on his face and nodded to me to come over. He leaned across the half-door through which he handed out the scissors, nodding his head as he spoke:

'Who fears,' he said, 'to speak of '98?' (This referred to a well-known Irish ballad celebrating the Wolfe Tone rebellion of 1798.)

Seán standing nearby overheard the remark and all three of us stood there laughing uproariously while the PO eyed us suspiciously.

Prison visits are one of the emotional highpoints of life inside. During the first three months Anne was able to come regularly on Appeal Visits. These were 'closed visits' lasting twenty minutes – meaning that prisoner and visitor were screened off from physical contact by a glass panel and metal grid. In theory, too, you could only discuss business connected with the appeal but any half-way decent screw wouldn't insist on that too strictly. We also received 'open visits' every four weeks.

After our appeal was finally rejected by the House of Lords there were only the regular visits to look forward to. They were like beacons on which you could fix your sights from one month to the next, counting the days as they approached. It was impossible, however, for them to live up to the emotional capital invested in them. For the first ten or fifteen minutes you were trying to get your bearings; for the rest, you were conscious of how soon the visit would be over.

Anne came once a month, sometimes on her own, sometimes for the first ten minutes or so with other friends and relatives. From September onwards, however, there was always at least one other person present – our son Seán who was born in August. He was a month old when I first saw him, but he would be six months old before I would spend time with him regularly and watch him grow and develop.

In mid-July I applied to join the English Literature Diploma class. But at about the same time I again got into trouble with the prison authorities. On 10 July the *Daily Sketch* and the *Daily Mirror* carried reports based on an article in the *Prison Service Journal* by the Catering Adviser to the Home Office, a Mr Belcham. These suggested that prisoners were enjoying gourmet meals, and described a typical meal as comprising hors d'oeuvre, mutton chops, peas and chips, pie, custard and tea. I wrote a letter to *Peace News* denouncing this nonsense and tried to smuggle it out through someone on an outside working party. Unfortunately, there was a search that day and my friend had to drop the note on the ground to avoid being found with it. As a result I spent another seven days on 'non-associated labour' and lost seven more days remission. I was fortunate that the case had been heard by the main governor, Hayes, and not by his deputy (an ex-Colonel), or the punishment might have been considerably more severe.

But next time I attended Bowering's literature class, Zeno was contemptuous.

'Dozens of "stiffs" [illegal letters] are smuggled out of this prison every week,' he said. 'It's sheer stupidity to get caught.'

I'm sure this confirmed Zeno's view that the people in the disarmament movement were not merely misguided but incompetent.

Fortunately, the episode did not stand in the way of my joining the Diploma class, and it was here that I became properly acquainted with George. Seán was also on the course, as were the young Americans imprisoned for handling cannabis. Zeno played a leading role in its activities, cajoling the rest of us from time to time into writing essays so that the organizers would have something to show for their efforts.

I had of course seen George regularly at the music class and the other literature class, but there was little opportunity during them for protracted discussion. The Diploma class was different. Once a week, on a Monday, we were given the whole morning off for reading and study. Our class was held in the Education Block, where we were supervised only by a blue-band trusty – usually Zeno.

Of course we did some reading – and we were always resolving to do so in a more disciplined way. Then, half-way through the morning, when we made coffee in the adjoining kitchen, inevitably the debates and discussions would begin. I don't remember them being about literature – though I do recall discussions on just about everything else from freewill and determinism to whether or not the police should be armed. George was firmly of the determinist school; he felt the forces of history and of the physical world were the ultimate arbiters of human destiny. He insisted, however, that he was not a fatalist in the sense of believing one should passively accept whatever happened – the participation of human beings was part of the process.

At the study session we would swop newspapers and journals and sometimes the debates would arise out of the articles we read. I received a range of political journals including *Peace News*, *New Statesman*, *Tribune*, *Freedom* (the anarchist weekly), *Anarchy*, a monthly journal, *War Resistance*, the monthly journal of War Resisters International, and *France Observateur*. After a time I got into the habit of lending some of these to Blake. He would keep them for a few days before returning them to me.

Like Pat – like most prisoners – I had been curious from the start about Blake. And like him I had no time for the espionage activities of East or West, or for repressive or authoritarian regimes of any description. The first political demonstration that I had personally initiated was a walk – which I ended up doing on my own – from Vienna to the Hungarian border in 1956. I carried a placard and leaflets in several languages calling on Soviet forces not to fire on unarmed demonstrators and expressing the support of Western pacifists for the Hungarian passive resistance. I planned to distribute this in Hungary – it was perhaps fortunate for me that I was arrested by Austrian police at the frontier and ordered to leave the country within two days!

Nevertheless, there were aspects of Blake's case which engaged my sympathy.

First, however much one might disagree with his espionage activities, we feel there was no question but that he had acted out of genuine belief and commitment as Lord Parker, indeed, had acknowledged at his trial. 'I am perfectly prepared to accept', he said, 'that it was not for money that you did this, but because of your conversion to a genuine belief in the communist system.'[5] The Prime Minister of the time, Harold Macmillan, also stated in the Commons that Blake had acted out of ideological conviction and that this was what made him a particularly difficult kind of spy to detect.[6] In this sense, Blake was a prisoner of conscience, however much one might disagree with what this conscience had led him to do.

Second, the 42-year sentence struck me as vicious. It was not as if the Attorney General, Manningham-Buller, who led the prosecution of Blake, or Lord Parker who sentenced him, rejected espionage *per se*, or had ever distanced themselves from the lies, disinformation, sabotage and assassination carried out by Western Intelligence Agencies. Despite the theoretical separation of powers within the British system, this smacked of revenge by the British Establishment on someone who out of political conviction had done for the other side what British Intelligence had trained him to do for them.

There was also the fact that Blake's trial and appeal had been heard *in camera*. No one could say exactly what he had done, and all there was to go on was rumour and speculation.

Finally, I knew that Blake had been active with the Dutch underground resistance during the Second World War, though I didn't at that stage know the details. It was impossible for me not to feel some sympathy for a person with that background and experience. Although my own position was essentially pacifist, my convictions stemmed from a rejection of *indiscriminate* warfare – including, most importantly, nuclear war, which threatened millions of lives and perhaps even human survival. I was not sure I could have adopted a pacifist position in 1939 if I had been old enough to have had to face up to the choice of fighting or not fighting in that war. Thus my pacifism did not preclude admiration for those with a courageous record of resisting Nazism. The Rev. Michael Scott, a leading member of both DAC and the Committee of 100, had been an RAF pilot in the Second World War, as had Dr Fergus King, another Committee of 100 member who gave evidence at our trial. And Claude Bourdet, editor of *France Observateur*, perhaps the best-known French advocate of nuclear disarmament, had been an important figure in the French wartime resistance.

Pat and I discuss in a systematic way the moral and political issues relating to espionage, and to our decision to help Blake escape, in the final chapter of this book; here the purpose is simply to indicate some of the thoughts and feelings that informed our attitude to him when we met him in prison in 1962.

I didn't for some time discuss spying as such with George, or express my own deep antipathy towards it. But by chance in late September, after I had got to know him rather better, *Peace News* published a review of a book about espionage which amounted to a blistering attack on the whole business and everyone connected with it. It was entitled 'The Stinking Net of Espionage' and read in part as follows:

> I am liable to run out of adjectives to express my loathing of the despicable trade which is the subject of a book just published under the title of *The Secret War* . . .
>
> This is an exhaustive study of spying in all its aspects, replete with details of the latest and most notorious trials; and the author has been blamed for giving away far too much 'vital' information. What he makes obvious is that that unsavoury creature, the spy —who deals mainly in trivialities and if he happens to supply useful facts is likely to find them distrusted and discounted – is now completely out of date, and the sooner he and his like are paid off the better for us all. The agent on the ground has been rendered redundant by the 'spy in the sky', and only blind obstinacy can still guarantee him employment . . .
>
> Is it too much to hope . . . that with the mechanization of espionage we may be able to rid ourselves of the unscrupulous tribe of liars, thieves, forgers, blackmailers, kidnappers, seducers, saboteurs and assassins employed by allegedly civilized Governments in the fraudulent racket of so-called security? . . .
>
> Although the author of *The Secret War* refrains from romanticizing the role of the spy, the assumption is accepted that whatever nauseating tricks the Soviet KGB or MVD may be capable of, the American FBI and CIA can outmatch them in villainy. From a Congressman 'in on CIA secrets' is quoted a reference to 'some activities which it almost chills the marrow of a man to hear about'. Here is an organization which acts as an invisible government with a secret uncontrolled budget and an unrecorded staff of tens of thousands of agents and 'has in fact become as direct a policy maker as the State Department through its political forays'.
>
> The CIA runs its own underground political offensives, takes upon itself the task of countering the spread of Communism and in the process makes a practice of bolstering up corrupt and reactionary regimes. It was responsible for the Cuban fiasco [i.e., the Bay of Pigs invasion] and for the U-2 overflights which embarrassed Eisenhower's Administration, scuttled the Summit Conference, and presented Khrushchev with a big propaganda opportunity of which he took full advantage. Inscribed on the wall of the main entrance of the CIA's elaborate building in Langley, Virginia, only ten miles from Washington is the motto of this official lie factory: 'Ye shall know the truth and the truth shall make you free' [Gospel according to St John].
>
> The innocent might assume that espionage could perhaps be justified

because it is directed against a wicked enemy. It would come as a shock to know that it is directed just as treacherously against one's friends. NSA (the National Security Agency), silent partner of the CIA, boasts that it has been eminently successful in spying on the allies of the United States and 'reading the codes of 40 nations'. Its gentlemanly tactics include subverting the code clerks in friendly embassies. Diplomatic privileges are openly abused. Every important embassy and consulate has its quota of CIA men who are given 'cover' rank but whose work escapes diplomatic discipline. In Washington the initials of the CIA are said to stand for 'Caught in the act' and when an expulsion takes place governments call in the noble principle of retaliation that permeates international policy, and a corresponding representative of the foreign country concerned is expelled. Thus international relations are poisoned under the cover of diplomacy . . .

The tragedy has its farcical side. Most of the 'secrets' lie wide open and are of little significance in any case. 'Intelligence' covers a monumental mass of stupidity. Even after the most elaborate sifting of recruits and the elimination of 'security risks', the small minority who are base enough to be employed as spies are usually immature, unbalanced, untrustworthy, unscrupulous and addicted to double-crossing. Hence the double agent paid by both sides and betraying the lot and the Communist defector who is described as a hero who has 'chosen freedom', and the defector from the anti-Communist side who is denounced as a traitor deserving to be shot . . .

How can one retain respect for anyone, however eminent, who allows himself to be entangled in the stinking net of espionage? The courage and initiative for which he might be given credit are prostituted to degrading ends.[7]

I was intensely curious to find out what George would make of the arguments, but because of the vehemence of the denunciation not simply of espionage as a profession but of all individual spies, I hesitated for a while to draw his attention to it. In the end I decided to do so, and he took away my copy of the paper promising to return it to me the next time we met.

When he handed back the paper I looked at him inquiringly.

'Well,' I said, 'what do you think?'

'I agree with every word of it,' he said simply. Then he paused. 'Unfortunately, as long as the world is divided into nation-states I suppose it is inevitable that espionage will continue.'

I respected him for that response; he could very easily have taken umbrage. At a personal level he gave the impression of being a thoughtful, somewhat diffident person. He clearly held strongly personal convictions to have risked his life working with the Dutch underground during the war, and later to have put his family life, his future and his reputation on the line in support of the Soviet cause. But he did not try to foist his views on people.

Sceptics will argue that Blake's demeanour was simply a front, a tribute to his professionalism and cunning. This was the conclusion that Seán Bourke himself reached after the escape and after living with George in Moscow:

> The George Blake that we had all known at Wormwood Scrubs had never really existed. It had been an elaborate and calculated pose with a long-term objective. In Moscow, with no more reason for posing, George Blake reverted to type.[8]

We don't believe, however, that you can keep up a pose week in week out, especially in the exposed situation of prison life. Moreover, George's willingness to help those less fortunate than himself extended to illiterates and semi-illiterates from whom he stood to get very little in return. Here is Zeno again:

> If I had his knowledge of languages and his patience as a teacher, I still could not give up hours a day of my time to teach any man who asked me to and who showed diligence and application. George does just that. He has a class of young cockneys to whom he teaches French, and he has brought them to a standard whereby one at least will shortly be sitting GCE 'A' level, and the others their 'O' levels. For years George devoted an hour a day to teaching a West Indian to speak German. This was particularly remarkable when I remember that I had the greatest difficulty in understanding the man's English. And yet steadily, and despite the hours he spends with his proteges, he is studying for an Honours Degree in Classical Arabic. Sometimes when I go to his cell I am greeted by cockney voices holding an animated conversation in French, or reading to each other from French newspapers or periodicals, and if this is the case I withdraw and return at another time. I may find him alone, standing as he sometimes does, and reading the Koran, which rests on a lectern made for him by one of his pupils. Or he may be seated at his table making notes, or again he may be lying on his bed reading a tale in Arabic from The Thousand and One Nights. Whatever he may be doing, if he is alone I am greeted with a charming smile of welcome, an offer to seat myself, and if the time is right an invitation to take a mug of tea.[9]

47

I can vouch for the authenticity of that account in that I knew one semi-illiterate prisoner in the bakehouse whom George was coaching with his reading and writing. Could all this really be a calculated pose with the long-term aim of finding people who would help him to escape? George didn't, after all, have to go to such lengths to make his point. The much more likely explanation is that he was indeed a gifted and dedicated teacher and derived immense satisfaction out of helping people whom society had cast aside as ne'er-do-wells and degenerates.

George's apparent calm puzzled even those who had got to know him well. One day Zeno, escorting me somewhere within the prison, turned to me and said:

'What do you make of old George?'

I wasn't quite sure how to take the question.

'He's a fascinating man,' I said. 'I like him.' But Zeno wasn't really interested in my opinion.

'I think', he said with the smile of someone speaking from experience, 'that the sentence hasn't yet hit him. One of these days it will.'

Zeno himself was much more friendly towards me during the last few months of my term inside – mainly, I believe, because of the debates we used to have on the Diploma study mornings.

I remember only one occasion on which I won a debating point at his expense. The group had been discussing the question of whether or not the police should be armed and Zeno put the clinching argument against doing so:

'If you arm the police,' he said, 'the criminals will also carry guns as a matter of course and the violence will escalate. You've only got to look at the United States to see what would happen.'

'You have just made an excellent summary', I said, 'of my argument for unilateral nuclear disarmament.'

George gave a long chuckle and Zeno too smiled. He soon came back, however, with the argument that once the escalation had taken place and both sides were armed it would be disastrous for one side to throw away its weapons.

At the end of one particularly stimulating study morning I commented:

'*C'est magnifique, mais . . .*'

George completed the phrase:

'*Mais, ce n'est pas l'étude*!'

The clearest evidence of how Zeno's attitude towards me had changed came at the beginning of one of the diploma classes. He was sitting next to me and leaned close so that our faces were almost touching:

'My trouble is', he said in a low, confidential voice, 'that I'm an arrogant s.o.b. The only good thing is that I realize it!'

He makes much the same point against himself in his autobiography but interestingly cites his friendship with George, and George's own example, as the reason he was able to some extent to overcome it:

> In my cell I find the humility I longed for when I came here first. Outside of it my stupid pride predominates. Years ago, when first I realized that if I were to serve my sentence with any degree of acceptance, I should have to learn humility, I denied that there was any person in the prison on whom I could model myself. That was true then, but I feel that it is no longer. I have found the model, and when I am in his company I am conscious that he has the humility I seek. His virtues create similar virtues in me. It is strange that he should be the man whom the law, by the very severity of the sentence it imposed on him, should have considered to be the greatest criminal of all.[10]

One other incident recorded by Zeno warrants quotation because of the light it throws on George's character and the regard in which many of the screws as well as other prisoners held him. It concerned a prisoner from Aden by the name of Abdul who was mentally unstable after suffering head injuries in a car crash, and particularly so whilst observing day-long fasts during the month of Ramadan. George was one of the few people in the prison able to get through to him:

> The next day, half-way through a meal, we heard a high-pitched yell, almost an animal scream, from some distance down the hall. There was an immediate silence, and everyone's head, screws and prisoners alike, turned in the direction of the sound. Abdul was standing with his hands above his head pouring out a volume of words, his eyes directed above the heads of the men seated in front of him. He broke off and went in a stumbling run for a few yards down the hall; then he started again. I looked at the screws as they stood round the desk, making no move, some of their faces concerned, others amused. I was pleased about this, for not many years ago Abdul would have been in the strongbox within

thirty seconds of his outburst . . .

I glanced at George, and his eyes met mine. He was uncomfortable, and I saw his hands tensed on the table. I realized that he abhorred anything that approached physical violence. I had suspected this before, and I appreciated suddenly that this was an interesting insight into his character. I muttered, 'You'd better have a word with him, otherwise *they'll* have no alternative.'

George stood up, forcing himself to his feet, and went down the hall to Abdul. I saw a look of relief on the screws' faces, for although they could cope with the situation they wanted it settled as easily and amicably as possible . . .

George got to Abdul, and from the thirty yards which separated us, those on our table could see him talking to the Arab, one hand resting lightly on his shoulder. Abdul was arguing, George being conciliatory. He succeeded, for the Arab turned away and moved towards his own cell with George following him. I realized how much George would underplay the whole incident, and smiled to myself at the prospect of his return. I looked across at Paddy opposite me:

'I'll lay a bet now that when George gets back he'll say that Abdul is a trifle disturbed . . .

After a few minutes George came back to us, first stopping at the desk to reassure the screws as to Abdul's condition. He sat down at the table again. None of us said anything. George looked up, his eyes passing lightly from one to the other of us. 'I'm afraid poor Abdul is a little upset' he said mildly.

The roar of laughter which burst out swung dozens of heads in our direction. George blushed, and his head jerked from one to the other of us in search of an explanation.

When the laughter subsided, I explained the joke. George was forced to smile a little himself.[11]

One other point of contact between George and me was that we were the only prisoners in Wormwood Scrubs that year to be taking GCE exams. I took 'A' levels in English Literature and Economic History and 'O' levels in French and Latin; he took 'O' levels in British Constitution and Russian. George had studied Russian at Downing College, Cambridge in 1947, and could speak and read it with facility, but I suppose he wanted to have the formal GCE qualification. At the next Monday morning study period after he had sat the exam I asked him how he had got on.

'It was reasonably straightforward,' he said, 'though there was a rather interesting essay question – "Where I would like to spend my summer holidays".'

He was holding back a grin and clearly dying to tell us what he had written about.

'Well – where did you choose?' I asked him.

His face broke into a broad smile.

'I chose Moscow!' he said.

I told the story to friends in *Peace News* after my release and there was a small item about it in the paper in mid March, together with the suggestion that I would be writing about some of my conversations with George.[12]

During all this time I had not forgotten the hasty conversation with Pat just before he left about helping George escape. But I had said nothing to George himself, and indeed there were normally other people around when I saw him. But once during the last ten minutes of one of the Monday morning study sessions all the other prisoners on the course had had to leave for one reason or another and for the first time George and I found ourselves alone. It was an ideal opportunity for me to refer to his conversation with Pat. I kept framing the words over and over again in my head, yet hesitated to voice them.

We sat in total silence. Did he, I wondered, have a sense of what was in the air? My heart was pounding because I knew that to say anything would be the first irrevocable step on a venture involving incalculable risks. But while I was still in this state of mental turmoil, the screw came in to take us to the midday meal.

CHAPTER FOUR

Best-laid Plans . . .

Narrated by Michael Randle

I kept in touch intermittently with both George Blake and Seán Bourke after my release from Wormwood Scrubs, though mainly in the form of sending them a card at Christmas. Then one day in the summer of 1964 to my astonishment I saw Seán's name featured in one of the tabloid newspapers. Seán, it appeared, had formed an attachment for the actress Yvette Wyatt, formerly of the hospital TV series *Emergency Ward Ten*, who had been working as a volunteer with the drama group at the prison. He had made a proposal of marriage and somehow the paper had got hold of the story.

Seán had been a member of the drama group when I knew him in Wormwood Scrubs. In fact, I still have a programme from a production the group put on when I was inside. It was a three-act comedy entitled *A Father in the Fold*, written by two prisoners identified as Pat and Fergus. Characters were listed in order of appearance, and Seán's name topped the bill.

I wrote to him asking about his release date, and told him I was at university and might well end up in a teaching job. I received a reply soon afterwards, cautioning me about the pitfalls of being a teacher. No doubt, like many others, I would start out with the best of liberal intentions; but I would probably still end up being regarded by the kids as a tyrant. He was, I suppose, thinking back to his own schooling at the hands of Christian Brothers in Limerick, and of the Oblates at the reformatory in Daingean.

We exchanged a couple of further letters, but the correspondence lapsed again, apart from my annual Christmas card to him and George. Then one day in mid May, 1966, I answered the phone and was surprised to find Seán at the other end of the line. He explained that he was on the hostel scheme and due for release in five or six weeks' time. (The scheme is designed to ease long-term prisoners back into the routine of normal life. Prisoners on it work in an outside job during the day and have weekends free, but have to return to the hostel inside the prison walls each evening.)

'I was wondering, Michael, if 'twould be convenient to come over and see you some time soon?' (Seán could be quite formal on occasions.)

'Certainly, I'd be delighted to see you. When had you in mind?'

'This afternoon, if you like' – and so it was agreed.

We were living at this time in Torriano Cottages, at the back of Leighton Road in Kentish Town; the house was part of a small co-operative housing venture.

He arrived not long afterwards. Describing the meeting in his book *The Springing of George Blake* – where he identifies Anne and me as 'Anne and Michael Reynolds', he says I looked 'rather pale and drawn'.[1] That was probably true. I had not been well and had been under a lot of strain working for my final exams for a BA in English at University College, London. Seán, however, looked no different than when we had last met some three years earlier.

We talked at first about his situation. He was working during the day at a factory in Acton that manufactured spare parts for cars, and was due for release on 4 July.

We recalled prisoners and screws we had both known and remembered incidents that had taken place, laughing again over Pat M's line 'Who fears to speak of '98'; the time we had burnt the bottom out of PO Ted's kettle, and the day we had topped him in effigy in the workshop lavatory. Seán himself had left the tailor's shop some time since, and had become editor of the prison 'house journal' *New Horizon* until joining the hostel scheme.

I asked after George, and Seán suddenly became very serious. It was precisely about George, he said, that he had come to see me. But it was a sensitive matter: even talking about it was dangerous.

George, he went on, had approached him one day last summer in D Hall. He was more serious than Seán had ever seen him and spoke slowly and deliberately, fixing his eyes on the ground. He had a proposition to make. After four years in prison he had given up all hope of being released in an exchange deal with the Russians. In the past, he explained, such deals had only occurred where the Soviet agent was not a British subject. Although he had been born in Holland of an Egyptian father and Dutch mother, his father held a British passport and he himself had taken British citizenship after settling in England during the war. He had come to the conclusion that his only hope lay in organizing an escape.

George had gone on to stress that after a lapse of five years he had no information that could be of any interest to Soviet Intelligence and that he would now be quite useless for espionage work. If he escaped from prison he would prefer to live in some neutral country – perhaps Egypt – rather than go to the Soviet Union. He had also emphatically denied that any Western agents had been executed as a result of his activities when he was working for the Russians. (Whether he would have even known what happened to Western agents he identified is a moot point.)

Seán had at once agreed to help him and they had worked out two or three possible plans, thinking of a date in late autumn when the days began to draw in. They had been able to continue to exchange notes, thanks to the help of a trusty whose work took him between the Hostel and the long-term D Wing. A few weeks earlier Seán had bought a pair of walkie-talkie sets and smuggled one in to Blake. Now they could again communicate directly.

The problem was money. It would not be an expensive operation, but several hundred pounds would be needed to buy a getaway car, to pay for a forged passport and for boat or airline tickets. Seán assured us he did not expect us – with two young children – to become closely involved; but if we could help with the finance, he would take care of the rest.

Our second child, Gavin, had been born in January 1964, which meant we now had two children under five; thus we were not well placed to undertake any high-risk project. But helping to raise money was another matter. We could see our way to that.

'We're with you,' I said and we shook hands solemnly.

'But we don't have any money ourselves – we'd have to try and raise it from people we knew,' I added. I also asked him if he knew what the penalty was for aiding a prisoner to escape. He said he had looked into this and the maximum was a five-year prison sentence.

'But do you think you can really pull it off, Seán?' I asked.

'My friend,' he announced, 'I can tell you one thing. Even if you are not able to help, George Blake will definitely be out of Wormwood Scrubs six months from now. There is absolutely no question about it!'

His confidence was unbounded. Still more impressive, however, was the amount of detailed planning that had already been put into the venture and the fact that he had successfully established radio communication with Blake and set up a small network of trusted helpers to smuggle in equipment. He told us too that he knew quite a bit about radio and had chosen walkie-talkie sets whose frequency could not be picked up by police-car radios. (This, incidentally, was in the days before every copper on the beat had a walkie-talkie set.)

I believe our meeting took place just before I was due to sit my Finals and I explained I would be unable to do anything immediately about raising money. Seán claims in his book to have already seen the published results of the exams in *The Times* when he met me, and says he congratulated me on my success. But here he is mistaken. I graduated in 1966 and even if I had just finished sitting the exams, the results would not have been published until the following July or August.

He was due back at the hostel at 9 p.m., and at last, after again thanking us both, he got up to leave. We couldn't offer him a lift as we still had no car, so he had to allow plenty of time to take the underground from Kentish Town to White City. We arranged to meet again in a few weeks.

In bed that night, with the two children safely asleep, Anne and I discussed Seán's visit. She had heard me many times talking about both Seán and George, and she shared my feelings about the 42-year sentence. We felt particularly close sharing this bizarre secret. But we knew too that if the plan did go ahead there would be many tensions in the coming months. Even so, we had no idea then just how deeply we would become involved, or the extent of the risks we would soon be running.

It was a hectic summer. After my exams I signed on – as I usually did during vacations – with a typing agency that supplied temps to businesses, and also started applying for a number of teaching and lecturing posts. By chance the agency sent me to the offices of Dictaphone Limited in West London. From time to time I would meet Seán immediately after work in a pub in the area.

Earlier in the year, in April, I had been to Rome to attend a War Resisters International (WRI) Conference and to take over the Chair of the organization. There was a strong American contingent there, and they urged us to make a priority of campaigning for US withdrawal from Vietnam.

In August I went with three other Committee of 100 members on a non-violent 'raid' on the USAF base at Wethersfield in Essex – the same base that had figured in the Official Secrets Act trial in 1962. We leafleted the whole of the married quarters and several of the barracks before being stopped by US military police. We were finally escorted off the base by local British police.

A second Vietnam project, however, was to take up much more of my time. This was the Volunteers for Peace in Vietnam project, an international initiative designed to put pressure on President Johnson to halt the bombing of Hanoi, Haiphong and other towns and villages in the Democratic Republic of Vietnam (North Vietnam).

Fortunately I was underemployed at Dictaphone. My immediate superiors didn't like it if they saw me reading a book when they had no work for me to do, but were quite happy so long as they could hear the typewriter in action! It was from there that I wrote to Ho Chi Minh in Hanoi about the project and to the Chinese Embassy in London regarding transit visas for the team. I often wondered what the reaction of my employers would have been if they had discovered just what their industrious temp was up to. As it was they asked me if I would consider signing on with the firm!

For a long time the Volunteers project remained at a standstill. Then one day I received a cable at my home address from the Vietnamese Prime Minister Pham Van Dong saying the team would be welcome. We eventually left just after Christmas, on 28 December. Our journey and meeting with Ho Chi Minh were publicized in Britain, Western Europe and North America – in fact the meeting with Ho Chi Minh featured as the main front-page picture of the *New York Times* in early January 1967. I believe that the project helped mobilize international opposition to the US war. (Unfortunately in the early 1970s I lent all my papers related to the project to a writer working on a biography of Ambrose Reeves, and lost track of them. If he should chance to read this, I would be obliged if he would return them!)

Meanwhile, Seán and George kept in regular contact through the walkie-talkie sets and settled on a definite escape plan. I cannot remember if Seán explained to us where George concealed his radio, though from certain passages in the book it appears that it was not kept in the cell all the time. There were occasional searches of the cells, usually following a tip-off or escape attempt. But I knew from my own period inside just how much contraband of one kind or another is successfully concealed and passed around in prison.

Seán describes the escape plan accurately and in detail in his book – and of course the event itself was extensively publicized at the time and has been analysed in many subsequent books and reports. For completeness I again summarize it here.

It is simplest to describe first the position and lay-out of the prison. Wormwood Scrubs consists of four oblong cell blocks A, B, C and D inside a compound, running parallel to each other with the narrow ends to the north and south. A twenty-foot high perimeter wall encloses the compound. To the north, at the back, lies Wormwood Scrubs Common; to the south – where the Forecourt, Main Entrance, Administrative Block and staff accommodation are located – is Du Cane Road. D Block is on the extreme right as you face the prison from Du Cane Road, parallel to the eastern perimeter wall. This wall runs alongside a narrow cul-de-sac, Artillery Road. Farther to the right, as you face the prison from the road, lies Hammersmith Hospital, fronted by a large visitors' car park.

Two features of the cell blocks are the twin towers at either end of the buildings, enclosing large gothic windows which provide the daylight for the halls. The windows start at the level of the second floor landing and extend to a point near the roof. (Confusingly, perhaps, this landing is referred to as 'the threes' – the ground floor being designated 'the ones'.) From 'the threes' landing George would make his exit through the gothic window at the south end of D Hall.

The windows are divided by cast-iron struts into panes eighteen inches high by six inches wide. Removing two panes of glass and one of the struts would provide an aperture twelve inches by eighteen, just large enough for a man of George's slight build to squeeze through. He had in fact made a wooden frame of that size in his cell and practised getting through it. Whether the frame was ever spotted in his cell, I don't know. But even if it had been, its significance might still not have been realized.

Immediately below the window is a door out of the wing with a pointed arch above it reaching the very spot on the threes where George would be making his exit. Once out of the window he could slide down the porch onto the roof of a covered passage that leads to the adjoining C Wing, and drop down into the yard below.

The escape was timed to take place between 6 p.m. and 7 p.m. on a Saturday evening when most of the inmates and staff would be at the weekly film show in the theatre adjoining the wing. There would be at the most two screws on duty in D Hall itself. As a rule they watched television on the ground floor at the extreme south end of the block. And because of the way the landings jut out from the

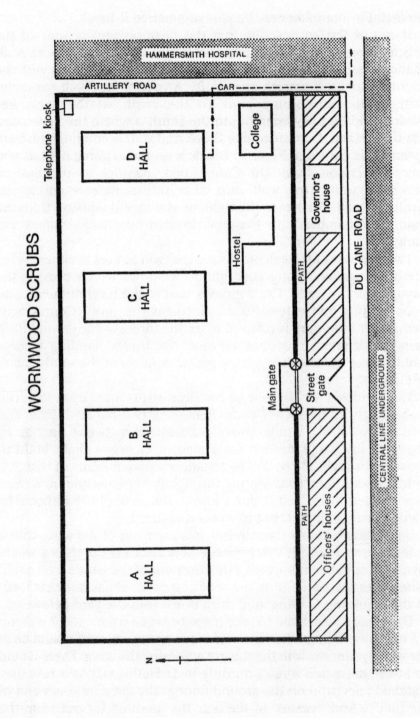

walls, their line of vision to the south window, and to anyone on that part of the landing, would be blocked.

Seán was to throw the rope over the eastern perimeter wall (which runs parallel to D Wing) at the point corresponding to the south end of the wing; it was easy to identify the spot because of the turrets that towered above it. He would park the getaway car on Artillery Road alongside the prison wall facing outwards towards Du Cane Road. Once George was safely over the wall, they would drive to the end of Artillery Road, turn left into Du Cane Road and away from the main entrance of the prison.

We knew that there were security patrols which went round the perimeter walls on the inside. However, Seán and George reckoned that the patrols passed any given point along the wall every twenty minutes or so which would allow enough time between one appearance and the next for the escape to be completed.

A more serious threat came from the watchman posted permanently at the corner formed by the eastern and northern perimeter walls. During the planning of the escape, we always assumed that the watchman and night-patrols were regular prison officers assigned this task. The Mountbatten Report, however, indicates that this was not the case, describing them as 'untrained watchmen', and recommending that wherever modern electronic devices were installed, regular prison officers should undertake night duty.[2] The watchman would be in a position to see the ladder coming over the wall and could dash to the wing to raise the alarm and then try to intercept George himself. However, George had some advantages. He could hide at the end of the wing until the ladder was thrown over the wall; he would know exactly when it was coming; and he would be only fifteen yards or so away from it, whereas the watchman would be about a hundred yards away.

Once the alarm was raised we expected a search party to set out within a few minutes. It was important, therefore, to work out the time it would take for a patrol setting out from the main gate of the prison on Du Cane Road to reach the point on Artillery Road where Seán and George would be attempting to complete their getaway by car.

To settle this point Seán took up jogging around the outside perimeter wall, timing every leg of the run with a stop-watch. He was still on the hostel scheme at this point and told the screws he wanted to get properly fit before being discharged. By his reckoning it would take them two to three minutes to reach Artillery Road from the main gate, and one could certainly double that to allow for the initial confusion and getting the patrol organized. Seán and George would not have much leeway, but if there were no hitches they should be able to drive into Du Cane Road and probably be some way along it before any patrol even started out.

Such then was the plan which had been decided upon by early summer and which would, with some refinements, be put into effect on the day of the escape.

Once I had finished my exams, I started to think seriously about raising money for the escape. In early July I obtained an initial sum of £200 from a personal friend. He paid me in cash, but to prevent any possibility of the money being traced back I went round a succession of banks in Central London exchanging £30 or £40 at a time for smaller notes before handing over the money to Seán. Some of the banks displayed notices apologizing for having to give customers used notes!

Seán was released on Monday 4 July and moved into a flat in Perryn Road not far from the prison. According to his account I handed over an initial £100 to him on 24 July which he used to buy a second-hand car costing £65, and other tools and equipment. The car was a 1956 two-tone Humber Hawk, registration number 117 GMX. He and George agreed that the tools needed for breaking out of the wing should not be smuggled into the prison until nearer the time in order to minimize the risk of discovery.

In August the pace quickened. I was now meeting Seán regularly, and at one of these meetings he told me that he and George had decided to bring forward the date of the escape. There were several reasons for this. On 6 June there had been a break-out by six prisoners from D Hall. They had sawn through the bars of a cell on the ground floor – 'the ones' – and stuck them together temporarily with glue. On the night of the escape they had climbed through the cell window and used a rope with an attached home-made hook to scale the eastern perimeter wall, the very wall that Blake planned to scale on his escape.

As a result of the escape, the prison had been visited by the Home Secretary, Roy Jenkins, on 7 June. It emerged later in the Mountbatten Report that the authorities had received prior warning about the escape but had not taken it seriously. The report also states that the Home Secretary directed that the physical security of Wormwood Scrubs prison and others should be studied urgently by the Prison

Department's Security Working Party. This study was undertaken and 'schemes prepared for improving wall patrolling at Wormwood Scrubs, Wakefield, Maidstone and Leicester Prisons; for the manning of the observation towers at Wormwood Scrubs during daylight by officers with VHF walkie-talkie sets, and for television coverage of the wall with powerful illumination at night'.[3] A night watchman shelter was put up immediately on the perimeter, later linked by telephone to the main office. Luckily, we did not know any of this at the time!

George feared that this demonstration of the weakness in the Scrubs' security system would lead the governor to recommend his transfer to another prison. The Mountbatten Report shows that the Governor had recommended George's transfer to a more secure prison in January 1966 but that this had not been acted upon.[4] On several other occasions, too, according to the Report, the question of transferring Blake had been considered. Mountbatten himself concluded that there were four occasions when he should have been moved: in November 1961 when the Security Services completed their interrogation of him and themselves recommended his transfer to Winson Green prison in Birmingham; in May 1964 when he was reported to have used a discharged prisoner to contact someone on the outside; in January 1966 when he was one of three prisoners the governor of Wormwood Scrubs had recommended for transfer to a more secure prison; and finally in June 1966 after the escape of the six prisoners.[5]

Then on 12 August three policemen were murdered in their squad car in Braybrook Street, just off Wormwood Scrubs Common. Sean thought at first that it might be connected with an attempted break-out – if this proved to be the case the present escape plan would have been abandoned, and the chances of setting up another one would be minimal. Although it was soon established that the murders had nothing to do with any attempted break-out, nevertheless for several days security in the area was intense. Sean had to cancel a planned radio link-up with George the day after the murders and it was with trepidation that he renewed it a week later.

In early August I proposed bringing Pat in on the project. I had considered this when Seán had first approached me about the escape, but had put off suggesting it, partly because Seán himself had sworn us to absolute secrecy. Seán had not met Pat, but when I explained that George had worked with him in the mailbag shop in Wormwood Scrubs, Seán was happy to accept my suggestion.

Greatly relieved, I phoned Pat at his printing works on Tuesday 9 August.

'Pat – look – I need to speak to you urgently but I can't talk to you on the phone. Can you meet me after work?'

Pat seemed to take it in his stride. 'OK,' he replied. 'Shall we say High Holborn tube station at six?'

As we walked out of the station we caught sight of the headline on the newspaper hoardings. It was about one of the wanted Train Robbers, 'Buster' Edwards, who was reported to have been seen earlier in the day near the spot where the robbery had taken place. I nodded towards the hoarding and said that the headline was not entirely unconnected with what I wanted to discuss.

The hint was unnecessary. As soon as I had phoned him, Pat had guessed what it was about. He told his partner, Doug Brewood, that he could think of only one thing that I would be unwilling to discuss with him on the phone – namely, a plan to free George Blake. And he was prepared, even before I met him, to help.

We asked ourselves frequently why it was that we both agreed so readily to help? Our immediate response was spontaneous though rooted in our own experience of prison life and political activity.

Motives are never entirely straightforward. Our first-hand experience of prison life had given us some insight of what the prospect of twenty-eight years in prison would mean. And there was a certain appeal in the idea of helping to free a prisoner serving the longest sentence ever imposed by a British court. Nevertheless, we would not have agreed to become involved if it were not for the conviction that that sentence was fundamentally unjust, and that helping him was the decent human response.

When Pat had first broached the topic in 1962 I was considerably more doubtful about it – though sympathetic in principle to helping George escape. Yet in 1966, when in many ways less well placed personally to do so, I had agreed. What had changed in the meantime?

First, the plan itself was more concrete. Pat's brief exchange with Blake had resulted in no more than the germ of an idea which we would have had to take the initiative in developing. Seán had come with a fully developed plan which, with or without our help, he was determined to put into effect. It was also to be an entirely unprofessional – almost one could say a DIY – affair without any involvement of the Russians or anyone else.

Second, since the role Anne and I were initially being asked to play was a secondary and supportive one we were not confronted at the outset with all the implications of our decision. Only as the venture developed did we become increasingly drawn into the planning and, in its second phase, the execution of the escape.

Finally, part of my hesitation in 1962 concerned the possible repercussions on the peace movement if two prominent activists in the direct-action wing of the campaign were convicted of plotting the escape of a man serving a prison sentence for spying for the Soviet Union. This objection would of course have applied most strongly if, as Blake had initially proposed to Pat, we had tried to involve the Soviet Embassy in the plot. (Pat, however, had ruled out that part of Blake's plan from the outset.)

But by 1966 the nuclear disarmament movement was a shadow of what it had been in the late 1950s and early 1960s, and the Committee of 100 could no longer claim to be in any sense a mass movement. More importantly, many of us in the movement had become deeply estranged from US and Western policies not only because of nuclear weapons but because of the US war in Vietnam – and the shameful silence about that war in Britain. We remained non-aligned in the East–West confrontation, but with a far more acute sense of the ambiguous or downright indefensible aspects of post-war Western policies.

The direct-action wing of the movement now tended to concentrate on smaller-scale, more daring and sometimes more clandestine actions, such as the 'Spies for Peace' episode in Easter 1963. This was undertaken anonymously by people close to the Committee of 100 and involved a clandestine raid on a secret underground bunker in Berkshire. Extracts from documents taken from the bunker were duplicated by the group and sent to all the national newspapers and journals, revealing for the first time the existence of a network of underground shelters which would serve as Regional Seats of Government in the event of nuclear war.

I was not personally involved with the operation and knew nothing about it in advance, but helped to draft an editorial for *Peace News* headed 'The Spies were Right'.[6] The authorities attempted to prevent that issue of *Peace News* from being distributed and warned that the editor and staff, and anyone handling the paper, could face prosecution under the Official Secrets Act. The paper's editor then appeared on television and said that he stood by the editorial and would be willing, if necessary, to go to prison for it. I have always felt that this was a turning point in the affair. His quiet but firm stance took the fervour out of the spy hunt that had followed the revelations.

However, even the Spies for Peace episode would not have the same repercussions as helping to free a British agent who had decided to spy for the Soviet Union. We knew that if our involvement was uncovered the media might use the occasion to throw mud not only at us personally but at the peace movement as a whole. They would imply that our first loyalty was to the Soviet Union or that, at best, we were Soviet dupes.

It was – and remains – important for us and for the peace movement as a whole to establish their independence of the Soviet Union – or for that matter of any state. But we also feel it is important not to run away from moral and human challenges out of fear of what the movement's detractors may try to make of it. That way lies endless retreat.

All four of us – Seán, Pat, Anne and I – met at our house in Kentish Town soon after I first contacted Pat about the escape. Seán took us through the plan step by step. It had now been elaborated and certain details changed. The cast-iron support on the gothic window was to be broken several days before the escape and taped back into position with black masking tape. The two panes of glass would also be smashed and removed in advance. The technique is simple and widely known. Tape or sticky paper is stuck to the pane to be broken so that when the blow is struck not only is the sound deadened but the splinters of glass are held by the tape rather than flying in all directions. Blake had a 'technical assistant' inside the prison to do this job and break the cast-iron support. Fortunately, there were already quite a few missing panes, so that the absence of another two was unlikely to be noticed. Seán had made arrangements to smuggle in a car jack to George so that his technical assistant could break the cast-iron strut quietly and efficiently without attracting the attention of the duty officer.

On the night itself George would watch television for a while with the screws on duty, and announce that he was going back to his cell to do some reading. The break-out would begin as soon after six o'clock as possible once George had received the message from Seán on the two-way radio that he was parked outside the prison wall ready to go into action.

Narrated by Pat Pottle

Hearing for the first time from Seán the preparations for the break reminded me of occasions sitting in the Nissen Hut at Ford Open Prison with twenty-four other prisoners, and listening to the stories of various 'jobs' they had done. Their present predicament was – if you could believe them – only a minor hiccup in an otherwise successful career. They all talked of the thousands they had stashed away from previous 'jobs' – even the ones in for robbing gas meters! When one questioned them closely about the way they organized their 'jobs' it soon became clear that no matter how clever the swindle or fraud or burglary, there was always some basic flaw which meant they were bound to get caught.

I was determined that if I was to get involved with the break it should not fail because of silly and obvious mistakes. If this meant being over-cautious, so be it. In my short time as a prisoner it was clear that the place was full of people who would lie in their bunks at night saying 'If only . . .' If we were to be caught it should not be the result of inadequate planning.

Michael's telephone call suggesting a meeting had come out of the blue at a time when I had put out of my head any further thought of trying to free Blake. After leaving prison towards the end of January 1963 I had started working almost immediately as one of Bertrand Russell's secretaries. I had mentioned the discussions with Blake about an escape to one or two people – not with any serious intention of doing anything about it, but, I'm ashamed to say, more as a conversation piece. I said nothing about it at any point to Russell himself.

While working for Lord Russell, I was approached by the Spies for Peace group who told me about the break-ins they had made at secret Regional Seats of Government (RSGs). They asked me if Russell would be prepared to donate £100 for a pamphlet about the RSGs and the government's draconian plans in the event of war. This was to be distributed on the Aldermaston march and simultaneously to the national press and media. Russell agreed, and I handed over £100 in cash to them in a pub in Sloane Square.

I mention this, because soon after I left Russell's employment in 1964 I contacted the Spies for Peace group and told them of my proposal for Blake's escape – this had been a more serious attempt to get something done. The group, though not hostile, stressed the practical difficulties. They pointed out that two years had now passed since my conversations with George, and that we had no way of knowing if the same prison routine was still in operation. Given that, and the fact that we couldn't contact George, the plan was pretty hopeless. This I accepted – I think even possibly welcomed – and I made no further effort on George's behalf.

Now, listening to Seán's outline of the proposed break, I was impressed. Clearly he and George had done a lot of preliminary work, including setting up a network of helpers on the inside. What impressed me most was Seán's touch of genius in smuggling in the two-way radios. But almost everything about the plans for the actual break-out from prison seemed professionally arranged.

Everything, that is, apart from one thing – the fact that the getaway Humber car that had been bought was registered in Seán's own name. Michael told me afterwards that he had understood that Seán would delay sending off the registration documents so that the ownership of the car would not be traced to him, but it was soon clear that Seán had not followed this plan. Perhaps this was because he thought the precaution unnecessary, perhaps because the person he bought the car from insisted that the change of ownership should be registered. (A third possibility, which did not occur to us till much later, was that Seán really wanted concrete evidence to fall into the hands of the police that it was he who had organized the break.)

The simplest solution to the problem of obtaining an untraceable getaway car would have been to steal one on the night – provided Seán wore gloves there would then be nothing to link the vehicle with him. But we ruled that out straight away. It would involve an injury to an unknown and innocent individual, and although we were prepared to break the law and to risk imprisonment we were determined that innocent third parties should not be made to suffer. Equally, we insisted that we would have nothing to do with the break if there was any question of weapons being used, and we received absolute assurance from Seán on this point.

However, the crucial weakness in the plan related to its second phase – i.e. the period after the break-out from the prison itself. What, in short, was to be done about hiding George and getting him safely out of the country once he had scaled the prison wall? In contrast to the detailed plans for the actual escape Seán had only the vaguest idea of what came after it.

It was this gap that had most worried George's mother and sister when Seán had approached them, at George's suggestion, to ask them for money for the operation. Seán had assured them that

George could lie low for a while and that he could provide him with a forged passport through underworld contacts so that he could slip out of the country when the excitement had died down. In his book Seán records the response of George's sister Adele as follows:

> There are a number of things I would require [before agreeing to help] . . . I would want to inspect the accommodation where you intend hiding George after the escape. I would want to see the passport. I would want precise details of how you intended getting George out of the country and I would want to be satisfied that these arrangements were fool-proof . . .[7]

Seán was, of course in a Catch-22 situation. He would have been running a serious risk to have approached any contacts about forging a passport for George until the latter was out of prison – and even then he could only do so if he first had the funds; yet George's mother and sister were unwilling to come up with the money until they had the evidence of the passport to reassure them. Nevertheless, they had accurately diagnosed the weak spot in the overall plan.

What surprised me was that George himself had not given more thought to this problem. He would never be permitted two shots at escaping, so he needed to be sure that the first one would succeed. Yet here he was putting his faith completely in Seán, without any clear idea of what would happen once he was over the wall. Even allowing for his desperation, this was an enormous gamble.

As Michael and myself became more deeply involved, it was this second phase of the escape that chiefly occupied our attention and for which eventually we were to take over full responsibility.

Narrated by Michael Randle
Going back to the break itself, one point we raised that evening was the design of the rope ladder. Seán proposed making the rungs as well as the uprights of rope. But this would make scaling the twenty-foot wall quite an athletic feat, and after four and a half years in prison George was not all that fit, yoga or no yoga. As he stepped on one rung it would drag the two vertical ropes closer together, increasing the difficulty of getting a foothold on the next rung. At best progress would be slow and difficult, and the chances of discovery would be greatly increased. Seán had considered making the rungs of wood. But that, he decided, would have made

the ladder both heavy and noisy. He might have had difficulty in throwing it over the wall, and, even if he had succeeded in doing so, it would have made a great clatter as it banged against the far side.

The suggestion of using knitting needles was probably our single most important contribution to the planning of the actual break-out. We proposed size 13 needles which would be strong enough to take a man's weight but nevertheless very light. We had one other idea which Seán did not follow up. The rope ladder proper would be twenty foot long – i.e. long enough to reach from the top of the prison wall to the ground on the inside; it would be attached to a simple rope which Seán would hold on to to take the strain as George climbed up. Our suggestion was that at the point at which the rope ladder proper was attached to this rope there should be a hook which George could place on the coping stone on the top of the wall so that he could lower himself down by the rope at least part of the way, and not have to jump the whole twenty foot into Artillery Road. Perhaps Seán decided that the idea was not practicable and that the hook might foul the rungs of the ladder as he attempted to throw it. However, my initial understanding was that he had incorporated this idea in the design of the ladder.

On 29 August (according to Seán's own account), about two weeks after this first full planning meeting, Seán went to a haberdashery in West London and to the amazement of the woman behind the counter ordered thirty steel knitting needles size 13. It had never occurred to us that he would try to get all the needles at once in the one shop! He bluffed his way out of the difficulty by claiming he needed them for working with avant-garde art students. The lengths of rope he bought from Woolworths.

We spent most time that evening considering the second phase of the operation – hiding George and getting him out of the country after the escape. We were tempted to go for a quick exit and we discussed the possibility of his travelling to Dublin on the night of the escape either in disguise or hidden in a vehicle. In Ireland there would be less risk of discovery, and if he should be arrested, he would be able to plead that his offence was a political one and that he should therefore not be deported to Britain. Meanwhile, Seán could arrange to get him a forged passport so that he could fly from Dublin or Shannon airport to some neutral country. Seán was the keenest about using Ireland as an exit route, because there was no passport control on the crossing from England, and normally no stringent security checks. He also had rather more confidence than either Pat or myself that George could successfully fight extradition if arrested.

Another possibility was to hide George in the boot of a car with a specially constructed false bottom and for me to take it on a cross-channel ferry the evening of the escape and drive to Hungary, Czechoslovakia or East Germany.

The obvious drawback to leaving the country on the evening of the escape was that all sea and air ports would be closely watched. George himself, when Seán put the proposition to him, was adamant that no such attempt should be made on the night of the escape or for some time afterwards. It was crucial, he felt, that he should lie low for a time – this made it all the more urgent to find him a safe hide-out in London.

In previous discussions, I had said that George could stay with me if nowhere better could be found. But this was very much a last resort. The fact that I had known George in prison and that we had attended several classes together would almost certainly come to light once inquiries began. Moreover, I had regularly sent him a Christmas card since my release and knew that the names of everyone corresponding with a prisoner are listed by the prison authorities. (Indeed, according to the Mountbatten Report, special arrangements were made for all Blake's incoming and outgoing correspondence to be sent to the Security Services for scrutiny.)[8] There was also the item in *Peace News* in 1963 mentioning my connection with George which might have been picked up by Scotland Yard or Special Branch (as it had been by one journalist at the time). Finally, Seán and I had corresponded while he was still inside, so if he came under suspicion, so might I.

Pat also offered to hide George. But though the authorities would have less reason to link the two of them, and though he had not even met Seán in prison, this was still far from ideal. If the police were to question me, and began to suspect a connection with Committee of 100 activists, they would almost certainly go on to question or search the homes of the five Committee of 100 people who had been in prison in 1962 over the Wethersfield demonstration.

A third possibility was for George to stay with Seán. This would mean our role could be closer to the one Seán had originally asked us to play – namely, to provide funds and talk through the escape plans with him. But in many ways Seán was the least suitable person for George to lodge with – he had only recently been released from Wormwood Scrubs, and his friendship with George would certainly have been noted by the prison authorities.

Seán's name, moreover, had been publicly linked with Blake's in July 1965, following an article in the *Daily Sketch* commenting on an issue of the prison journal *New Horizon* which Seán edited. This contained an editorial written by Seán entitled 'The Morality of Spying'. According to the *Daily Sketch* report the editorial read in part:

> After all what is a spy but a soldier in civilian dress? It is both desirable and inevitable that the spy should be ruthlessly hunted down. But one thing we should all be spared is the hypocritical facade of righteous indignation.
>
> Every intelligent man will realize that the angry politicians who decry the activities of the spy in the morning, will, in the afternoon, calmly vote a million pounds to their own espionage service – to be used partly for procuring foreign citizens to betray their own countries.[9]

The July issue of *New Horizon*, according to the *Daily Sketch*, carried several letters commenting on the editorial and an article attacking religion entitled 'Knaves and Fools' by George Blake. In fact the original by-line had attributed the article to 'The Humanist Group' and Seán had complained about the *Daily Sketch* report to the Press Council, which subsequently upheld the complaint. We learned about it from Seán himself, but it is referred to also in the Mountbatten Report which disclosed the fact that the copy of *New Horizon* received by the *Daily Sketch* had been doctored so that the 'Knaves and Fools' article was attributed to George Blake.[10] Given this publicity and Seán's known friendship with Blake, the likelihood was that he would be a prime suspect – perhaps *the* prime suspect – once the escape was discovered. What we really needed was a hide-out where there would be no links at all with George, and thus nothing to put the police on his trail.

Over the next few weeks, Seán, Pat and myself met regularly, sometimes at Torriano Cottages, more often at Pat's flat at Willow Buildings, Hampstead. Little by little we formulated a plan for providing George with a hide-out. This involved George staying with Seán but only after elaborate precautions had been taken to throw the police off his track.

First, Seán would sell the Humber car and buy another one. He would again pay for it in cash, but this time would register it under a false name and address. Thus, if the car was spotted during the break-out, or was identified afterwards, there would be nothing to trace it beyond the previous owner.

Next, Seán would quit his job, give up his flat in Perryn Road, and let it be known amongst friends and workmates that he had decided to leave England for good and settle in his native Ireland. In fact, he would move in with Pat while he located a suitable flat not too far from the prison. He would rent this under the assumed name of Michael Sigsworth – a name he chose himself – and give his occupation as that of journalist. Once the flat had been found, he would fly to Limerick, stay there with his mother for a week or so and generally make his presence known. Finally, after claiming that he was going to Dublin to find work and lodgings, he would fly back to Britain – using yet another alias when buying the ticket. If everything went according to plan Seán, alias Michael Sigsworth, would have a safe base in London which would also provide a hide-out for George.

Should the police later attempt to trace Seán's movements, their investigations would lead down a blind alley to Limerick and Dublin.

We do not have an independent note of the exact dates when Seán began to put this plan into effect, and rely here on his own record of dates and times. Some of these – such as the date he first rented the bedsit where Blake was taken after the escape – are corroborated by press reports that appeared within two or three months of the escape. According to his account, the four of us met on 4 September and finally fixed the date of the escape for 22 October. No doubt it was at this meeting that the plan for him to sell the car and travel to Ireland was worked out, for Seán notes that it was then that Pat offered to have him stay with him as soon as he left Perryn Road and before he travelled to Ireland. Seán gave notice at work and at Perryn Road on 9 September and moved into Pat's flat two week's later on 23 September.

Meanwhile he continued to maintain radio contact with George. From early August onward he had conducted these conversations in the greater comfort and safety of the Humber car. Parking the car in the forecourt of Hammersmith hospital, he would conceal the walkie-talkie in a bunch of chrysanthemums, and pose as a visitor about to see a sick friend or relative in the hospital.

At one of our evening meetings he announced that he had something to show us. He produced a portable tape recorder and switched it on. First came Seán's voice.

'This is Fox Michael calling Baker Charlie, Fox Michael calling Baker Charlie. Come in, please. Over.'

There was a pause and crackling, then George responded. His voice was much less distinct, but there was no mistaking the precise, clipped enunciation, the somewhat guttural vowels.

'This is Baker Charlie calling Fox Michael, Baker Charlie calling Fox Michael. Can you hear me? Come in please.'

'Stone walls do not a prison make

Nor iron bars a cage. Over.'

'Minds innocent and quiet take this for a hermitage. Over.'

'Richard Lovelace must have been a fool. Over.'

'Or maybe just a dreamer.'

We already knew this was the call sequence. However, hearing it – and the subsequent discussion – on tape like this brought the whole venture out of the realm of fantasy. In just a few weeks' time the escape we had been so feverishly planning really would take place! The idea of making the recordings, like that of communicating by two-way radio in the first place, was an inspiration for it meant we could eavesdrop on the discussions and hear at first hand George's reactions to details of the plan. Perhaps even at that stage Seán was looking ahead to the time he would be writing about these events.

Seán had in fact been recording his conversations with George from the start, but had not told us this. He must have sent the tapes of these early discussions to a friend or relative, or perhaps left them with someone in Ireland during his visit in October, because the first time we knew of their existence was when the *News of the World* published some of the transcripts in January 1969.

Seán had worked out the call sequence. Fox Michael was the code for the letters F.M. and stood for Finn McCumhaill, the legendary Irish giant and leader of the original Fenians; Baker Charlie was the code for B.C and stood for Finn's lieutenant Baldy Cannan. The verse was from Richard Lovelace, the seventeenth-century poet whom Seán and George had studied on their literature course in the prison. Such, in the penal context, are the uses of literacy.

There were, however, setbacks. In mid-September Seán learned that two prisoners had been caught trying to saw through one of the cast-iron supports in the south facing window of D Hall – the same window George would be using. Their attempt was foiled, but when

Seán next made contact with George on 17 September he learned that metal grids were being put on the outside of the windows of all the wings. Grills had already been fitted to A and B wings (the young offenders' wing) and C Wing (the wing for short-term offenders where Pat and I had been held); even allowing for the inefficiency of the prison works office it was scarcely credible that D Hall would not be protected by the proposed escape date. George therefore asked for wire cutters to be smuggled in to deal with the metal grid, in addition to the jack which Seán had already agreed to get to him. But we decided to leave this until shortly before the escape so that there would be fewer things to conceal.

The logical thing, of course would have been to have fitted the grilles first to the long-term D Wing. But this, as Seán remarked at the time, would have been too much of an affront to the bureaucratic mind.

It was around this time that we discovered an apparent flaw in the escape plan. Seán had explained to us that two patrols went round the perimeter fence inside the prison throughout the night in opposite directions. According to their observations the patrols would pass any given spot every twenty minutes, giving Seán and George ample time after a patrol had passed the agreed spot to effect the escape. I had left Pat's flat late one evening after we had once again gone through all the plans, and was waiting for a tube at Hampstead Underground when something began to trouble me about the patrols.

Suddenly I realized what it was. If they were moving in opposite directions, the length of time that elapsed between a patrol arriving from one direction and one coming from the opposite direction would vary at different points along the perimeter fence. At the two points at which the patrols converged and crossed, the interval would in effect be zero, though once they had started moving away from the point there would be the maximum interval before the two patrols crossed there again. Only at the two points where the patrols were at the maximum distance from each other and were about to start converging would the intervals be regular. Those intervals might indeed be of twenty minutes but unless Seán and George had timed the patrols passing at, or very close to, the point where the ladder would come across, their calculations could be completely out.

I hurried back to Pat's. Luckily Seán was still there.

'Hello – what have you left behind this time?' Pat joked. (I am notoriously forgetful and always leaving things behind when I go anywhere.)

'No, no, it's not that! I've discovered a flaw in the plan.'

We sat down again at the table and I drew a sketch to illustrate the problem. We looked at one another thinking how dumb we had all been and then Pat said:

'Of course! It's so obvious! How the hell did none of us think of it before?

'There's no serious problem,' Seán said after mulling over the issue for a few minutes. 'I can easily smuggle in a stop-watch along with the other tools' and get him to re-time the patrols. I'll talk to George about it when we next make contact.'

Surprisingly George seemed quite unable to grasp the problem. When, a day or two later, Seán brought us the recording of the conversation in which he had told George that he would be smuggling in a stop-watch and wanted him to re-time the patrols, it showed that George was completely baffled.

'I thought we'd been through all this, Fox Michael,' he said. 'I really don't see the point of the stop-watch.'

Seán did smuggle him in a stop-watch – or at any rate told us he had – but my hunch *is* that because George saw no point in it, the patrols were not re-timed.

Money continued to be a headache. Pat, Anne and I went through lists of friends but most had little or no money and could be ruled out straight away; others we eliminated because we thought they would not support the venture. There was never any question of involving any peace or political organization as such, nor, despite the rumours that circulated after the publication of Mr Montgomery Hyde's book in 1987,[11] did we in fact receive monetary or other support from prominent CND or Committee of 100 members. Pat and I did approach two or three people in all, either singly or together. None wanted to have anything to do with it. One said sharply that he never wanted to hear the topic raised again in his presence.

In retrospect, it is easy to understand why the people we approached acted in this way. For those who had never met George he must have appeared as an unknown and sinister figure, convicted of spying for a totalitarian state, and serving a very long prison sentence. Some were also concerned at the possible effect of Pat's and my involvement on the peace movement if our role was ever discovered.

Even more worrying than the refusals was the fact that every individual we approached was one more who knew what was afoot. We were terrified that the plan would leak out through a careless remark and decided for the time being not to approach anyone else. The essential equipment, including the car, had already been bought with the money I had raised earlier and enough was left over to cover some of the ongoing expenses. For the moment, the operation would have to go forward on a shoe-string with all of us pooling our limited resources.

The solution to the money difficulties came quite unexpectedly. A young woman, Bridget, who was a good friend of ours approached me one day to say she had inherited some money and wished to donate it to a deserving cause; as a socialist, she did not believe in inherited wealth. Could I suggest a suitable project or organization where the money would be put to good use?

I did not immediately suggest the project we were engaged upon, or even tell her about it, though I knew we could rely upon her absolute discretion. None of us can remember for sure whether we told her what we were planning before the escape, or waited until after it had happened. We do know that we didn't receive the money from her until some three weeks afterwards.

It was a piece of extraordinary coincidence that Bridget approached me about disposing of her inheritance when she did. But the coincidence is not quite as strange as it first appears, given that we moved in political circles where people who came into any money would be likely to consider how it could be put to good use. To protect her, we are not able to reveal her real name or give any details about her beyond saying that she had been a family friend for some years – and that she is not Vanessa Redgrave! But we do want to record that without her generosity and unselfish support, the project might well have ended in failure.

As the day of the escape drew closer we spent more and more time trying to figure out the best way of getting George out of the country. The idea of hiding him in a car boot with a false bottom was reconsidered and rejected – none of us had the skills in metalwork to manufacture the false bottom and we could not start touting around for someone else to do the job. We were not convinced either that it could be done successfully – half the available boot space or more would have to be used up, even in the case of a car with quite a large boot, and unless the design was very ingenious the alteration would hardly escape even the most casual of inspections.

Seán remained confident that he could obtain a false passport from his underworld contacts. If George lay low for a while and travelled in disguise to Ireland, he ought not to have too much difficulty flying on from Dublin or Shannon. But the success of this plan rested not only on finding a safe house but also on providing George with a convincing disguise.

We did at one point consider theatrical make-up and I even paid a visit to a friend, Chris, who was involved in the production side of a play in the West End. He was more than a little surprised when I told him we were planning to break someone out of prison and wanted advice on how to provide him with a convincing disguise! (I did not tell him who the person was.) He wasn't quite sure at first whether or not to take me seriously, but in any case he couldn't help; theatrical make-up was something he knew very little about.

So we abandoned this idea. It would be galling indeed if all the planning that had gone into getting George over the prison wall was to be cancelled out because of a bungled attempt at disguise. Grease paint, false beards and moustaches were probably the very things that Customs and immigration officers were trained to spot. If George was to be disguised, we had to come up with something better than that.

We eventually hit upon a novel solution – we would turn him black!

The idea came to me when I recalled a review I had read of a book called *Black Like Me* by an American writer, John Howard Griffen.[12] It tells the true story of how a liberal white American had taken drugs and a course of treatment to change his colour pigmentation temporarily so that he could experience at first hand the discrimination and humiliation faced by blacks in the USA.

I talked first to Pat about the idea. He was highly enthusiastic. As he recalls, the idea hit him 'like a sledgehammer'. He knew all about the book, which had been serialized in a national newspaper, and was convinced that it would solve at a stroke the huge problem facing us once George was out of prison. Seán too was taken by the notion.

I located the book in the local library. The author did not name the drug, but said it has to be taken orally in conjunction with a course of treatment under an ultra-violet lamp. The treatment is used clinically to treat vitiligo, a disease which causes white spots to appear on the face and body. Normally it would take six weeks to three months to darken the skin pigmentation to the necessary degree, but Griffen took larger doses to accelerate the process, and in only a week he was able, with the addition of stain, to pass himself off as black. Thereafter the pigmentation continued to darken while the treatment continued.

Griffen points out, however, that the drug can attack the liver. He himself had regular blood tests during the treatment to make sure his health was not being impaired. It was clear therefore that if we were to pursue this option seriously we would need medical advice – first to find out the name of the drug, second to get information about dosages and a safe course of treatment.

Pat made an appointment for us both to see a doctor friend of ours. We explained to him first that the issue was highly confidential. He nodded to the phone to warn us it was probably bugged (he too was involved in the Peace Movement) and then to the electric light bulb in the ceiling, which apparently was also suspect. We then trooped out into the garden to continue the conversation.

Once safely outside, we explained that we wanted to use the drug and course of treatment described in *Black Like Me*. We gave him no more details than that, nor did he ask. He knew our political record, and the idea itself appealed to him greatly. He promised to make inquiries among his colleagues and to have the information we wanted within a few days.

The day we returned it was wet and cold, so the traipse round the garden wasn't much fun. However, he had done his homework and was able to give us all the information we required. The drug in question was meladinin, and he advised us on dosages and the time the patient would need to spend each day under the ultra-violet lamp. The principal difficulty was that we would need a prescription or doctor's note to obtain the drug. He did not want to risk providing us with one since if it came to light he could be struck off the medical register. However, he was prepared to show us how to write the formula for any given quantity of the drug in case we wanted to write out our own prescription. Finally, he warned us again about the serious hazards to the patient if the treatment was not properly monitored.

We decided to forge a doctor's note. Seán and I would then make a shopping expedition a few days before the break to buy the meladinin and the ultra-violet lamp. Pat printed the letterhead, inventing a fictitious name, address and telephone number. He used letterpress rather than litho to give a more impressive finish, and he chose a stylish typeface and quality paper. And although the address was non-existent, it was non-existent in the smartest district – Harley Street, in fact.

Pat took elaborate precautions when printing the letterheads. He bought a packet of quality paper of a kind he did not stock himself and wore surgical gloves to avoid leaving any tell-tale fingerprints – we had read reports that the fingerprints of Buster Edwards, the train robber, had been found on a newspaper at their farm hideout. He counted out twenty sheets and put the figures one to twenty on the top one, crossing out a number each time a sheet went through as he adjusted the inking and impression. When he had twelve good copies he made sure all the sheets had been accounted for, and burnt the unwanted proofs, together with the remainder of the packet. He then stripped down the machine bed where any impression could have been left and burnt it. He also broke the type down and destroyed not only the letters used in the printing but all the remaining type fount in case any flaws in the characters were repeated.

By this time Seán had moved in with Pat who tells below what it was like living with him, and of his growing suspicion that Seán had departed in one crucial respect from the agreed plan.

Narrated by Pat Pottle
Seán moved into my flat in Willow Buildings, Hampstead on 23 September. We got on well together. He was full of confidence and seemed absolutely fearless. If ever I queried anything or showed any sign of worry he would simply say 'George Blake will be sprung from prison on the 22nd, Patrick, and that's a fact!' His confidence was infectious. Come what may, he was determined to go ahead.

It was during the fortnight he stayed with me that he completed the first stage of smuggling the wirecutters, jack and stop-watch into the prison. According to Seán's own account, George had suggested that they should be hidden in an empty house in the prison forecourt that had formerly been used by the prison chaplain. It was in the process of being renovated by a works party from inside the prison, and George had learned from a member of the party that there was a loose floorboard just by the toilet with a cavity underneath. If Séan could deposit the tools there, the contact on the works' party could pick them up later and bring them into George.

Séan goes on to describe how one night he hid the tools under the floorboard.[13] However, as Michael and I clearly recall, and as the tapes show, George later informed Seán that their contact had found the wire-cutters and the handle of the jack in the hiding-place, but not the jack itself. This is hard to explain if Seán had placed it there himself. It seems more likely that he gave all the tools to someone on the hostel and that this person failed for some reason to put the jack in the hiding place with the other tools.

Interestingly, in his book Seán not only makes no mention of the hiccup over the jack but falsifies the account of his discussion with George over the walkie-talkie about the smuggling in of the tools. Seán's version of the discussion goes as follows:

> 'Well', I said, after we had hurried through the identifying code, 'did the goods arrive?'
>
> 'Yes.' Blake sounded pleased. 'It is as well you sent the cutters because the grids have now been fitted to B and C Halls. With three more weeks to go before the event, our own window simply *must* be fitted with a grid. Over.'[14]

Compare this with the transcript taken directly from the relevant tape on page 93 – a tape that was in Seán's possession from November or December of 1968 after his return to Ireland from the Soviet Union. Moreover, in January 1969 the *News of the World* published extracts from the tapes, including the exchange about the tools.

During the two and a half weeks he was staying with me, Seán tried without success to rent a self-contained flat within a reasonable distance of Wormwood Scrubs. His problem was references. Although he told prospective landlords that he was a freelance journalist who had spent the last ten years in Australia and so was unable to give reference's, they wouldn't buy it – without the references he couldn't have a flat.

He told us that when he approached the landlords and agencies he wore a disguise of a large black beard and plain glass spectacles and used his best English accent. Whether this hid his Irish background I doubt; as my mother would have put it, he had the map of Ireland printed all over his face. Michael and I were also worried that an amateurish disguise might arouse suspicion. But whenever I raised such doubts with Séan he would dismiss them airily.

'Amateur dramatics, Patrick,' he would retort, 'amateur dramatics!'

When Seán left for Ireland on Monday 10 October, he had still not managed to find a flat. This was a major headache for all of us. He was due back the following Saturday, 15 October, which would leave him less than a week to find somewhere. However, he was confident that if he lowered his sights he would be able to find one without much difficulty. None of us were happy about the situation but there was nothing else we could do.

He had had more success, however, in changing the getaway car – or so, at least, it appeared. He told us that he had sold the Humber for a reasonable price and bought a replacement which he was confident would be suitable. As agreed, he had used a false name and address when buying it so there would be no leads to him if and when it was discovered after the break. It was now 'in a garage being serviced'.

This all sounded very reasonable. Yet I remained uneasy. Neither Michael nor myself had seen the new car, and Seán was vague when I asked him about the make and model. Neither could he remember the name of the garage where it was being serviced. I asked to see the log book. That, he told me, was in the car.

After he left for Ireland and I was once again alone in the flat, I thought about his answers. They struck me as having a false ring about them. What was particularly worrying was that on one occasion after we had decided the Humber should be sold he had given me a lift in it and I hadn't taken the precaution of wearing gloves. I was worried that my fingerprints might be on it. Moreover, if Seán had kept the Humber and was planning to use it for the break, the whole trip to Ireland became a farce. We had to assume that the getaway car would be spotted on the night itself, or found soon afterwards, and if it was registered in his name no amount of subterfuge would put the police off his track. But I had no concrete evidence that Seán was lying to us and for the time being I said nothing to Michael about my fears.

Seán returned from Ireland on Saturday 15 October, reflecting that it had been a lovely trip, seeing all his family and friends, even if he had felt guilty telling them he was leaving for Dublin when in fact he was on his way back to England. First thing Monday he would pick up the car and renew the search for the flat.

When he came back to Willow Buildings on Monday evening he was jubilant. He had found a self-contained flat in Highlever Road, not half a mile from the prison and had been to see it with the landlady. She was foreign – German he thought – and lived in a house nearby. He had paid her two weeks in advance and told her he would be moving in the following day.

He had also picked up the new car and had been driving around in it all day. It was ideal for the job, and even more reliable than the Humber. The one disadvantage was that, unlike the Humber, it didn't have a fitted aerial. However, he had bought an aerial that slotted on to the top of the side window and was sure this would work satisfactorily.

It seemed, then, that our two outstanding problems had been solved in a single day. Yet somehow the doubts remained. When I suggested to Seán we should go and look at the car, he said he had parked it in another area of London to prevent anyone seeing it near Willow Buildings. He had also decided, on the same grounds, not to use it for moving his belongings to Highlever Road the following day. Such caution was so out of character for Seán that I became more than ever convinced that he had never sold the Humber. I resolved finally to raise the matter with Michael.

We met at my print shop the following day, but Michael couldn't believe that Seán would deliberately lie to us about the car. Nor could he believe Seán would have gone through the expensive business of creating an alibi which would be rendered useless as soon as the car was discovered after the break. It would mean the trip to Ireland had been a charade, intended to deceive not the police but us.

I had to agree that I had nothing more to go on than a hunch. I also shared Michael's reluctance, just a few days before the break, to accuse Seán of deceiving us when we had no hard evidence. Nevertheless, Michael agreed to raise the matter with Seán when we met that evening at my flat.

Narrated by Michael Randle
When Pat first voiced his suspicion that Seán had held on to the Humber I dismissed it out of hand. It seemed inconceivable that he would put so much at risk by lying to us, and that he would go through with the trip to Ireland, if the Humber was still in his possession. It was true that he had at first been reluctant to part with it, I suppose because he had got used to it and didn't want the trouble of having to sell it and find another. But having agreed to sell it, and having told us he had done so, it had never crossed my

mind to doubt that he was telling us the truth.

In the end I didn't raise the matter with him, for that Tuesday evening brought an unexpected new worry – the missing jack. We listened in silence to the tape Seán produced. After the usual identifying code, Seán begins:

'Well, now, my friend, obviously the first question I have to ask you is this: did you receive the tools and are they suitable? Over.'

'We did *not* receive it. Only the handle was found at the appointed place and the cutters. But not the jack itself. That is the position at the moment. Over.'

There was a long pause. Then Seán came back, sounding deflated:

'Well, this is very regrettable. I'm meeting him again tomorrow night at seven o'clock. That's the earliest I can discover why you haven't had them. Over.'

Again there was a pause. From George's next comment it seemed as if he had not properly heard, or at any rate not fully understood, Seán's response:

'Do you know where he put the jack – because it wasn't with the other stuff?'

Despite this hitch, Seán's recording ends on an optimistic note. 'I hope,' he said, 'in four days time it will be just like the words of the old Irish song: [he sings]

> I'll walk beside you in the world today,
> While dreams and songs and flowers bless your way,
> I'll look into your eyes and hold your hand,
> I'll walk beside you through this golden land.

'Follow that if you can,' Seán concludes triumphantly.

This time there was an even longer silence; George, we think, didn't quite know how to respond. Finally he said:

'I'm looking forward very much to hearing you sing Irish songs very shortly. I don't see any difficulty at all. So come and get it over on Saturday and I hope everything will be all right, because the waiting is getting a little bit nerve racking as it must be for you too.'

It was a flamboyant gesture of Seán's, singing to George over a two-way radio when any moment could bring discovery, and it was further evidence, despite the hitch over the jack, of Seán's unshakable confidence in the success of the project. Listening to the tape, however, he wasn't too happy about the quality of the reproduction. Several times that evening he broke into snatches of the song to show us the tape didn't do him justice!

Although our own confidence was now high, we couldn't help thinking about the consequences for us and our families if we were caught. Even if everything went smoothly on the night itself, and we managed to get George safely out of the country, the security services might discover our involvement in the weeks and months that followed. Pat recalled reading about how a team of plain-clothes detectives had been used to follow Lonsdale and find out who he was meeting. One day a team of detectives would follow him a certain distance and then break off contact; the next an entirely new team would watch out for him at the point at which their colleagues the previous day had stopped. This procedure continued until his destination was discovered, and virtually ensured that he would not suspect he was being followed. If the security services were to investigate the escape with that kind of thoroughness, we had to face up to the fact that their investigations might lead to us.

We went through our reasons for being involved and how we would put them across in the event of an arrest and trial. We decided that if it came to it we would not deny our involvement, or shelter behind a legalistic defence, but would concentrate on the moral and political issues involved.

We also discussed the kind of sentence we could expect if convicted. Seán's researchers had indicated that a five-year sentence was the maximum for assisting an escaped convict. However, we knew that if we were convicted of conspiracy, there was no statutory limit to the sentence that could be imposed and the length was likely to be influenced by the prevailing atmosphere, and the temperament of the trial judge. We could, however, offset the disaster to some degree by writing up the story; this would help to defray the legal costs and provide some minimal support for Anne and the children if I was in prison. It was agreed that Seán would leave the taped discussions between him and George with me before the day of the break so that these could be used to support any written account, whether in the form of a book or newspaper articles.

The last week was mainly taken up with practical details and with a final review of the plans. On Wednesday 20 October Seán bought a set of clothes for George and the following day he bought a second-hand television for the flat in Highlever Road. That evening he gave George a detailed briefing on the procedure to be followed on the night of the escape, and later on we gathered at Pat's flat to listen to it. It was a model of clarity, one which would have done credit to a Squadron Leader about to embark on a mission – or to a Chief Marshall on the eve of an Aldermaston March. We were highly impressed, and our confidence in Seán was fully restored.

The tape began – after the identifying exchange – with a discussion between Seán and George's technical helper inside the prison. The latter said that they still had not received the jack, but that it didn't matter; he had already broken the cast-iron bar with a kick, and had now strapped it back into position with tape as planned. He had also smashed out two panes of glass, using paper and tape to deaden the sound. The wire cutters Seán had provided would not, he said, have been any use – it would have needed bolt-cutters to deal with the metal grid if this had been in position. But again, fortunately, this didn't matter since the grids were still not in position and there was now no possibility of them being erected before the weekend.

George then took back the walkie-talkie and Seán began the briefing:

Seán: On the night of the operation I will drive you to a particular spot. On the way there you'll undergo a change of clothing. [Actually a raincoat and hat to hide George's prison garb.]

I'll hand you three items: a brown envelope, a piece of paper and two keys on a ring. One is a Yale key, one an ordinary key. In the envelope there will be some money for emergency use. [The paper had Anne's and my telephone number on it written in a simple code; each digit of the number was advanced by one.]

When I stop the car I'll name a particular street, a particular house in that street. You will enter this street, walk up to the front door of the house in question with the Yale key, let yourself in through the front door. You must approach the house confidently. You are my guest.

Lock the door behind you. You'll find yourself in a long narrow passage. Walk down to the end of the passage – literally to the end and you'll see a door. You cannot go any further. With the second key you will let yourself into this room. Have you got that?

George   All clear so far. Continue please.

Seán   You will lock the door behind you and lie on the bed and wait for me. If I fail to return that night, you can assume I have been apprehended, in which case the emergency instructions will be carried out. You will stay in the house the night and the following day and leave the following evening. [The arrangement was that if Seán was arrested, George would phone us and he would then stay either with us or Pat].

There will be a wireless set in this room and a television set and you can keep in touch with developments. If you hear an announcement that a man is assisting the police with their inquiries you can take it that man is me. I'll not be assisting them with their inquiries. You'll find on the table in this room an A–Z map of London plus an Underground plan to enable you to find where you have got to go.[15]

George then confirmed that this was all clear. There was always, he concluded, an element of luck in these matters, and they would just have to hope that it would be with them on this occasion.

On Friday afternoon – the day before the escape – Seán and I met in Central London to buy the meladinin and the ultra-violet lamp. I had with me in an envelope the forged doctor's note which Pat had made out and signed with a gloved hand. As far as I remember we ordered three ounces of the drug, though I cannot be sure about this. [The note would not enable us to get the drug on the National Health Service, but we were quite happy to pay for it ourselves.]

From early September I had been doing two or three hours part-time work each day at Princeton College off Red Lion Square, teaching English as a Foreign Language to young adults from various countries. It was agreed that I, rather than Seán, would order the meladinin – we did not want to put him at any risk over a secondary issue when success or failure of the main operation rested on his shoulders.

We went first to a large and prestigious West End chemist that our doctor friend had told us to try. I wore a pair of thin white gloves to avoid leaving fingerprints on the doctor's note. I assumed that the chemist would keep it and feared that if things went disastrously wrong with the escape the meladinin might be discovered in the flat and the chemist shop traced; in that event the doctor's note would certainly be subjected to rigorous forensic examination. I also wore Séan's reading glasses and pork-pie hat as a rudimentary disguise.

Seán waited outside while I entered the shop. This time the attempt ended in an anti-climax. The man behind the counter said he was sorry. That particular branch of the firm couldn't supply meladinin; I would have to go to another branch in Central London.

Seán and I made our way there by tube and I again donned the gloves, hat and glasses and went into the shop. The glasses made me giddy and the shop was a blur as I walked to the counter, I fumbled for the envelope with gloved fingers and handed the doctor's note to the man in the white coat waiting to serve me. He looked at the note and seemed surprised.

'This is a very large dose,' he said, looking at me intently. Then his eyes strayed down to my gloved hands and he added in a more sympathetic tone:

'You've really decided to give this treatment a try, have you?'

I could only nod assent.

He returned five or ten minutes later with the package. To my relief he also handed me back the doctor's note; in the event all our precautions had proved unnecessary.

But if obtaining the meladinin was simpler than we had expected, there was an unexpected complication with the ultra-violet lamp. That too, we discovered, required a prescription or doctor's note, and we did not have a spare forged letterhead with us. Eventually Seán persuaded a chemist at the top end of Tottenham Court Road to let him buy one anyway, promising he would being in the necessary prescription after the weekend. This time I was waiting outside the shop, and Séan handed me the receipt, remarking how simple it had been. Then he whipped the receipt back out of my hand and threw it nonchalantly over his shoulder.

We had a cup of coffee together and I walked with him down to Tottenham Court Road tube station. We were due to meet again that evening at Pat's place for a final review of the plans.

After Seán had left I started to worry about the receipt. Suppose things went wrong and the police located the Highlever Road flat and decided it was important to trace the shop which had sold Seán the lamp? They might issue an appeal for any chemist who had sold a lamp of this kind within the last few days to come forward. Wasn't it then just possible that they would find the crumbled receipt directly outside the shop, a receipt that would have not only Séan's finger prints on it but mine? All this verged on paranoia; Séan would certainly have so regarded it. But then, I argued, why take even the smallest risk when such a simple action could remove it altogether? Thus I walked back past the chemist's shop, scouring the pavement for this scrap of paper. Surprisingly, it was still there. I pocketed it and later burnt it.

That evening we all met for the last time before the escape. Each had brought a list of queries which we went through systematically, sitting round a table with a large-scale map of London on it. We rehearsed the timings again, satisfying ourselves that even if the screw in the look-out booth spotted the rope ladder coming over the wall, the getaway would still be feasible. Seán traced the route the car would take from Artillery Road to the flat on Highlever Road. He had made more than one dummy run in the car and reckoned he could reach the flat within a few minutes of the break. His route would take him along Du Cane Road to the traffic lights at the junction with Wood Lane. There he would turn left into Wood Lane, then right a hundred yards or so farther on, into North Pole Road. He would go under the railway bridge, turn right again almost immediately into Latimer Road, then left into Oxford Gardens, and left again into Highlever Road. Number 28 would then be fifty or sixty yards on his right.

The map overleaf shows the route. Turning down Latimer Road appears on the face of it to be a diversion as North Pole Road intersects Highlever Road higher up. But there is a roundabout there which doesn't allow access to the lower part of Highlever Road where the flat was situated.

Seán also emphatically repeated his assurance that he would not carry a gun or any weapon during the operation. If anyone tried to stop him and George he would not give up without a struggle. But other than that he did not plan to use any violence.

We agreed that George would be given my telephone number to ring in an absolute emergency. (Pat wasn't on the phone at home). However, that contingency apart, Pat and I would temporarily end all contact with Seán after the break, and would not visit him or George at Highlever Road. We would, however, continue to help out with money and with our efforts to raise the necessary funds to see the project through to a finish. Seán would get in touch with us about this within a few days.

The last thing we did that evening was to burn the map and all the notes we had been making. We even burnt several pages below the

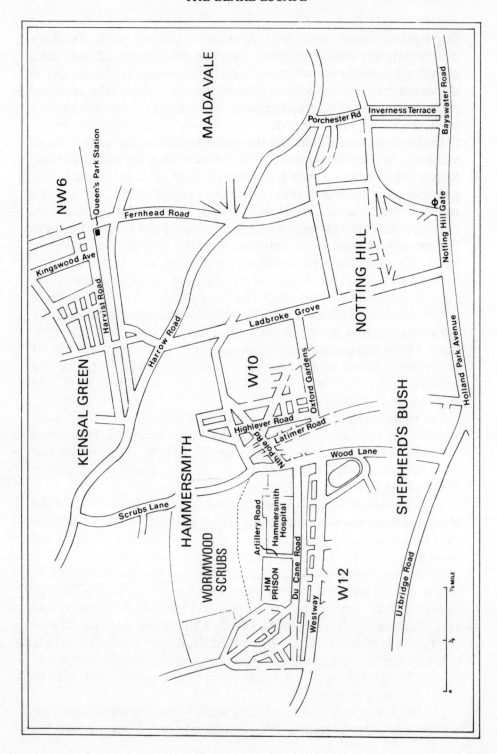

last used sheets in case any impressions had remained on them. This again seemed to border on paranoia, and we laughed at ourselves as we were doing it. But many years later I saw a TV documentary about police forensic work which showed that impressions could be traced through quite a number of seemingly blank pages. In retrospect our caution was not so misplaced.

Seán, Anne and I left together and walked to Hampstead tube station. No one said much; we were all thinking about the day ahead. The train we wanted came in first and we waved Seán goodbye as it started to move over of the station. He now had the really difficult and dangerous part of the whole operation to perform. In less than twenty-four hours we would know whether or not he had succeeded.

CHAPTER FIVE

. . . Gang Aft Agley

Narrated by Michael Randle

I slept little that Friday night, dozing off towards dawn and then waking up to find it was broad daylight. I lay there for several minutes not wanting to move. As the haze of sleep cleared I suddenly recalled what day it was and what plans were afoot. Instantly I was wide awake, a knot tightening in my stomach.

Downstairs I picked up the *Guardian*. 'One hundred and fifty feared lost in Welsh landslip' the headline ran, over the horrendous story of the slag heap in Aberfan that had engulfed a school and much of the village. There were pictures too of the wrecked buildings protruding from the black mountain of slurry and waste. All day the radio and television carried further details of this gruesome tragedy. By comparison our own anxieties over the escape seemed trivial.

In other respects it was a perfectly ordinary Saturday morning. We walked down to Kentish Town to do the weekend shopping, buying a few extra items because Anne's parents and younger sisters were driving down from Luton in the afternoon. At the bottom end of Leighton Road on the corner with Kentish Town Road two kids had a makeshift guy propped up on the pavement.

'Penny for the guy, mister,' they called out.

'You're a bit early, aren't you?' we replied, but gave them a few coins anyhow.

'Can *we* have some fireworks?' one of our children asked.

'Later,' I said. 'On Guy Fawkes night.'

Anne's family arrived as planned in the afternoon. We had said nothing to her parents about the escape or the part we were playing in it. Her young sisters, aged eleven and thirteen, played with our two children and kept them amused.

From four o'clock onward I hovered near the phone. I was waiting for the call Seán had promised to make before setting off. At about half-past it came.

'Everything's ready,' he said. I'll be leaving shortly.' His voice was clipped and tense.

'Are you all right?'

'Well, my friend, let me put it this way – I've seen better days. But yes, I'm all right.'

The break was due to take place at six o'clock, but Seán planned to set off well in advance to avoid the possibility of getting stuck in traffic jams.

'Why don't you slip down to Kentish Town and buy a few fireworks?' Anne suggested. We both felt guilty at having said no to the children in the morning. The fireworks would be a treat for them, and with luck we too would have something to celebrate before the evening was out.

As I walked down Leighton Road I felt strangely light-headed, almost as if I hadn't eaten for a day or two, and as though there was a screen between me and the world outside. On the way back it began to drizzle, and I thrust the bag of fireworks under my coat to prevent it from getting damp.

By half-past five the rain was coming down heavily.

'Can we have the fireworks now?' the eldest boy demanded.

'When it's dark, I told you!'

'But it is dark, it is dark!'

He was right. The sky was now completely overcast – this at least would work in Seán's favour when he threw the rope-ladder over the wall. At a quarter to six we let the fireworks off, setting them close to the house so they wouldn't get wet. The Roman candles flooded the small garden with bright orange and green light. It was time then to light the sparklers, which our two held in excited awe. Then we went back inside in time for the children to catch the beginning of *Dr Who*, which started at ten to six, and for us to prepare the tea for our two boys. Later on one of the neighbours would be coming in to baby-sit, while the rest of us went out for a meal.

As soon as six o'clock had passed I sat tensely in front of the television, expecting at any moment that the programme would be interrupted. I glanced at the time: only five past six. If things were going according to plan George should be out of the wing by now and dropping down into the yard below. At any moment he and Seán would make radio contact and Seán would fling the rope ladder over the wall. My heart was beating fast. I was quite oblivious

91

of the other drama that was being played out on the television screen a few feet away.

Ten past six – still no interruptions to the programme. But at this stage no news was good news; it meant that the escape hadn't yet been discovered. But it must come soon. The watchman in his telephone booth at the corner of the northern and eastern perimeter wall, even if he missed the rope coming over, must surely see George Blake scrambling up it. I got up and brought in the telephone from the hall table, setting it down close to me so that I would be ready to take Seán's call.

The theme music of *Dr Who* broke into my consciousness. Six-fifteen. Still no news flash.

'Evening all!' said the familiar uniformed figure of Jack Warner from the screen, playing Dixon of Dock Green. I smiled as he touched the peak of his helmet. No one was particularly watching the programme now, but we left the set on.

By 6.30 I was becoming anxious. Had something gone drastically wrong? Surely if the escape had gone ahead as planned it must have been discovered by now – and surely the alarm would be sounded as quickly and as publicly as possible when it was? And why hadn't Seán phoned? He and George ought to be together in Highlever Road by this time. Then I recalled that Seán had to dump the getaway car after dropping George off, and travel back on foot or by public transport.

By seven o'clock anxiety was giving way to depression. Something had gone wrong. Perhaps George had been spotted trying to break out of the wing. Or perhaps he and Seán had both been caught at the next stage when the rope ladder came over the wall. By seven o'clock the prisoners would be back in D Hall from the cinema, so for better or worse the escape attempt must now be at an end.

By seven-thirty there was still no news and we were convinced that the plan had failed. There was nothing for it but to set out for the restaurant as planned.

Then, at last, the phone rang. I grabbed it eagerly.

'Yes?'

'I'm just calling to say that I have been to the party and thrown the bait to our friend, who has taken it hook, line and sinker.' It was Seán, his voice unsteady. 'I have him here now standing beside me.'

I was too overcome to speak and sank back on to the sofa. Anne hurried over in alarm.

'Are you all right?'

'Yes, yes, I'm fine. Everything's OK!'

Then to Seán:

'It's great news – fantastic. I can hardly believe it.'

'There is one small problem,' Seán continued. 'Our friend has hurt his wrist. We're hoping it's only a sprain but it may be broken. If it is we'll have to get him to a doctor. I'll phone you again in the morning.'

This was an unexpected complication. In all the hours of planning we'd never once thought that George might injure himself jumping off a twenty-foot wall! I beckoned Anne to follow me up to the bedroom and told her the news.

'Seán seems to think it's only a sprain. The main thing is he's done it. He's actually done it!'

We drove to Tottenham Court Road and ate at the nearby German Restaurant, Schmitt's. We still kept the escape secret from Anne's parents, but there was none the less an atmosphere of celebration. Her stepfather and I drank pints of draught lager before the meal, and we all had wine with it. On the way home we turned on the car radio for the news. The report, as nearly as I can remember it, went as follows:

'Tonight, George Blake – serving a 42-year sentence for spying – escaped from his cell at Wormwood Scrubs prison in London. The Prime Minister, Mr Wilson, who is spending the weekend at Chequers with other senior cabinet Ministers, was informed immediately. All ports and airports are being closely guarded.'

The announcement, straightforward as it was, hit me like a blow to the stomach. We knew – had known for months – what was going to take place that night, and what a furore it would cause. Yet the public announcement of the escape still came as a shock. It was like wakening from an exciting but frightening dream to find it was actually happening.

Back at the house, the phone rang again. It was Terry Chandler, one of the 'Wethersfield Six', who had been in Wormwood Scrubs with us in 1962.

'Mike, I don't know if you've heard the news – George Blake has escaped. We've formed a 'Keep Blake Free Committee' and I wondered if you would be interested in joining?'

I was nonplussed, and stammered weak apologies down the phone.

I could hear the disappointment in his voice. Mike, he would perhaps be concluding, had gone respectable. Absurdly, I felt ashamed.

Soon afterwards the phone rang again. This time it was a journalist – I don't remember from which newspaper. In 1963 a *Peace News* account of prison conversations I had held with another spy, John Vassall, about his evidence to the Radcliffe Tribunal had received national publicity, and I suppose this is what had prompted the journalist to phone me.

'I'm trying to get information about the escape of George Blake, and I believe I'm right in saying you were in Wormwood Scrubs with him some years ago. Do you have any suggestions as to who might have helped in the escape?'

My mouth went dry.

'What did you say?'

'George Blake, the spy. He escaped tonight from Wormwood Scrubs. I thought you might know something.'

'I'm sorry,' I stammered. 'I can't help you at all.'

I put the phone down, and found myself trembling.

Half an hour later a second journalist phoned with the same question. This time I was taken less off-guard, though I prayed that the phone wasn't being bugged.

'I know nothing whatever about it,' I said, hating myself for having to lie in this way. One thing at least the calls confirmed; we had been absolutely right in deciding not to have Blake stay with us after the escape. If journalists could make a connection between him and me so too could the police.

Next morning the escape was splashed across the front of every newspaper, and continued to be the lead item in all the radio and television news broadcasts.

'Double Spy Blake Escapes from Gaol' was *The Sunday Times* headline, which also published a picture of a much younger George wearing a beard and looking remarkably like Pat. The Home Secretary, Roy Jenkins, said the report, had immediately been informed of the escape, and police from Hammersmith and She-pherd's Bush had been rushed to the prison to begin an 'inch by inch' search of the buildings and of the grounds with dogs. The report summarized Blake's career, noting the 'highly valuable' work he had done for the Dutch Resistance up to 1943.

The *Observer* gave the story even greater prominence, and published a more up-to-date prison mugshot of George without a beard. Inquiries in the prison, it reported, had lasted all night; police forces throughout the country had been alerted and all airports and south coast harbours, as well as 'Communist embassies' in London, were being closely watched. This report too summarized his career, noting that he was 'the most difficult type of spy to detect'; there was no evidence that he spied for money, and his motives seemed to have been purely political. As senior Intelligence officer in Berlin, he had had free access to the most confidential documents, and in addition to the damage he had done to Western Intelligence in Eastern Europe, 'almost the entire British Intelligence network in the Middle East, built up over years, had to be withdrawn'. However, 'informed circles' did not believe that he had any further useful information to give the Russians.

The reports had still not lost their ability to shock. But it wasn't simply the prominence given to the story of the escape that was so unnerving as the evidence that our little band of amateurs, working on a shoestring budget and still without the means to see the project through to its conclusion, was the object of one of the country's biggest ever manhunts. Suddenly getting George over the wall began to feel like the easy bit. At least previously we'd had the advantage of surprise. Now Britain's whole security apparatus was on the alert and would use all its skills and experience to track down Blake and his helpers. Now it struck home that the task of keeping Blake hidden and successfully spiriting him out of the country was fraught with peril.

But at least, I reflected, Seán hadn't phoned back, so perhaps the problem with George's wrist hadn't turned out to be too serious.

Just then I heard the garden gate open, and looking up saw the familiar stocky figure of Seán coming down the path. This was contrary to all our plans, yet I was delighted to see him. We opened the door and greeted him with hugs and congratulations.

'I'm afraid, Michael, I have serious news,' he said as soon as we had sat him down in the front-room. 'The wrist is much worse than we thought. It's bent at an odd angle and he can't straighten it. George is in agony. We're going to have to get him to a doctor or hospital straight away.'

'We can't possibly take him to a hospital,' I said in some alarm. 'His picture is everywhere.'

'Prison mug shots!' he said contemptuously. 'No one would recognize him from them. I'm prepared to go with him myself to the hospital – unless, of course, you know of a doctor who might come out to him. That's really what I came to ask you.'

I tried to think of anyone who might help. The doctor who had told us about the meladinin was abroad, and in any case might not have wanted to become directly involved in this way. For the moment I could think of no one else.

Anne brought in tea, and we persuaded Seán to tell us what had happened the previous evening.

'Bad and all as things are,' Seán began, 'they were very nearly a lot worse. We almost didn't make it!'

'I arrived at the spot in Artillery Road soon after six o'clock and got through straight away to George on the radio. I told him to get his helper to remove the loosened bar from the window. In three minutes – three minutes, mind you! – he was back on the air to say it was done. It seemed almost too easy.'

'Then a van turns into Artillery Road and drives past me to the far end and then right into the gated track at the bottom that leads to a sports pavilion. I decide he must be a groundsman or a patrolman, and I tell George to hang on. Five minutes later the van drives back down and pulls in just ahead of me, and a man in a donkey jacket gets out and stands there staring straight at me. He had security written all over him, but I sit there sniffing the chrysanths and hoping I looked like a hospital visitor. Then what does the bastard do but get a bloody great Alsatian out of the back and stand there again facing me with it?'

' "Jesus!" I said to myself – "I'm off. If I stay here we'll all be nicked." '

'I couldn't even let George know what had happened. To tell you the truth, I thought it was all over – for that night or for any other.'

He paused, overcome with emotion as he relived the trauma.

'I kept thinking of George inside there waiting for the signal to come out and wondering what had happened. And I thought – ' "How am I ever going to tell Pat and Michael?' And will they ever believe me anyway?" '

'So I drove in a wide circle, past the front entrance of the Scrubs again and back into Artillery Road. The van had gone but there was a car parked where it had been. I wondered if it was a police car, but I drove past it anyway, did a U-turn at the end of the road and drove back down behind it.'

'Can you believe what it was? – a courting couple! I did what the security man had done to me – I got out of my car and stared straight at them. It did the trick, and a few minutes later the man started the car, did a three-point turn and drove off.'

'I called George again on the radio. He was getting desperate – the men were starting to come back from the cinema. "OK," I told him, "go ahead!" '

'I had no sooner given the signal than another car turned into Artillery Road and parked just inside the entrance by the hospital wall. There I was, blinded by the lights, and deafened by George's voice coming over the radio saying – "Throw the rope now! Fox Michael. Throw the rope now!" '

'I told him he would have to wait a bit longer. But as soon as that car switched off its headlights yet another car swung in and parked just opposite the first, right by the prison boundary wall. This one kept its lights on. In desperation I left the car again and walked right up to it with the pot of chrysanths in my hand. Finally as I drew level with it the headlights were switched off and the occupants got out.'

'It was five to seven when I got back to the car, and I knew it was our last chance. I had left the radio on the car seat and I could hear George's voice, in a panic, saying: "Fox Michael, throw the ladder! There's no more time!" '

' "It's coming over now," I told him. I climbed on top of the car to throw it, and then jumped down to hold the rope securely. Then I waited. Jesus, I thought the man was never going to come! At last I felt the strain of his weight and then saw him peering over the top of the wall. As he lowered himself onto his hands another car pulled into Artillery Road. They were all coming now because it was visiting time at the hospital.'

' "Jump!" I shouted to him – at the same time positioning myself to catch him to break his fall. That was the mistake. He fell awkwardly and hit his head on the gravel path. He was lying there unconscious while the car cruised closer. Then it stopped and reversed back down near the other one on the prison side of the road. Fortunately, we were shielded from view by my car and by the rear door which I'd left open for a quick getaway.'

'George came to, dazed and moaning, and I dragged him on to the back seat. I drove off as if the devil was on my tail and turned left into Du Cane Road with no interruptions. George had recovered a bit and kept saying, "Take it easy, Seán, take it easy! Don't spoil it all now!" But I just kept going.'

'Then as I went to wipe the windscreen clear of condensation, I realized the cars in front had stopped at the level crossing just by the front entrance to the hospital. I slammed on my brakes, but banged into the car in front. When the traffic started moving again he pulled into the side and signalled me to stop. "You'll be bloody lucky!" I said and drove on past.'

'George put on the mac and hat I had laid out for him and at Highlever Road I went with him into the house. He looked a sight, I can tell you, with cuts and bruises on his forehead and blood trickling down his face. I couldn't have him going into the house on his own looking like that.'

'After I'd taken him to the flat, I went back to the car and drove it for half an hour or so before abandoning it on the side of the road. When I got back I rang you.'

He finished his tea. Telling the story had taken his mind off the immediate crisis for the moment. But still he was distraught.

After Anne and I had questioned him further, I returned to the subject of Blake's injuries.

'How bad do you think the wrist really is?' I asked.

'If you want my view, it's broken. Something will have to be done very soon. If you don't know of a doctor, he'll have to go to a hospital.'

'That would be suicide!' I said.

I thought finally of two friends I could phone – Matthew and Rachel, whom Pat and I had approached earlier for help, and who would therefore know what I was talking about. They had no medical knowledge themselves, but they might know of a doctor prepared to help.

Matthew answered the phone and I said simply that I had a friend in need of a doctor. Without asking any further questions, he told me to come down and see him straight away.

We arranged for Seán to return to Highlever Road and to ring Anne from the call-box in the house. He could not remember his number to give to us so he would have to make the initial call.

We walked together down Leighton Road to Kentish Town tube station. His last words to me were:

'Remember, if your friends can't help, I'm sure there'd be no problem about going to a hospital.'

'Seán, be patient', I urged. 'We'll get something fixed up.'

I travelled by tube and bus to Matthew and Rachel's house, arriving some forty minutes later. Rachel knew a doctor, a friend of the family, who she thought might be willing to help. It turned out, however, that he would not be able to see us until early evening. I needed to let Anne know this, but went to a call-box in the street, preferring not to use the phone in the house. The number was engaged. I waited five minutes and tried again. Still no luck.

Back at the house we sat round drinking coffee and talking anxiously. I was on the edge of my seat, desperate to get through to Anne. After twenty minutes I tried again from the call-box. Unbelievably, it was still engaged. Who on earth could Anne be talking to all this time?

I tried going through the exchange. They too got an engaged signal but on checking the line found that the receiver had been left off the hook. All they could do was to put a buzz on the line.

For the next few hours it was the same story every time I tried to ring. I couldn't sit still, but kept jumping up and pacing about the room. We had more coffee, and later Rachel prepared lunch. Matthew put on Beethoven's piano concerto No. 5 – the Emperor. We talked a little about music, and I remember he said that he found it a satisfying form because it suggested the struggle between the individual and the State.

But I couldn't concentrate on the music, thinking only of what might be happening back at Highlever Road. If I could not get through to Anne, probably Seán could not either. At some point he would give up trying and attempt to persuade George to go with him to the hospital, regardless of the risk. The one hope then would be that George would refuse to go. But if he did go along with Seán's plan, I was convinced he would be recognized and arrested. Given the state Seán had been in, the worst might already have happened.

'Are you feeling very nervous?' Rachel asked.

'Very,' I acknowledged. 'I'm afraid if we can't get help soon it will be too late.'

My chief anxiety at that point was not about the safety of Anne, Pat or myself, but that within twenty-four hours of the escape George would be back in custody. In that event he would not only have lost several years of remission, but would certainly never be given another chance to escape.

My mind kept going back to the time in prison in 1962 when I had been caught trying to smuggle a note out to *Peace News*, and

Zeno's contemptuous comment that this was proof of sheer incompetence on my part. He would be doubly contemptuous now if we bungled this attempt to rescue George.

I finally got through to Anne in the early afternoon. Our phone was on a shared (or party) line and it was the other subscribers who had not replaced their receiver properly. Anne had been driven half crazy because every time she picked up the phone all she could hear was the sound of kids playing in the house of the party line. We did not know their name and address, and thus had no way of getting in touch with them. Anne phoned the Exchange from a neighbour's house and got them to put a buzz on the line. But this had no effect either – at least for some time, and the Exchange said there was nothing more they could do.

When I finally managed to get through to Anne I learned that Seán had contacted her just before me, after repeated attempts. He was distraught, and had insisted that George be taken at once to a hospital; however, he had not yet taken that irrevocable step. Anne had done everything she could to reassure him, and would do so again when he was next in touch. But I still had no definite news. The doctor could not see us until after six o'clock, and even then there was no guarantee that he would be able – or willing – to help.

Shortly before six, Matthew, Rachel and I set off by bus to the doctor's house. Montgomery Hyde described him as a 'CND doctor' – a description subsequently used by journalists. We do not know, even to this day, how he regards CND; however, we can state categorically that he has never held any position within the organization.

'Well,' he said, 'how can I help?'

'I'll come straight to the point,' I said. 'A friend of ours escaped yesterday from prison.'

'George Blake, I presume,' he interrupted, seeming neither surprised nor impressed. 'I heard it on the radio, though normally I don't listen to it.'

'Yes. He's hurt his wrist badly jumping down from the wall. We think it's probably broken, but we dare not take him to a hospital.'

He heard me out and was silent for perhaps half a minute.

'I have no time for the communists,' he said at length. 'I can never forgive them for what they did in Spain. However, I understand that this man worked with the Dutch resistance during the war. Working with an underground resistance in an occupied country can do terrible things to people. To that extent I can have some sympathy for him.'

He asked me about the nature of the injury and I told him what little I knew. From my description he thought it was broken. By rights he should be taken to a hospital for an X-ray and proper attention.

'Some people, however,' he went on, 'have an aversion to going to hospital. Now, on the understanding that your friend is one of those people I will come and see what I can do.'

That left one major problem – the doctor had no plaster at home to make a cast for the wrist and no way of getting any until the following morning. But just when this complication seemed to put the whole operation at risk I had an idea. A friend of mine worked in the wardrobe or make-up department at BBC Television Centre in Wood Lane, only a short distance from Highlever Road. I knew they sometimes used plaster bandages on actors with supposedly broken limbs, and if we called by my friend might be able to get me one.

At the BBC Television Centre the doctor drew up inside the forecourt. Ten minutes later my friend had brought us a box containing the plaster of Paris we needed. The doctor and I then set off on the final leg of the journey to Highlever Road.

Meanwhile earlier in the evening Pat had rung our number to check if we had heard any news. Anne could say little on the phone, but Pat understood at once that something was seriously amiss. He now takes up the story.

Narrated by Pat Pottle

I made several trips to the phone-box at Hampstead underground station that Sunday to try to contact Michael, but each time I rang I got the engaged signal. I finally got through at about 6 o'clock when Anne answered and told me that Michael was trying to contact a doctor because an old friend of his had been injured, and that his other friend was very nervous and agitated. I immediately decided to go to Highlever Road to try to help.

The last twenty-four hours had been nerve-racking enough without this new twist. The previous evening I had invited myself to dinner at my twin brother Brian's flat in East Finchley. Brian was completely unaware of my activities, but I needed to be with people between the hours of six and seven o'clock to establish an alibi in case one was ever needed.

Brian shared the flat with a Spanish friend of his, José. When I arrived that Saturday evening I found Jo's parents were also there, staying with them on a visit from Spain. I was left alone with them while Brian and Jo prepared the meal – an awkward situation, because they spoke no English and I spoke no Spanish. We sat in the room together in silence with the television switched on. Jo's father had been watching it all day and had managed to pick up the phrase 'Black and Decker' from the ads. So whenever I looked towards him he would say:

'Black and Decker, Black and Decker, Black and Decker!' – it was infuriating!

I left following dinner, soon after seven o'clock, and arrived home at around 7.45. I switched on the television at once to see if there was any news of the break, or – worse still – of any attempted break that had been foiled. But there was nothing.

Most people old enough at the time remember what they were doing when President Kennedy was assassinated. I remember with equal clarity down the years the film I watched on ATV that night; it was called *The Springfield Rifle* and starred Gary Cooper.

It was not until ten o'clock that programmes were interrupted by 'news flashes' announcing Blake's escape. I poured myself a drink and, raising my glass towards the TV set, I wished Seán and George 'Good luck.' I had often said to Seán that I would never have the nerve or courage to perform his part in the escape, so I raised my glass to him again.

I had trouble sleeping that night because I had begun seriously to doubt whether we would be able to keep George hidden and eventually get him out of the country. We had told ourselves beforehand that there would be enormous publicity and a huge police operation when Blake's escape became known, but living through the reality of such publicity was quite a different matter. For the first time I began to realize what an incredible task we had set ourselves.

I started wondering what sentence we would get if we were caught. Three years? Five years? I finally settled on twelve years, which with remission would mean serving eight years. I'd be thirty-five by the time I was released. I lay there wondering whether life was over at thirty-five. It seemed so far away.

As the bus approached Highlever Road I became increasingly nervous. Had Seán and George already been caught? Was I walking into a trap? Why the hell hadn't we thought about the possibility of one of them being hurt? We seemed to have allowed for everything except Sod's Law – if it's possible for something to go wrong, it will.

The bus took me to the top end of Highlever Road and I walked down it looking for No. 28. It was dark and foggy, and raining steadily. The time was around seven o'clock. Suddenly a figure emerged from the fog, walking up the middle of the road. It was Seán.

'Pat!' he called out. 'I've got him!' Then louder still: 'Over here!' I nearly died.

'Where's Michael? Where's the doctor?' he shouted.

He was in a highly excitable state, and looked physically shaken. His tie was askew, the top button of his shirt was open, his raincoat undone. He was drenched, and the rain was dripping off him. I tried to calm him and said we shouldn't discuss things till we were indoors. The door of No. 28 stood wide open.

He led me into the flat – or rather the small bed-sit, as it turned out to be. It was a small room at the end of a long, narrow passage. George was sitting in a chair, a forlorn figure in his prison vest and with his arm in a makeshift sling. His head and forehead were cut and there was congealed blood on his scalp; one eye was puffed out and nearly closed. He was obviously in great pain. I was shocked into silence at his appearance, and it was he who spoke first:

'Pat! I had no idea you were involved,' he said, smiling weakly.

I tried to reassure them both that Michael would be along shortly with a doctor. But within minutes of my arrival, Seán had rushed out into the street again.

'You've got to try and restrain him,' George said, looking agitated. 'He's been in and out of the house all day, and if he's not careful he's going to draw attention to himself.'

After my own encounter with Seán, I had to agree. The broken wrist, coming on top of so much else, had clearly unnerved him. George told me that Seán had kept insisting that they should go to the casualty ward of a hospital if a doctor could not be found quickly to attend to the injury; he, George, had never been prepared to entertain that idea.

Between us we managed to keep Seán in the flat until Michael and the doctor arrived. Despite his broken wrist, George seemed chiefly concerned about his head wound. Seán had cut some hair away in order to dress the wound, and George was worried that it wouldn't grow again.

I sat there with my gloves on, unable to feel the cigarette between my fingers, and trying to fight off the despondency which was settling on all of us. Looking round the small, dingy room, I thought that apart from the police walking in, nothing else could now possibly go wrong. We sat, mainly in silence. George was clearly in pain and didn't feel like talking. I needed a drink. There was only whisky in the room, which I've never been able to stand – but I had some anyway. After a couple of glasses I felt a little less depressed and settled down to wait for the arrival of Michael and the doctor.

Narrated by Michael Randle
It was after 8.30 when I arrived with the doctor. I rang the doorbell. It was answered almost at once by Seán, who took us to the room. I was surprised and pleased to find that Pat was there. But I was shocked by George's appearance; the half-closed eye and the lacerations on his forehead gave him a particularly battered look, like a dummy on a shy-stall, and he was extremely pale. He smiled wanly at me and nodded.

'Hello, Michael.'

'Hello, George. I've brought someone to look at your wrist.'

The doctor put down his bag on the floor.

'I understand,' he said, repeating the phrase he had previously used to me, 'that you are allergic to hospitals and want me to treat your injury here.'

George nodded his confirmation and thanked the doctor profusely for his help. The doctor didn't respond at all but began examining the distorted wrist.

'It is broken,' he said in a matter-of-fact way; 'what I call a spoon fracture.' There was indeed an ugly bump at the wrist not unlike the bend at the end of a spoon handle. The hand was set at an odd, ungainly angle.

The doctor examined briefly the nature of the injury, and said he could do an emergency bone-set that should deal with the immediate problem.

'But I have to tell you that this is an operation I have not performed for some ten years, and it's bound to be a makeshift job. I would strongly advise an X-ray and proper attention at the earliest opportunity. The bone, indeed, may have to be broken again and reset to avoid a permanent distortion.'

He turned to Seán.

'I'll need some warm water,' he said.

'Yes, doctor,' Seán responded at once, and went to fetch a bucket of warm water from the bathroom in the passage outside. Seán treated the doctor with extreme deference, responding promptly to his requests.

There was a small wooden table in the room. We covered it with the day's newspapers and George sat by it with his left arm stretched across it. The doctor washed his own hands and forearm thoroughly in the sink located in the corner of the room, diligently assisted by Seán. He gave George a local anaesthetic, getting Seán to hold the arm steady while he did so. It would not, he warned, eliminate the pain altogether, but should reduce it. He then manipulated George's hand and wrist, while Seán gave George physical and mental support by holding tightly to his shoulder and upper arm. We could see George gritting his teeth to stop himself crying out. Beads of sweat appeared on his forehead.

When the doctor was satisfied that the bone was back in the correct position he wrapped George's wrist and arm firmly in the bandage and then wet it thoroughly to set the plaster.

At 9.20 we switched on the television for a short news bulletin. The lead story was still the escape and the massive hunt to recapture Blake. The doctor, however, showed no reaction, but carried on with the dressing. When he had finished he told George he would give him another injection as protection against infection.

'You're going to have to drop your trousers, I'm afraid,' he said.

George was embarrassed. He had a puritanical streak, springing from his strict Lutheran upbringing. I dare say, however, that any of us would have been somewhat embarrassed in that situation. Seán, Pat and I congregated at one end of the small room, and stood with our backs to George, facing the french window that overlooked the back garden. Soon the injection had been administered and the doctor prepared to go. He left sleeping tablets for Seán and George and brushed aside our repeated thanks. Not long after his departure Anne arrived.

By now the major crisis of the day was over. We drank whisky and ate chunks of bread and butter, while George and Seán relived the adventures of the previous evening.

'I was quite sure', George said, 'when I was waiting in the prison yard and had lost contact with you again that the game was up. I couldn't climb back into the Wing and I was more or less resigned to being picked up by the patrol. I almost switched off the walkie-talkie altogether but kept it on just in case. I was astonished when I heard your voice coming over it again – and mightily relieved, I can tell you!'

'To tell you the truth, I thought the game was up much earlier than that when the patrolman or whatever he was got the Alsatian out of the back of the van.'

The conversation, however, quickly turned to the immediate situation.

'There's one problem about this flat,' Seán acknowledged. 'Every Wednesday morning the landlady and her assistant come in to clean up the room and change the bed-linen . . .'

That wasn't the only problem. Seán had described the room as a self-contained flat, when it was clearly nothing of the kind. It was just another bed-sit with shared facilities, and all that that implied in terms of the lack of real privacy and anonymity.

As you came into the house there was a staircase immediately opposite you to the right, with a door into the front room on your left. Seán's room, as Pat noted, was at the far end of a long, narrow passage. To the left as you went down the passage was a shared toilet with a frosted glass panel above the door, and two other doors with similar frosted panels above them. Today they lead into a kitchen area, though we think at the time these were two separate small rooms, one of them a shared bathroom.

The room itself was small – perhaps 12ft by 13ft with a single bed in it. The door was in the extreme right-hand corner of the room, and we think there was a gas cooker or gas ring to the far left as you entered.

We did not tax Seán concerning the inadequacy of the room. He had after all just performed the crucial – and the most dangerous – feat of the whole operation. Moreover, given the difficulties he had had with agencies and landlords needing references, and the absolute need to find some refuge in the week before the planned break, we could not blame him for settling for a bed-sit.

Seán claims in his book that Highlever Road 'was never meant to be anything more than a temporary hiding-place, somewhere to go straight from the prison in order to get out of sight as quickly as possible.'[1] This was not so. Seán had told us it was a self-contained flat, and never mentioned the possibility that we would have to move out within a day or two. Had he told us at the outset that Highlever Road was a bed-sit, we would have had eight or nine days to look for alternatives. Now it was clear that we would have to move George out, and move him out fast.

The second problem was the car. Seán had told us that he had driven it for about half an hour and dumped it in a small street some miles away.

'Can you remember the name of the road?' Pat asked him.

'Yes, it was Harvist Road.'

Seán still had the *A–Z* he'd been working from in the room and we looked up the whereabouts of Harvist Road. If Seán had driven for half an hour after dropping George off at Highlever Road, then he had been driving round in circles, for Harvist Road, Kilburn, is no more than a mile away, and virtually at the back of Wormwood Scrubs Common.

'I think we should move the car,' Pat said. 'It's the one bit of real evidence the police could lay their hands on. I know a tip in North Wales; we could drive it there and dump it.'

Seán looked uncomfortable.

'We can't do that,' he said, 'because I ditched the keys after I'd abandoned the car. In any case, there's no problem; I wiped it clear of fingerprints before I left.'

The information about the keys brought our discussion to an abrupt end. We could only hope that if the police found the car they would not realize its significance, and treat it as just another abandoned vehicle cluttering London's streets.

George then raised another question.

'Assuming we can get over the immediate difficulties, what had you in mind for getting me out of the country?'

Pat grinned.

'We think you'll like this, George. We plan to turn you black and get you out on a forged passport!'

George joined in the laughter, but looked unsure. We then explained to him about the meladinin and the ultra-violet lamp, pointing to the latter which was still in its box in the corner. If anything George looked more uncertain at the end of the explanation than at the beginning.

'Obviously,' Pat said reassuringly, 'we wouldn't think of starting the drug treatment until you've recovered somewhat from your injuries.'

Anne, Pat and I left in time to catch last buses and tubes. As we walked down the road Pat resurrected an old worry.

'Mike,' he said, 'I'm still bothered about the getaway car. I can't believe Seán ever sold the Humber. And if he didn't, sooner or later the police are going to get on to it. It's registered in his name, after all. Once they find out it belongs to Seán, it's ten to one they'll give it a proper examination and discover it was the getaway car. George's fingerprints are very likely still inside it – and maybe mine too.'

This time I was convinced Pat was right. But it would be difficult to raise the matter with Seán for it would mean accusing him of lying to us and of having risked ruining all the efforts to lay a false trail to Limerick and Dublin. Obviously if he had indeed thrown away the keys, there was nothing to be done. But we suspected he might be saying that to try to prevent us from discovering that he had held on to the Humber.

Despite these worries, finding George and Seán another refuge had to take priority. If we were to avoid the risk of George being in the room when the landlady next came to clean it on Wednesday morning, we had no more than forty-eight hours to find alternative accommodation.

Next day the Blake escape continued to be front-page news in the papers and to dominate the radio and television news bulletins. 'Clue of the Pink Chrysanthemum' was the *Daily Express* headline, referring to the pot of chrysanthemums which Seán had finally abandoned at the foot of the wall; the *Daily Mail* led with 'Blake Hunt Clue of 20 Knitting Needles'; both ran editorials demanding that heads should roll for the security lapses that had allowed Blake to escape. The *Express* also ran a lead feature article by Chapman Pincher headed 'Indictment' in which he listed 'five blunders in a scandalous saga of espionage'. Forty detectives, according to the *Mail*, had questioned two hundred prison officers in 'the biggest escape-probe team to work in a British jail', and the Director of Prison Administration at the Home Office was reported in a number of papers to have instituted a special inquiry into the escape. *The Times* reported that the hunt for Blake was being led by Chief Superintendent T. Butler, head of the Flying Squad, while Commander Evans Jones, head of Scotland Yard's Special Branch, was in control of inquiries into possible international political links with the escape. The *Guardian* focused on the 'knitting-needle ladder' used in the escape and said Blake was 'no small-time spy' but one who ranked with Maclean, Burgess and Philby.

Of more immediate concern was the report in several papers that the flat of an official of the British Communist Party who had known Blake in D Hall had been searched – if this was the beginning of a systematic investigation of people who had been associates of George in prison it might not be too long before the police came knocking on our door. However, there was some comfort for us in the press speculation that Blake might already be out of the country, and perhaps have reached the Soviet bloc. The *Guardian*, for instance, reported that Intelligence circles feared that Blake could have reached a vessel in the Thames before the alarm was given at the prison and was now on his way to the Soviet Union. The *Express* too ran a piece suggesting that Blake could have been smuggled across to the Continent within twelve hours of the escape in a fishing-boat or small vessel. These were only the first of many theories to be aired in the aftermath of the escape.

It was clear that the police did not altogether discount theories that Blake had flown out of the country straight away, and were casting their net very wide. Thus the *Evening Standard* of Tuesday 25 October carried a report that police and security men had surrounded an aircraft landing in Sydney from Bangkok after a tip-off that Blake was on board. All ninety-five passengers 'were vetted for wigs, dyed hair, false beards and other disguises'.

The jockeying for political advantage by the Conservative Opposition started from day one of the escape. *The Times* of Monday 24 October reported Lord Butler (who had been Home Secretary at the time of Blake's imprisonment) as stating that it was 'quite extraordinary' that Blake should have been held in Wormwood Scrubs, and that he should have been sent to Parkhurst.

A major row erupted in the Commons after the Home Secretary, Roy Jenkins, announced the setting up of an independent inquiry into prison security to be headed by Lord Mountbatten. His Conservative critics, led by Quintin Hogg (Lord Hailsham), Edward Heath (Leader of the Opposition) and Duncan Sandys, a former Minister of Defence, said that this was not sufficient and demanded, in Hogg's words, 'a specific investigation, with a report, into this specific instance [i.e. the Blake escape] either independently of, or as an integral part of the Mountbatten inquiry'. Heath described 'the escape of this particular prisoner as 'a matter of the greatest national importance and international significance', and said that responsibility for his escape had to be pinned down. A furious Emanuel Shinwell then accused him of trying to make political capital out of the affair and demanded that in his investigation Lord Mountbatten should refer to the number of escapes from prisons during the thirteen or fourteen years of Conservative rule. An attempt by Hogg to secure the adjournment of the House on a matter of urgent public importance was refused by the speaker on technical grounds.[2] Later in the evening the Opposition put down a Motion of Censure against the Home Secretary.

The Commons row helped to keep the story on the front pages the following day, and both *The Times* and the *Guardian* ran editorials arguing that the Blake escape was sufficiently serious to warrant a particular investigation. *The Times* also published the terms of the Mountbatten Inquiry which had been released by the Home Office after a meeting between Jenkins and Mountbatten. The purpose of the Inquiry would be: To inquire into recent prison escapes, with particular reference to that of George Blake, and to make recommendations for the improvement of prison security.[3]

The key demand of the Opposition was met by this wording. Despite this, it decided to press ahead with the motion of censure.

On the Monday, some papers, forgetting that Lonsdale had been exchanged two years previously, suggested Blake, despite having spent the last five years in prison, was in a position to jeopardize British security. Thus the *Evening Standard* 'Londoner's Diary' column cited an unnamed senior Intelligence officer as saying that it was 'absolute nonsense' to suggest that Blake was of no further use to the other side; he could inform them of what he had told British Intelligence, and about British interrogation methods.

Chapman Pincher in a front-page story in the *Daily Express* headed 'Spies May have to be Recalled' stated that the Secret Service might have to consider 'immediate withdrawal of key British agents behind the Iron Curtain'. His thesis was that some of the British agents who had been pulled out of Germany, Poland and Russia after Blake's arrest in 1961 might have been redeployed there if it was thought that Blake had not had time to pass on their names to Soviet Intelligence. Now such people would have to be withdrawn again in case Blake had already reached the Soviet bloc and was making further revelations.

Theories also began to circulate about the manner of Blake's escape and about who was behind it. The *Guardian* on 25 October reported a theory being propounded in Canada by a journalist, Philip Deane, a former correspondent of the *Observer* who had spent thirty-three months as a fellow-prisoner of Blake in North Korea in the early 1950s. Deane argued that Blake was a 'double-double agent' who pretended to spy for the Soviet Union but continued in reality to work for British Intelligence. The escape, he argued, had been organized by the British authorities to delude the communists.

Later in the week, on the Friday, the *Evening News* prominently reported Deane's theory, and on 1 November it ran a long piece by Deane himself in which he not only denied that Blake was a traitor but asserted that the man who had served five years in prison and had been sprung by MI5 was probably not Blake at all. Deane said that he was another Intelligence officer who had agreed to serve time in Blake's place on the understanding that he would be released after a few years. Part of his reasoning was that Blake was 'not the sort who jumps eighteen feet unharmed on to concrete'. (Deane was mistaken in thinking that someone other than George had escaped from Wormwood Scrubs and in implying that the path immediately under the prison wall was a concrete one. But he was closer to the mark than perhaps he realized when he said that Blake could not have jumped eighteen feet *unharmed*.)

For Deane, however, the conclusive evidence of MI5 involvement was the pot of pink chrysanthemums found at the foot of the wall:

> The crowning touch, in my view – the trademark of British Intelligence – is the pot of pink chrysanthemums. What makes Britons such marvellous commandos or secret agents is their mischievousness. They are pranksters to a man and this characteristic has always served them well, since it baffles more stolid nations like Russia or Germany.
>
> So pink chrysanthemums it had to be.
>
> Any other secret service would have used a paper bag with stones in it or an old can or something one commonly sees thrown away in open spaces.
>
> The British secret service *would* use a pot of pink chrysanthemums.

'As for Blake,' the article concludes, 'I wish him luck, happiness and health, wherever he is, whatever shape his nose is, in whatever colour he dyes his hair'.[4]

However, on Tuesday 25 October John Le Carré was quoted in the *Daily Mail* as rejecting as 'romantic nonsense' the theory that British security services released Blake. Le Carré could see no realistic point in employing him, neither could he believe that the British authorities would have deliberately risked the scandal.

This last is, of course, the clinching argument. Nevertheless, the idea that Blake was released with the connivance of British Intelligence dies hard. Thus when Pat and I were publicly named by *The Sunday Times* in October 1987 as having assisted in the escape, the columnist Ted Oliver, writing in the *Daily Mirror*, suggested that the escape had been too easy, and that it smacked of a deal between Russia and British Intelligence. Seán Bourke, who was cheap and available, was chosen for the job and 'misguided CND supporters were flattered when asked to help'.[5] (Why it was necessary in the first place to involve 'CND supporters' in an operation masterminded by British Intelligence is not explained.)

Le Carré rejected too the idea that Blake had been sprung for money by the criminal fraternity; this was highly unlikely, he argued, because of the prison taboo against spies, and because members of that fraternity would know that no amount of money would make it worth their while to become involved with so 'hot' a property as Blake. He concluded finally that the escape was 'inspired or organized by the Russians' for propaganda reasons. They would realize, he argued, that as a British traitor he had no prospect of being exchanged in a deal, and that escape was the only option if he was to avoid serving out his sentence. Le Carré also linked the escape to a trend he detected in Soviet policy to spotlight the role and contribution of spies in Soviet history.[6]

Le Carré was wrong, however, in his estimate of the reaction fellow-prisoners would have to George and to his escape. It is true that spies are commonly held in particular contempt in the criminal fraternity: it is a measure of Blake's personal achievement that he overcame that. Here is Zeno again.

The chimes of Big Ben, always nostalgic, come to me over the radio, and I half listen to the news reader announcing himself. And then I am alert to a degree I have seldom achieved in my life. I am sitting up on my bed, my heart pounding and my breath held.

George Blake, serving forty-two years for spying . . . missing from his cell in Wormwood Scrubs . . . rope ladder over the wall . . . police alerted . . . watch on all air and sea ports.

For the moment my thinking is completely limited, narrowed to the projection of a single thought, almost as if I am trying to reach out and encourage him by the strength of my will . . .

A growing murmur of sound breaks into my thoughts . . . the men with radios are shouting the news to those without. The excitement in the voices I hear is unbelievable. There must have been nearer a hundred than fifty escapes in the years I have spent here, but I have never known a reaction like this. By concentrating, I can distinguish words and snatches of conversation.

'Blake . . . Blake . . . over the wall . . . George . . . had it away. Good old George.' Cowboy yells of 'Yippee', only once or twice sheer savagery, directed against authority more than in support of Blake's escape. 'He's fucked 'em . . .' And then, far away and faintly from the south end of the prison, singing, 'For he's a jolly good fellow'.[7]

Even more remarkable, as Zeno records them, are the reactions of many of the screws:

My door is unlocked, pushed quietly open, and I look up. A screw is standing in the doorway, looking at me. This is unusual, for the majority of the screws simply unlock the door and push it in an inch or two . . . I continue to look at him, a blanket half-folded in my hands. He's a decent screw, but I wonder what's coming. Suddenly he grins, raises his shoulders in a silent laugh and walks on to the next cell . . .

A dozen men come to my cell before I go down to breakfast, all of them hoping that I haven't heard the news, and that they will be the first to give it me. Their happy grins make me warm to them as little else could. On the landings I see screws standing, some a little sheepishly, but none with an expression of anger, or displaying the venom of the defeated. And now my heart warms to the screws as it has never done before. They *are* human. They cannot feel anger or regret that a man they *know* to be kind and considerate may not have to complete another twenty-three years of imprisonment . . .

When the screw arrives at our table to check the roll, he counts the nine of us and starts to move off. Paddy says, 'Only George to come.' The screw smiles and goes on. It's extraordinary. I could never have forecast such a universal reaction within the prison. I liked George from the moment I met him, and over the years I have become more and more attached to him. I have always known of his popularity, but until now I had never appreciated the extent of it.[8]

With so much public attention focused on Blake it was the worst possible time to ask anyone new to take the risk of hiding him and Seán. Pat and I decided, therefore, that I should sound out Matthew and Rachel again – they at least were already in the know.

However, they were extremely reluctant to take on this new responsibility. They had no sympathy for spies and spying, and were sharply critical of the Soviet political system. In practical terms, too, their house was not suitable. Not only was it small but they already had a middle-aged couple as lodgers in a room on the first floor. Moreover, because the couple were also personal friends they were in the habit of dropping in from time to time for coffee and a chat. Thus it would be very hard to have someone else in the house – much less two people – without them becoming aware of it.

Nevertheless, to help us out of the immediate problem, Matthew and Rachel agreed to put up one person – which logically had to be George – for a strictly limited period of say two or three days. They also asked for a specific assurance from him that it was not his intention to continue spying for the Russians after he had left the country. Obviously they knew, as we all did, that George could hardly refuse to give that undertaking – and equally that there would be no way of holding him to it. But it was a way of emphasizing a political point – that we had no more time for Soviet espionage than we did for that of the West.

Tuesday's post brought a welcome morale-booster – a note from Chris, the theatre man whom I had approached some weeks earlier about disguises. I had given him no hint as to whom we were planning to break out of prison, but his card had one word on it: 'Congratulations.'

On the evening of Tuesday 25 October I borrowed a car from another friend, 'Bernard', and, having warned Seán we were coming drove with Anne to Highlever Road.

When we arrived both Seán and George had packed their few personal belongings and were ready to go. I had to explain to them that George would be leaving on his own.

Seán and George looked at me in consternation.

'It would be a great pity if we had to be separated,' commented George 'Is there really no possibility they could take us both?'

'No chance at all. But it's only a temporary move. We're doing everything we can to find somewhere more permanent for both of you.'

Seán put a brave face on it.

'As long as I'm not named, and my photograph isn't published,' he said, 'I'm not in any danger. Obviously George must go if your friends can't take the two of us.'

I now had a final task to perform. Turning to George, I explained:

'The friends I am taking you to are sympathetic in the sense that they are opposed to the sentence you were given; for that reason they are prepared to help. But they are against espionage and have asked me if you could give them an assurance that when you do leave the country you will not resume espionage work for the Soviet Union.'

There was a shocked silence. But George quickly recovered his self-control.

'After this lapse of time,' he said, 'I can assure you that I have no information that could possibly be of any interest to the Russians. Moreover, having been arrested and imprisoned, I would be of no further use as an agent. So no, I will not be resuming work of this kind. I would also prefer, as you know, to move to a neutral country such as Egypt.'

We drove to Rachel and Matthew's place without incident. Once, however, at a set of traffic lights, I almost turned left into a one-way system. I had traced our route on an *A–Z* without realizing that there was a one-way system at that point. It caused us no serious delay. But I broke out into a sweat thinking what might have happened if in the highly tense state I was in, I had turned left into a one-way system and caused an accident. At another junction the traffic was being controlled by a policeman on point duty. As he waved us on Anne remarked that he would never know how near he had come that night to earning promotion!

When we arrived I introduced George – whom we had agreed to call David – to Rachel and Matthew. They shook hands but the atmosphere was strained.

'The first thing we have to do,' Rachel said, 'is to cut up your prison clothes so that we can dump them in the municipal incinerator. I've brought along several pairs of scissors.'

George unwrapped his bundle of clothes, which smelled dank and stale after the drenching they had had the previous Saturday. Soon we were all hacking into them with the scissors, some of which were blunt and made thumbs and fingers sore. Anne and I had to go after half an hour to return the car – but I wasn't sorry to miss an evening of this work.

The following evening, Wednesday 26 October, Pat and myself met Matthew by arrangement in the café inside the Festival Hall. Matthew was agitated.

'We need to know how long David is going to be with us. The house is really quite unsuitable and he has already bumped into our two lodgers on the stairs. I don't think they suspected anything, but that's not the point. Now that David is safely parked with us I don't want you to start to relax and think everything's OK. It really isn't. We said we'd help out for a day or two, but we can't do more than that.'

He was absolutely right. We *had* heaved a sigh of relief when we had installed George in the house, and, would probably have been content to leave things as they were for the time being. Clearly that was not on, and we undertook to move George by the weekend. But it was one thing to say that and another to think of someone who might help.

After leaving the Festival Hall, Pat and I crossed Hungerford Bridge and strolled to the Aldwych, racking our brains to think of someone suitable. At length we came up with Will's name. He had quite a large house in a fairly central area and would probably be sympathetic. We tried phoning him from a call-box near Aldwych but got no reply. I said I would try him again the following day.

'I'm almost as worried about that bloody car', Pat said, 'as I am about moving George.'

'You're right – we've got to do something about it. I'll tackle Seán and press him about the car keys. If he has them, and I can persuade him to hand them over, I'll move the car right away.'

We had arranged to meet Seán the next morning outside Goodge Street underground station. That would be a good opportunity to raise the matter.

I slept little that night, aware that our options were narrowing. As I lay awake, turning from side to side and longing for morning, I was seized by a new obsession. Pat at that time had a full black beard and it struck me how similar he looked to the photographs the Press had published – and in some cases were continuing to publish – of George as a much younger man when he too wore a beard. I began to worry that someone might mistake Pat for George, tip off the police and quite by chance put them on our trail.

Pat arrived first at Goodge Street that morning. It was convenient for him, as his printing works were on the far side of Euston Road in a small side-street. Oddly enough, the worry about being mistaken for George had struck him. He made up his mind there and then, before I had even had a chance to express my own fears, to shave off his beard when he got home.

When Seán arrived the three of us walked up Tottenham Court Road and stopped at a café for a cup of coffee. We had to confess to Seán that we could not give him any definite news about a new hideout, though we had thought of several people to approach.

Pat and I had decided beforehand that it would be less embarrassing for Seán if I raised the matter of the car when I was alone with him. So after a time Pat left us, saying he had to get back to his printing work, and Seán and I started to walk back down Tottenham Court Road together. I broached the topic as tactfully as I could.

'Seán, there's something I have to raise with you. We know that you didn't sell the Humber car, and that you used it for the break.'

We walked on in silence. Seán made no attempt to deny it.

'You may have been right,' I continued, 'it was the car you had got used to, and had fixed it up with the aerial for the two-way radio. But if it's discovered the police will be straight on to you, since it's registered in your name. There may be fingerprints inside it too – George's and perhaps Pat's as well.'

'I wiped it down for fingerprints,' Seán said emphatically.

'Even so, there's still the registration. Pat and I think we should move it and dump it in a quarry somewhere. Do you still have the keys?'

Seán had been uncomfortable from the start of the conversation. Now for a moment a look of panic crossed his face.

'I haven't got them,' he stated vehemently. 'I threw them away as far as I could after I left the car. In fact I dropped them down a drain in the street.'

'Seán, no one is blaming you. But if the police find the car they'll release your name and photograph and everyone will be in danger.'

'I think', Seán argued, 'that it would be foolish to attempt to move the car now. The police may well be aware of it already and keeping it under observation.'

'There's a risk,' I replied, 'whatever we do. I would prefer the risk of moving it than the risk of leaving it where it is.'

There was silence again.

'Very well,' he said at length. 'I do have a spare key. We can meet tomorrow if you like and I'll give it to you. But you're making a big mistake.'

We arranged to meet the following morning, and I walked back up Tottenham Court Road to where Pat was waiting. We travelled together to see Matthew at his place of work. I had tried phoning Will's number several times that day but still could get no reply. However, we knew he sometimes went away to the country for a few days, and thought Matthew might know the telephone number there. Eventually, with help from Matthew, we were able to track down the number. I rang him and told him that we had two people who urgently needed a place to lie low in for a few days. With all the publicity about Blake I assumed he would guess to whom I was referring.

He was entirely amenable and told me I should go to his house and pick up a spare key from an elderly female relative who lived in the downstairs part of the house. She was, he explained, deaf as well as elderly, and that was why we had got no answer to our calls. There was a spare bedroom where our friends could sleep, and they would have the run of the upstairs rooms. He hoped to see me on the Sunday evening.

Seán and I met as arranged at Goodge Street Station the following morning.

'I have good news, Seán,' I said cheerfully. 'We've found somewhere where you and George can be together. You can both move in at the weekend.'

'Well, I certainly look forward to that,' he said. But he looked intensely worried. 'I've brought you along the key but I think what you're doing is suicidal. You could be arrested as soon as you unlock the car door.'

'We've been through that.'

'Very well, my friend – but you know what I think.' Seán handed me the key, and explained where the car was parked. (It was only when his book was published some four years later that we learnt that he had informed the police of the car's whereabouts three days before he handed over the key to me – the Tuesday evening when we had moved George to Matthew and Rachel's house. We discuss later what might have led him to act in this extraordinary way.[9])

In the afternoon Bernard picked me up and drove me to Harvist Road. Seán had described the spot where the car was parked, yet we drove the length of it without finding it. I simply refused to believe that it had gone, and got Bernard to drive back down the road again, while I scanned both sides in case Seán had made a mistake about which side it was on. This time there could be no doubt. The car was no longer there.

At that moment, for the first time since the escape, I was really frightened. I could hardly believe that the police had identified the car and towed it away when it was innocently parked among so many others at the side of the road. But if they had we were in deep trouble.

Bernard dropped me off at a tube station while he went back to work. I was looking for a phone-booth to ring Seán when I caught

sight of the headlines in an early edition of the *Evening Standard* –
'Blake's Escape Car Found'. I bought a copy and raced through the
story with a pounding heart. Police, the report said, had found a car
which after forensic examination they were almost certain had been
used in the escape. It had been parked for some days in Harvist
Road, Kilburn. The police were 'anxious to interview the car's
owner'.[10] (By way of compensation, as it were, there was a major
feature inside suggesting the flights George could have taken on the
night of the escape that would have meant he was on his way to
Frankfurt at 6.30 p.m. – twenty minutes before his absence was first
spotted at the prison – and safely in Berlin by 9.30 p.m!)

This was the disaster we had feared. I cursed myself that we had
not confronted Seán over the car the night after the escape. If I had
driven it away that night, it might never have been found. The one
redeeming feature was that (so far at least) the police had not yet
named Seán or released a picture of him. But that must surely be
only a matter of days, if not hours, away.

I phoned Seán immediately and told him the news, warning him
to stay indoors. I would borrow Bernard's car again and move him a
day earlier than planned to the new hideout. He expressed no
surprise.

'It's exactly as I expected,' he said. 'Exactly what I had warned
you would happen.'

Next I went to see Pat, now clean-shaven, at his printing works.
The news was hardly less serious for him than for Seán. We agreed
that we should break off all contact for the next few days. Assuming
that the car had already undergone a thorough forensic examination, the police would probably interview Pat almost immediately
or not at all.

The discovery of the car also increased the chances of the police
interviewing me, for the prison authorities would have a record of
the fact that I had corresponded with Seán. Their records would
also show I had kept in touch with Blake. Thus Seán's explanation
in his book that he informed the police of the whereabouts of the
car, to draw fire towards himself and away from anyone else,
doesn't add up. That may indeed have been his intention, but in fact
he was putting us all in jeopardy.

Later that evening I moved Seán to Will's house. The first-floor
lounge was spacious and well appointed, with high ceilings, long
sash windows, and a splendid marble fireplace. There were also
comfortable armchairs, and a TV set – an altogether different

situation from the cramped quarters at Highlever Road. Seán was put in an end bedroom on the same floor which he would share with George when we moved him the following day.

On Saturday the morning newspapers highlighted the discovery of the car, confirming that it was a 1955 'two-tone' Humber Hawk which had last been seen in the vicinity of Wormwood Scrubs at 6.30 p.m. on the night of Blake's escape. The police were looking for an Irishman who was the legal owner of the car and had recently been released from prison. Several papers carried a photograph of the car issued by Scotland Yard. It had been discovered, according to *The Times* at about 9.45 p.m. on Tuesday evening. This tallies with Seán's claim in his book that he phoned Scotland Yard and informed them of the car's whereabouts on Tuesday, soon after George had left with us to go to Matthew and Rachel's house.

The most likely explanation for the delay by the police in releasing news of the discovery is that they kept it under observation in Harvist Road for a couple of days. This would have made sense if the police believed – as Seán says he assumed they would – that the tip-off had come from someone in the underworld. If the police did keep the car under observation for two days or more, we escaped detection that Friday afternoon by a hair's breadth.

The *Daily Express* report also stated that Scotland Yard were now no longer convinced that Blake was sprung by arrangement with a foreign power or that he had left the country. 'New evidence', the report stated, 'indicates that the escape was plotted by a small-time Communist . . . helped by a group of sympathisers.' Two Scotland Yard detectives, the report stated, had flown to Dublin the previous day. Seán was not, in fact, a communist. Nevertheless, this story was much too close for comfort.

The evening papers carried further details about the suspect. He was, the *Evening Standard* reported, aged thirty-three from Limerick in the Irish Republic; police thought 'he could lead them to Blake's whereabouts'. The *Evening News* carried a similar report, adding that he had served a seven-year sentence for causing bodily harm, and that police throughout Britain had circulated a description of him which said he was heavily built with only a slight Irish accent.

On Saturday evening Bernard dropped the car round to Torriano Cottages so that I could move George. We all had experienced panic at various times that week. That evening was Bernard's turn.

He had seen the reports in the papers and on radio and television, and was convinced the police were on to us.

'It's all over,' he said. 'It was a brave effort but it hasn't worked out. There is nothing for it now but to throw yourselves on the mercy of the Wilson Government. Special Branch will be installed in one of the houses at the back, keeping this place under watch.'

He said it as if it were not a matter of speculation but of fact. At that moment I could almost feel their binoculars trained upon us.

'They'll be waiting to follow you,' he continued, 'so that you can lead them to their man.'

'What I cannot understand,' I said, is why the police have not been round to interview us, as two journalists phoned me up on the night of the escape.'

'They probably thought too highly of you,' he replied.

It was intended as a simple observation, but it cut me to the quick. It was a sharp reminder that Bernard did not approve of what we had done or understand why we had done it. I had tried to explain it to him on earlier occasions, and we had gone step by step through the arguments. But he was not convinced; his help had been given solely out of personal friendship. I valued it all the more for that.

I picked up George and moved him without mishap. By now the lacerations on his forehead had dried up and the swelling under his eye had almost disappeared; he looked much more like the George I had known in prison.

George greeted Seán warmly when we arrived at Will's house – though still only with a handshake. He was never demonstrative.

'It's good to see you again, my friend,' he said,' especially in such congenial surroundings.'

At Matthew and Rachel's house it had been necessary for him to live under the most restricted conditions. Seán indeed attributes to him some ungracious comments on these conditions. According to Seán, he complained that he had been locked in his room all day, had had his meals brought up to him on a tray and had had to perform his natural functions in a bucket which he was not allowed to empty into the toilet until one o'clock in the morning. His hosts had even insisted that he stay in bed all day to avoid the possibility of alarming the neighbours. It had been considerably worse than solitary confinement because at least with solitary confinement you had an hour's exercise a day.[11]

Seán's account does not refer to the fact that there were other people living in the house – so it was not a question of alarming a next-door neighbour but of arousing the suspicion of someone in the next room. Given that, the house rules were absolutely necessary. Matthew and Rachel also told Pat and me that George was in the habit of doing yoga exercises in the room, sometimes directly in front of the window, and that it was this particularly that had worried them.

I stayed for a while and watched the TV news. The report confirmed the newspaper reports that two senior detectives had flown to Limerick, and added that they would be visiting the mother of the Irishman they were seeking. There was also speculation that Blake himself might be hiding out in the Irish Republic.

'At least,' Seán said, 'they still haven't published my name, or photograph – even if the whole of Limerick knows who they're looking for.'

'Not only the whole of Limerick,' George said, 'but every police station in this country. You, my friend, are going to have to lie low from now on.'

By now, only a week after the escape, all our carefully laid plans for sheltering Blake and organizing his exit from the country were in tatters. The 'self-contained' flat where he was to hide out with Seán had proved to be a myth, and now the discovery of the car meant that the police were hunting for Seán as well as George. It only needed the police to find Pat's fingerprints in the Humber to have them hot on our trail.

That weekend I went to see Matthew and Rachel. Between us we came up with the notion of smuggling George into the grounds of the Soviet Embassy, and dumping the problem in their lap. It would surely not be too difficult, we reasoned, if George could be got in without the British authorities knowing about it, for the Embassy to smuggle him out again in the back of a car and arrange for his flight back to the Soviet Union. Matthew and Rachel said they would take a stroll the next day in the Kensington Palace Gardens area – where the Embassy is situated – and see what possibilities existed.

I think it was about this time that another minor crisis occurred to add to the problems: I discovered I had lost my address book, which contained not only my name and address at the front, but those of Matthew and Rachel, and Will and Mary. I could have lost it anywhere – at work or on my way to work or it could be buried somewhere in the house. My nagging worry was that I might have

George Blake with his mother after his release from captivity in Korea, 1953. (*Topham Picture Library*)

George Blake, pictured at Gatow Airport, Berlin, in 1953 on his arrival from Moscow after his release from a North Korean internment camp. (*Topham Picture Library*)

DAILY EXPRESS

No. 18,992   TUESDAY JUNE 20 1961   3 a.m. forecast: Sunny   Price 3d.

40 AGENTS BETRAYED

AND ALL BY THIS MAN ➤

New shock over spy Blake

By CHAPMAN PINCHER

GEORGE BLAKE, the Secret Service agent who spied for Russia, betrayed the names of at least 40 other British agents to the Communists, I understand. My investigations over the last 12 weeks also reveal that many of these agents have disappeared and several are believed to have been executed.

The unprecedented sentence of 42 years' jail on Blake was confirmed by the Appeal Court yesterday. By coincidence, it works out at about one year for each agent he betrayed.

Blake also revealed the methods used by agents to acquire information and get it back to Britain.

As a result, some of the most important sections of the Secret Service behind the Iron Curtain and in the Middle East have been ruined at a time when intelligence about Russian missiles and troop movements matters so much.

Blake had access to the names of British agents in several overseas networks because he worked in various departments of the Secret Service.

This enabled him to learn the names of James Swinburn, James Zarb, and other Britons

RHODESIA : DAY OF DECISION

— A SON

GEORGE BLAKE'S wife, Gillian, 28, gave birth to a son—their third child — 10 days ago. If Blake gets full one-third remission he will be 66 years old and his son 24 before they meet in freedom.

slipped to be agents operating in Cairo. He passed these to the Russians who later gave them to Nasser.

The result: almost the entire British intelligence network in the Middle East, built up over years, had to be withdrawn.

Yet it is believed that part of Blake's work when he was posted to the Foreign Office College of Arabic studies in the Lebanon in September 1960 was to help re-establish this network which he had helped destroy.

I can also reveal that when Blake was freed from imprisonment in Korea in 1953 he was not screened by M.I.5. the experts in this procedure, but by his own colleagues in M.I.6.

In Berlin

They decided that after six months' rest Blake should go back to Secret Service duty.

Later he went to Berlin—and saw the Russians photographs of every secret document passing through his offices.

The offices were locked by a security man during lunch-time. Blake used to hide so that he was locked in—and could then use his camera freely, knowing nobody could enter for an hour.

Blake was the most difficult, the most able, the most difficult type of spy to detect. He apparently never became unstable. It proved just as easy for his British interrogators to induce him to confess his crimes as it was for his Korea interrogators to convert him to Communism.

How long is 'life'?

By FRANK GOLDSWORTHY

FOR 38-year-old George Blake, waiting in his cell at Wormwood Scrubs yesterday, 13 words in the Court of Criminal Appeal ended hopes of a cut in his 42-year sentence.

Mr. Justice Hilbery said : "This application is refused. The court will give reasons at a later date."

For three hours—including 37 minutes behind closed doors—Mr. Justice Hilbery, Mr. Justice Ashworth and Mr. Justice Paull had listened to a plea for reduction of the sentence, which is the highest within memory passed by a British judge and which Blake's counsel. Mr. Jeremy Hutchinson, Q.C., called

▶ PAGE TWO, COL. FOUR

Torchlight police hunt for nature boy Tony

TREATING THIS AS A CRIME, THEY SAY

Express Staff Reporter

A DOZEN senior detectives tramped Indian file through bracken and undergrowth late last night searching for 13-year-old "nature boy" Tony Tomlin.

Leading the way was a man who has told police he saw Tony on Saturday, the day he disappeared from his Southend home.

Police combed the five-square-mile National Trust Danbury Common, Essex, by torchlight.

The man assisting them wore dark glasses, a dark suit, and open necked shirt. He pointed out the spot where he saw Tony on Saturday.

2 am: Miners in 'grave danger'

Express Staff Reporter

FOUR miners trapped below ground were lying unconscious at the pit face early today, while rescue teams fought to reach them.

As the rescuers were heading back by the gas a coal-box official said : "These men are in grave danger."

Nine men were working in Silkstone seam of Cortonwood colliery, Wombwell, Yorkshire, when a tremor shook the seam and released the gas.

Five of the men managed to stagger choking for two miles through the fumes to the bottom and were hauled safely.

At 8 pm. officials managed to get through to the other four through the underground telephone. They were unhurt.

Three rescue teams from Mines Rescue Station at Rotherham started out to try to reach the men. But even with the aid of breathing apparatus the wall of gas forced the first two teams back to the surface.

And by midnight—with third rescue team going in—there was silence from the four trapped men.

One of the five men escaped said he would remember

Blake loses appeal

▶ FROM PAGE ONE

"inordinate, unprecedented, and manifestly excessive."

The sentence by Lord Parker, the Lord Chief Justice, at the Old Bailey, was of three consecutive terms of 14 years—and Mr. Hutchinson said he founded the appeal against it not on a claim that it was illegal but that it was wrong in principle.

The original case at the Old Bailey was mainly in camera. Now, said Mr. Hutchinson, he wanted as much as possible to be heard in open court, subject to the Attorney-General, Sir Reginald Manningham-Buller.

Mr. Justice Hilbery intervened to say : "What difference does it make to him (Blake) whether it is in public or private ? "

Mr. Hutchinson : "This man's mitigation and the whole circumstances of the case so far are unknown and there have been all sorts of speculation as to what he has done and has not done."

THE LAW.

Mr. Justice Hilbery : "We are not concerned with Press conjecture. We are solely concerned to administer the law. We are not here to scotch some rumour. It does not matter to Blake or anybody else whether certain things are made public. What matters is between the accused and this court."

The hearing continued in public until an intervention by the Attorney-General. Then the court was closed until the brief announcement of dismissal.

Mr. Hutchinson's plea was that an Act of 1889 dealing with these sort of offences fixed life imprisonment as the maximum sentence. Subsequently this was changed to 14 years.

"Never has a life sentence been literally interpreted," said Mr. Hutchinson. Today's actual serving time is about nine years.

"It is wrong in principle," said counsel, "to sentence a person to the aggregate of determinate sentences longer than life, because it robs him of statutory protection, the Home Secretary's right to review the sentence every four years."

In the silent crowded court Mr. Hutchinson turned to the case of another self-confessed traitor—Klaus Fuchs, the atom scientist sentenced to 14 years in 1950 on similar charges.

His conduct had been described as doing "irreparable and incalculable harm to this country and the United States" —but Lord Goddard, then Lord Chief Justice, had said to Fuchs : "The maximum sentence Parliament has ordained is 14 years and that is the sentence I pass upon you."

Mr. Justice Hilbery said :

"How much of that sentence did he serve ? And did he not, immediately after his release, go over to that other country and give them his services ? "

Mr. Hutchinson : "Is it to be believed that that great judge (Lord Goddard) did not appreciate or know that he could have passed consecutive sentences which would exceed 14 years ? Either he did not know, or he knew it was wrong in principle."

NO LIMIT

Mr. Hutchinson quoted the Prime Minister as telling the Commons "that Blake's disclosures will not have done irreparable damage to our interests and he did not have access to defence or nuclear information."

"Once this sentence has been upheld," said counsel, "there will be no limit in principle on the passing of consecutive sentences."

He said that evidence given to a Royal Commission suggested that only a superman could suffer 20 years' imprisonment and retain his soul.

The sentence of 42 years on Blake, said Mr. Hutchinson, "is so inhumane that it is alien to all the principles by which a civilised country will treat its subjects."

The making of a myth. Chapman Pincher's front page story. *Daily Express*, 20 June 1961.

Pat Pottle (*Photo: Tom Blau*)

Seán Bourke, circa 1968. He masterminded the Blake escape.

Michael Randle at the Press Conference for the Support Czechoslovakia action organized by War Resisters' International, September 1968. (*Daily Telegraph*)

The prison wall, Artillery Road, 1989. (*Photo: Michael Randle*)

The authors outside Wormwood Scrubs Prison in February 1989. Pat pointing to the spot at which Blake dropped down from the prison wall.

(*Above*) The Humber car used in the escape. (*Topham Picture Library*)

(*Below*) The back of the getaway car. (*Topham Picture Library*)

28 Highlever Road, W10, 1989 – the first hideout.

Willow Buildings, Hampstead, 1971. Pat Pottle's flat which provided Blake with a 'safe house'. (*Drawing by Sydney Arrobus, c. 1960s. Reproduced by courtesy of Hampstead Museum*)

Interior of van used to smuggle George Blake to East Germany. The child in the photograph is Michael Randle's son Gavin.

The Harz Mountains near Goslar. Return journey. Children with van in the background, 22 December 1966, four days after Blake was dropped off in East Germany.

The D.I.Y. Passport

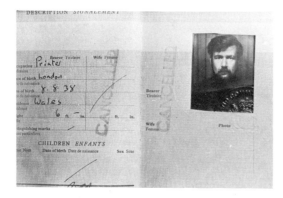

1 Steam off old passport photo being careful not to damage portion with embossed stamp

2 Mix plastic cement as instructions on packet.

Place in container and leave to stand for a few minutes. Sprinkle talcum powder on face of photo. Press embossed part of photo face down into plastic cement. Leave until cement has set hard.

3 Carefully raise photo from hardened mould. The embossed stamp is now clearly imprinted into cement.

4 Place new passport photo face down onto mould. Scribble over back with a hard pencil or ball point pen as if doing a brass rubbing.

5 After a few minutes of careful rubbing the embossed stamp will be transferred onto new photo.

6 Stick new passport photo in position, making sure it is aligned with the embossed stamp on page.

NB This technique is no longer possible on new passports which have a laminated strip running the full length of the photo.

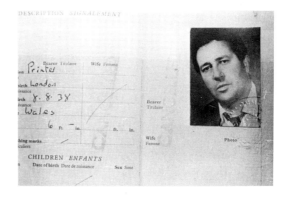

Anne and Michael Randle with their two children Seán and Gavin. Spring 1967
(*Sunday Telegraph*)

Blake in a carefree mood in the Soviet Union in 1967. He is pictured in the Carpathian Mountains where he was joined by his mother. (*Topham Picture Library*)

George Blake being interviewed on Soviet television for the first time in 1988. (*Topham Picture Library*)

Michael Randle on the shore of Lough Dan, Co Wicklow, 1987.

Pat Pottle at his London home, October 1987. (*The Times*)

dropped it on the pavement in Highlever Road on one of the trips there and that it would be handed in to the police. I felt vulnerable without it, and afraid that it would give the police some of the leads they needed if Pat and I came under suspicion. The upshot was that Matthew and Rachel agreed to go to Highlever Road and stroll down it with their arms around each other scouring the pavement. As we expected, they found nothing.

Speculation about the escape again dominated the Sunday papers. The reports said that Scotland Yard now believed Blake had used a two-way radio. The *Observer* reported that Blake had been a popular figure in Wormwood Scrubs and that the police inquiry team there were meeting a 'wall of silence'. It quoted one prisoner as stating that the atmosphere in the prison the day after the escape was 'like Christmas Day after Father Christmas has been'.[12]

On Sunday I arranged to meet Will's wife Mary, who had returned home before her husband from the country. We met in Central London, near Cambridge Circus. She looked upset.

'Who are these two people you have brought to the house?' she asked me, 'and why are they having to hide?'

I was astounded. Had Will not understood who they were? My hints had been as broad as I could make them on the phone, and news of the hunt for George was in every newspaper and on every radio and TV bulletin.

'Well, one of them,' I said, 'is George Blake . . .'

She stopped dead in her tracks.

'George Blake!' she cried out, her voice rising almost to a scream. I tried hurriedly to quieten her, terrified that she would attract the attention of passers-by. She lowered her voice, but was clearly in a state of shock.

Later that Sunday night I went to Will and Mary's house to talk through the situation with them.

'When you said, Michael, that you had two people you wanted me to shelter, I assumed they were American deserters or something of that kind. I never dreamt for one moment that you were referring to George Blake. This house really is not safe for him and his friend. The old lady isn't a problem, but I have a secretary who works here during the day, and there are frequent visitors. I am prepared to help out for a couple of days – but you'll have to find them somewhere else after that.'

This was a further blow. I didn't know anyone else to approach and I began for the first time since the break to consider going back to the original idea of having George stay with Anne and me.

But there was still the possibility of smuggling George into the grounds of the Soviet Embassy. On the way home that evening I called in on Matthew and Rachel. Their news was encouraging. The Embassy was enclosed by a walled garden, and there was a secluded and apparently unguarded area at the back where someone could be hoisted up over the wall.

Armed with this information, I called on George and Seán the following morning. I took a circuitous route from the tube station, checking at corners to see if I was being followed. When I came into the lounge George smiled and said they had been watching me coming down the street. I could rest assured that I was not being trailed.

We discussed the latest reports about the escape. The morning papers reported that the police had found an aerial in a cupboard in Perryn Road – the house where Seán had lodged prior to staying with Pat. Special Branch detectives had visited Limerick and had spoken to the mother of the Irishman they were seeking. The police had also announced the discovery of fourteen wrappers from £100 bundles of banknotes in the Humber Hawk car, and a microhead for a tape recorder.

The banknote wrappers were a mystery to us all. Seán said he knew nothing about them, and on this point we believe him. Certainly in all the time we spent with him he indulged in no spending sprees or showed any signs of having that kind of money at his disposal. The only explanation he could think of was that money had been concealed in the car at some point by a previous owner and that the wrappers had been left behind. Whatever the explanation, the discovery was a lucky break for us; it could put the police on the wrong track by giving the impression that the escape was a much more high-powered, professional operation than it actually was, and thus strengthen the belief that George had been whisked abroad within hours of the escape.

Finally, I broached the idea of smuggling George into the grounds of the Russian Embassy.

George stared at me, pale and disbelieving. Seán too looked shocked.

'I would be completely and utterly opposed to that!' he said, with more vehemence than I had ever heard him express before.

'But we've checked it out,' I continued. 'It would be perfectly feasible. There's one area where the garden wall is unguarded and where you could climb over without difficulty.'

He had jumped up in great agitation and paced up and down the room.

'That's not the point. I'm the last person the Embassy would want dumped on them. It would create a major diplomatic incident once the British authorities found out I was inside. The Russians might even be forced to hand me over as a fugitive from British justice. Besides, I didn't go through all this just to do a Cardinal Mindszenty [the Hungarian who took asylum in Budapest's United States Embassy for fifteen years]–to exchange one prison for another. I would have been better off staying in Wormwood Scrubs than doing that.'

'But why would the British authorities have to find out? And if they didn't, what's to stop the Russians smuggling you out in a month or two in the boot of a car?'

'Believe me,' George insisted, 'Special Branch would know about my presence within days, perhaps even within hours. No, no – this is a counsel of despair!'

The room fell silent. After some minutes George continued in a more conciliatory tone.

'If it's impossible for you to cope any longer and you wish to involve the Embassy, it would have to be done quite differently. You would have to go there in person and explain the situation. I think it's most unlikely they would be willing to become involved, but if they were they would take charge of the whole operation and you would have to await their instructions.'

It was this phrase 'await their instructions' that struck a sudden chill inside me. Our earlier plan would not have involved any direct contact between me and the Embassy staff. The proposition that they should take over and that I should take instructions had entirely different implications.

'I couldn't do that,' I said. 'Let's drop the idea altogether.'

Seán's account indicates that it was myself rather than George who proposed entering into negotiations with the Soviet Embassy after he had declared himself absolutely opposed to being smuggled into the Embassy garden.[13] But on this point he is mistaken. From the outset we had resolved at all costs to avoid having any dealings with a foreign power. Seán also attributes to himself a speech warning me of the consequences of involving the Soviet Embassy.

The thought may have been going through his mind, but he didn't contribute to the discussion in any way. Nor after George's words was it necessary to do so.

Not long afterwards George leaned against the elegant marble mantlepiece.

'Tell me,' he said in a detached, matter-of-fact way, 'what were you planning to do with me? You must have had *something* in mind when you got me out of prison?'

For several seconds I was in a blinding rage. I could have hit George at that moment – and Seán too.

'You know very well', I replied hotly, 'what we planned to do. But things have gone badly wrong.'

I turned to Seán, who looked acutely embarrassed. Without him there would have been no escape. But the present crisis was entirely of his making.

George said in a placatory tone, 'Yes, yes, of course, I understand that.'

I left them to do my two or three hours of teaching, agreeing to come back that night. By now I had begun to think seriously about moving George to our place in Torriano Cottages. Over a week had passed without the police showing any interest in us, so perhaps we would not be questioned after all. I decided it would not be too difficult to make a false partition under the stairs, or even to dig out a mini cellar there just big enough for George to squeeze into. He could then retire to this 'priest's hole' every time there was a knock on the door. We had a student lodger with us during the week but I didn't consider that an insuperable problem, and after all we could not go on shunting George from one place to another. What we desperately needed was a period of tranquillity to set the plans in motion for getting him out of the country.

I returned in the late afternoon with an *Evening Standard*. It featured a photograph of the house in Perryn Road, and of a young-looking landlady carrying a toddler. At least after Seán's trip to Ireland in October, we knew that there were no leads from Perryn Road to Highlever Road, much less to the present address. The main story in connection with the escape was that the Prime Minister would be making a statement on it in the Commons later in the day. In the evening there would be a debate on the Opposition's Motion of Censure on the Home Secretary.

Wilson's statement was reported on the early evening news by BBC television. (Seán states that this bulletin carried a report of the censure debate itself, but this is a mistake. The debate didn't start until just after a quarter-past seven, and ended in the division lobbies around ten o'clock.) Wilson stated that Blake had had no access to official information since September 1960 and emphasized that 'there was no suggestion at all of any risk to national security' arising out of the escape.[14]

It was some time later in the evening, when George, Seán and I were having a discussion in their bedroom, that Will came into the room.

'There is just one thing I feel I should mention to you,' he announced. 'My wife is undergoing a course of analysis. This requires her to be absolutely frank with her analyst and not to conceal anything from him.'

We looked at him blankly.

'Are you saying', George asked, maintaining his composure with a visible effort, 'that she has told him about *us*?'

'Yes,' Will replied.' Everything. There's no point in it if she isn't completely frank. You must understand, of course, that what she says to him is in the strictest confidence.'

George had gone very pale. (I'm sure I had too!) His voice was thin and reedy as he struggled to retain his self-control.

'And what did the analyst say when she told him?'

'Oh, he said that she was imagining it, and that it was because there had been so much publicity about the escape of George Blake.'

For several seconds no one spoke. Will's casual announcement had transformed this comfortable haven into a trap.

'In view of what you have just told us,' George said at last, speaking in a clipped, taut voice, 'I think it would be advisable if we left immediately and went back to our previous address.'

Seán dived down to grab his suitcase from under the bed and began piling his clothes and belongings into it. I was too shaken to say anything.

When we all had time to recover, we reached two main decisions. First Seán should return at once to Highlever Road until I could find somewhere else for him. None of us were happy about this, especially after all the publicity there had been in the last few days. But at least his photograph had still not been published, which meant that he wouldn't be recognized by the man in the street. Seán himself couldn't get out of the house quick enough; I think he would have roamed the streets in preference to spending another night there. George, we decided, should stay put for one more night.

Next day I saw Pat for the first time since the car had been discovered. I told him breathlessly of all that had happened, and of our decision to move George into our house and build a 'priest hole' for him under the stairs. Pat shook his head.

'No, no. That's as good as to say that if the police came to the house looking for George they wouldn't be able to find him. That's nonsense. They'd only come in the first place if they were suspicious. It's obvious what the solution is: he must come and stay with me.'

It was a real tonic to be with Pat again. He had stayed in his flat in Hampstead since the news of the car's discovery and, as agreed, had simply stopped seeing or phoning us for a few days.

By now it was obvious that one of us would have to harbour George. Pat's bachelor flat was certainly more suitable than our house with two children and a lodger, and with neighbours in the housing co-operative in the habit of calling by. There was still the risk that the police would find Pat's finger-prints in the Humber car, but given that they had known its whereabouts for almost a week, this, Pat argued, was unlikely.

After more than a week of successive alarms, I felt a sense of enormous relief at Pat's offer. Perhaps at last we would have a respite from the constant chasing around and a chance to focus our energies on getting Seán and George out of the country. We agreed that Seán could stay in Highlever Road for a few more days, and that Anne and I would move George to Pat's place the following evening.

CHAPTER SIX

Safe House

Narrated by Michael Randle

The removal of George to Pat's flat was a turning point in the second phase of freeing George Blake. It marked the end to a period of acute uncertainty, punctuated by moments of panic and near desperation. It was also the point at which Pat, Anne and I recognized that we had to throw caution to the wind and take full responsibility for hiding George and organizing his flight from the country.

The Monday and Tuesday of that week marked another watershed – the collapse of the Tory Opposition's attempt to make political capital out of the escape. The censure motion in the Commons on Monday 31 October was defeated by 331 votes to 230 in what was hailed in the Press next day as a notable victory for the Home Secretary, Mr Jenkins, and a crushing defeat for the Conservatives. 'A Triumph for Mr Jenkins over Critics' was the *Guardian*'s front-page headline. The report by its Parliamentary reporter, Norman Shrapnel, opened:

> If sound and fury could bring back George Blake, the Commons would have managed it last night. In fact Mr Quintin Hogg would have done the job single handed.
>
> He piled into the Home Secretary with a vehemence that aroused successive bursts of anger and ridicule from the Government benches as well as a charge from Mr Jeremy Thorpe that the censure motion was thoroughly hypocritical.
>
> If Mr Hogg or anybody else expected Mr Jenkins to be contrite they soon changed their mind. He did more than defend himself successfully. He demolished his attackers and had them speechless by the end. He held off the indignant Mr Hogg with one hand and felled an even more furious Mr Sandys with the other.[1]

The Times was still more forthright:

> With imperious contempt, and a flow of invective rarely heard in the House of Commons these days, Mr Roy Jenkins, Home Secretary,

tonight swept aside an Opposition censure motion on his refusal to set up a specific inquiry into the escape of George Blake.

The voting figures were 331 to 230, a Government majority of 101. But the figures scarcely mattered. The cruel slashes of Mr Jenkins' verbal sabre, lacerating the Opposition Front Bench while his cohorts roared him on to greater bloodshed, told the whole story.

Mr Heath, castigated as a procedural incompetent, so obsessed by personal pique that he failed to read the terms of reference of the Mountbatten inquiry before framing the motion, never stood a chance. His shoulders seemed to shake with laughter at the end, but he might well have been sobbing.

From the outset it had been only too clear that this was a censure motion that should never have been – and to all intents and purposes never was. Mr Hogg had led with a long and flimsy speech of consummate oddity, battered by jeers and laughter as he tried to sustain the case that an inquiry into Blake was all that mattered; that prison security was for the Home Secretary alone . . .

Mr Hogg did have one point of substance: that a warning of Blake's possible escape was given in 1964, that special restrictions were imposed and that had they not been lifted he would never have escaped. The same theme, that the Government were warned and should have acted, was later rubbed in with even greater force by Mr Enoch Powell.

Unfortunately for both of them, Mr Jenkins revealed that the warning had been false, and that the then Home Secretary, Mr Brooke, had put no extra curbs on Blake whatsoever . . .

But the one simple point that won the day for Mr Jenkins, beyond his slaughter of Mr Sandys for doubting the loyalty of the police force, and above all his merciless scorn of Mr Heath, lay in the Mountbatten inquiry itself. He had been asked by the Opposition to put a specific instruction on the Blake escape into the terms of reference, and this he had done. He had been asked for a speedy inquiry, and this one would be completed by the end of the year. What more did they want?

What the Opposition wanted, it was very plain, was a strong helping of sweet revenge for the events of last Monday. They wanted the head of Mr Jenkins on a pikestaff, and that of Mr Wilson as well. In the event they got neither, and nor did they deserve it.[2]

Wilson's statement earlier on Monday that Blake's escape would cause no further damage to national security was also prominently reported.

On Tuesday the Opposition tried to retrieve something from the wreckage when Quintin Hogg challenged the accuracy of a key passage in Jenkins's speech – namely, his denial that the former Home Secretary, Lord Brooke, had instituted any special restrictions on Blake when the alleged escape plot of 1964 was reported. Jenkins insisted that his account was correct, though he had to concede that his version of Lord Brooke's Minute at the time – 'It would be a pity if Blake escaped' – was a paraphrase; Brooke's actual Minute read that the escape of Blake would be 'as disastrous as if another of the train robbers were to get out'. However, in authorizing the Home Office to release the text of Lord Brooke's Minute, Jenkins caused further embarrassment and humiliation to the Opposition; it revealed that Brooke did not even know at the time in which prison Blake was being held!

But we had little time that Tuesday to relish the discomfiture of the Opposition – the preparation for moving George that evening to Pat's place in Willow Buildings, Hampstead took up all our energy. He now takes up the story.

Narrated by Pat Pottle
Willow Buildings in Willow Road, Hampstead – now known as Willow Hall – had originally been built as army barracks but over the years had become working-class tenements. Set back from the road behind a high brick wall, you could easily walk past them without realizing they existed; only when viewed from Gayton Crescent opposite did they emerge in their true Victorian splendour. They looked like something out of Dickens – dark, dreary and damp. Friends would refer to them as 'Bleak House'.

My flat, 4c, was on the first floor, up an unlit flight of stone stairs. It had three bedrooms, a sitting-room, a kitchen and a lavatory, but no bathroom. The rent was £6 per week. All the other flats were occupied by sitting tenants who paid on average £1 per week. The Buildings were dilapidated, and desperately in need of modernization. Outside long grass and weeds grew in abundance. However, compared to others, my flat was in a reasonable state, apart from the lavatory which was damp, and where some kind of dark brown fungus was flourishing.

Two of the bedrooms were tiny, about nine foot by five – smaller in fact than the room George had been occupying for the last few years. Jokingly I thought to myself, 'a few days of this, and he'll be yearning for his old cell again'.

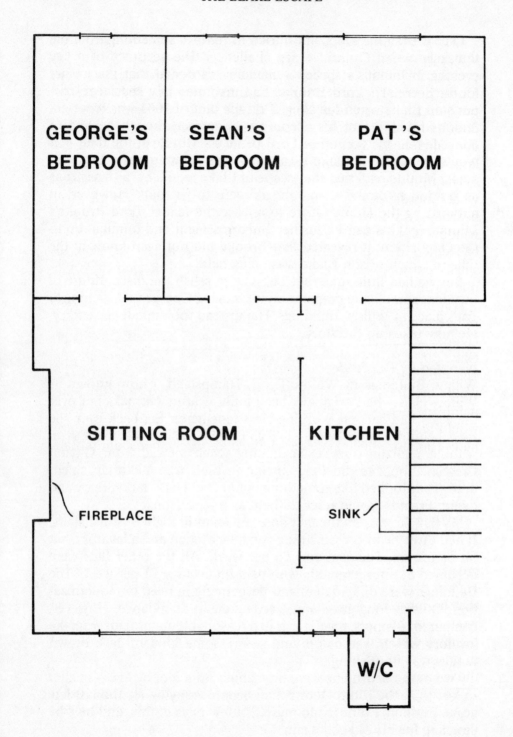

I spent the whole of that Tuesday – 1 November – acquiring the things I needed to get the flat ready for George's arrival in the evening. I bought net curtains for the windows, and six stout bolts for the doors. The front door was secured only by a Yale lock, so I put bolts on it, top and bottom. I did the same with the sitting-room door and with the back bedroom where George would sleep. This door already had a mortice lock on it, but I figured that with two large bolts as well it would take an awful lot of kicking down.

The thinking behind these defences was that they might somewhat improve George's chances of escaping out of the back bedroom window if the police arrived. Immediately below the window was a brick wall dividing the flats from the gardens which backed on to them. You could step straight on to the wall from the small bedroom window and then turn right or left and drop into one of the private gardens on the other side.

How much help the bolts would have been if the police had come is questionable. Clearly if they had had reason to believe that George was hiding in there they would have covered all possible exits. But if their inquiries had been of a more routine nature, the delay in their getting into the flat, and into the room where George would be hiding, might just have made a difference. (On the other hand, the discovery of a room in the flat bolted from the inside would have done nothing to allay any suspicions they might have had!) I suppose the main effect of the bolts was to boost our morale. It may not have made the situation more than marginally safer, but it made all of us *feel* more secure.

At about six o'clock Michael, accompanied by Anne and their two young children, Seán aged four and Gavin aged two and a half, arrived with George. George was wearing an overcoat which was rather too big for him, and conjured up images of Russians in heavy greatcoats. He had a trilby hat pulled down low over his forehead. He was as usual impenetrably calm, showing no signs of the strains that he must have been under during the previous ten days. The wounds on his forehead had dried up, and were well on their way to being healed, and he looked much more like the man I had known in prison than the battered figure I had last seen at Highlever Road the evening after the escape.

'You've turned this place into a fortress,' he said with a laugh after he had examined the bolts on the doors. 'You know, it's the first time I've felt really secure since I escaped.'

'I'm afraid your bedroom is somewhat cramped,' I replied. He smiled again.

'I think I'll feel all the more at home in it,' he joked.

All of us, in fact, felt much more confident now that George was no longer being farmed out to someone who had not been in on the original planning and had been pressurized into taking him. For the first time since the escape we felt that matters were under our control.

Michael and Anne did not stay for a meal, as they had to get home to feed their children and put them to bed. But I made mugs of coffee and they sat with us for half an hour to discuss the situation and the outstanding problems.

The most urgent of these was what to do about Seán. No photographs had yet been published, but we had to assume that police forces would have been issued with one. And aside from the danger that he would be spotted by an alert policeman, we were all uneasy at the thought of him being foot-loose in another part of London.

'What bothers me,' I said, 'is the thought of Seán strolling into one of those pubs in the vicinity of the Scrubs and being recognized by an ex-con, or one of the screws.'

The others agreed.

'He seems quite oblivious sometimes of the risks he could be running,' George said. 'I couldn't get him to stay indoors when we were together in Highlever Road.'

I looked around the small flat, weighing up in my mind whether to offer to have Seán move in. Two fugitives in the flat hardly represented a greater risk than one, provided Seán could be kept indoors. But living conditions would be cramped, and Seán wasn't the easiest person to have around.

'The obvious solution', I said at length, 'is for him to come here. George will be around to keep an eye on him during the day and I'll be here nights and on a weekend.'

Michael looked troubled. I think he was concerned that I was taking on the responsibility for looking after both Seán and George.

'That would be terrific,' he said. 'But do you think you can really manage with two extra people in the flat?'

'Of course!' I answered. If I was making the offer there was no point in being half-hearted about it.

We agreed that Michael would arrange to put the plan to Seán as soon as possible, but that we would retain Highlever Road as an emergency bolt-hole. Thus if the police came to question Michael – which would probably mean I was next on their list – Seán and George could immediately move back to Highlever Road.

A hardly less urgent problem was money. After we had used up the £200 Michael had raised earlier in the year on such things as the car, Seán's visit to Ireland, tools, rent and food, we had chipped in whatever money we could personally spare. It was difficult enough scraping by from week to week in this way; but if we were to get George out of the country we needed a substantial sum. As soon as we had firm plans, and knew approximately how much it would cost to implement them, we resolved that Michael should speak to Bridget about putting up the money.

Finally there was the question of starting the treatment to turn George black.

'How do you feel about it at this point?' Michael asked. 'Are you fit enough yet, do you think, to start on the course of meladinin?'

George looked uncomfortable; clearly, he still had some reservations about the whole idea.

'My wrist is still painful at times,' he said, 'and the head wounds have not completely healed. I think it would be better to delay taking powerful drugs for a while longer. But I could start the sessions under the ultra-violet lamp.'

The lamp had accompanied George during the last hectic week, but it had remained in its packing-case. On its own it probably wouldn't do much more than darken George's pallid prison hue. Still, that itself would be a start.

Michael and Anne left soon after six-thirty.

'Is there anything at all we can get you?' Anne asked George as they were leaving. 'Any particular books you would like?'

George paused to reflect.

'Well, there is just one thing,' he replied diffidently. 'If you can manage to get hold of a copy of the *Koran* in Arabic that would help me in my study of both the language and the Islamic religion. But only if you can get one without too much trouble.'

'We'll see what we can do,' Anne promised.

George and I were now alone together for the first time since the escape. We had a simple meal of chops and salad with a bottle of red wine; I had been too busy that day to think of cooking anything more elaborate, and anyway cooking was not my strong point. That evening, and during the next few days before Seán joined us, we had the opportunity to talk in a more direct and frank way than later on when there were three of us in the flat.

'I believe I owe you half a bar of chocolate,' I said.

He looked puzzled.

'You remember – the one you used to conceal the escape plan in when we were together in the mailbag shop at the Scrubs.'

'Oh, that!' He chuckled. 'I think we can call it quits on that one.'

'I'm sorry,' I continued, 'that I wasn't able to follow up the plan. I was never in favour of approaching the Russian Embassy, but I didn't have the chance to discuss things with you before I was moved to open prison.'

He brushed aside my apology.

'I doubt anyway if the Embassy would have been willing to help. It was always a long shot, and I never really expected anything to come of it.'

The discussion turned towards his personal situation. George's main concern was for his wife, Gillian, and their three children, aged ten, seven, and five.

'Our youngest, George, was born soon after my trial in 1961,' he explained, 'and the other two were still very young. James was a toddler of two when I was arrested, and the oldest boy Anthony was five. Being separated from them and my wife has been the hardest thing for me over the past five years.'

His escape would not bring them together. His wife had visited him regularly while he was in prison, but recently he had started divorce proceedings. This was not because they had grown apart but because he did not think it fair she should be tied down for perhaps another twenty years or more while he was in prison.

'Will you attempt to contact her at some point?'

He shook his head.

'Later, perhaps. But you know she also works for British Intelligence – they encouraged us to marry within the Service. It was a complete shock to her when I was arrested, but I think she and the boys had adjusted to the fact that I was in prison. Now all the publicity will make things very difficult for them again. Fortunately, Gillian's father – who is an ex-colonel – will be able to protect her to some extent from the intrusions of the Press.'

'Do you have any regrets?'

'About the family, yes. I have destroyed something I loved very much. My hope now is that when this is all over Gillian will remarry and the boys will settle down in a new situation. As far as my work as an agent is concerned, I have no regrets at all.'

I did not question him about his espionage work, not wishing to give the impression that we were prying into that side of his life or that we thought, having helped him to escape, we were somehow entitled to know about it. From time to time George would reveal a little of what it involved, though without saying anything about the information he gave to the Russians. He said, for instance, that when he had material to pass on he would take the underground line that links West and East Berlin and leave the package at a prearranged spot where later a contact would pick it up.

'I only ever felt apprehensive', he said, 'when travelling, on that underground. Aside from that it was all fairly routine.'

Once George had settled in we worked out a simple code for the doorbell – two quick rings, a pause, then another two quick rings; any other pattern, and the door would not be opened. George also suggested a signal to warn me of any danger when I returned home each evening. Normally the net curtains on the left-hand window were to be left half drawn; if they were fully drawn, I would know something was amiss. I passed these simple signals on to Michael.

George's wrist was still in plaster, so I volunteered to be cook. At George's insistence, we left the washing-up each evening; he said it would be something to occupy him the following day. We soon got into this routine, and kept it up when Seán arrived. Once George's wrist had healed he took charge of making puddings. A particular favourite was apple pancakes with cream – something he wouldn't have seen much of during his five and a half years in prison!

One of our chief concerns was Seán. I told George of the suspicions I'd had about the Humber car not being sold, and how I was kicking myself for not having questioned Seán more closely about the matter. I also wondered how anyone in their right mind could have chosen the bed-sit in Highlever Road as a hideout.

'Well, at least it was close to the prison,' George responded. 'That could have proved important.' He was always very protective towards Seán.

I agreed. Still, I felt he should have told us what the situation was before the escape, not waited for us to stumble on the truth after the event. In a sense George's injury was a lucky break for us because if it hadn't occurred Michael, and I might not have gone to Highlever Road, and the landlady and her assistant might have become suspicious about the stranger in Seán's room.

None of us could work out why the police hadn't named Seán as the Irishman they wished to interview, or issued his photo to the Press. With the Humber in their possession they now had concrete evidence of his involvement in the escape – strong enough evidence, indeed, for them to have sent detectives to Dublin and Limerick and to issue a verbal description of Seán. We wondered if they were holding back for fear that publication of Séan's picture would prejudice any subsequent trial of him for aiding and abetting George to escape. If so it was an extraordinary miscalculation, for it meant running the risk of letting their main quarry slip away.

If they had issued Seán's picture at that time the Highlever Road address would certainly have been located almost at once, for when Seán's picture was finally published in *The Times* in early January the landlady immediately went to the police. This would not necessarily have meant the recapture of George and the arrest of Seán and the rest of us, but it would have made this outcome very much more likely.

Narrated by Michael Randle
Sean and I met on the evening of Thursday 3 November at the entrance to Great Portland Street tube station. We crossed over into Regent's Park, walking up the pavement on the left-hand side of the Outer Circle. (Seán mistakenly places us in Albany Street, which runs parallel to the Outer Circle but is busier and brightly lit.) We were able to ascertain at once that we were not being followed. The pavement was deserted and had the added advantage of being in semi-darkness. All the lamp-posts were on the opposite side of the road. They were made of cast-iron with the bulb housed in a lantern-shaped box on top that threw pools of light nearby but left the side of the road where we were walking in almost total obscurity. To our left was the even deeper blackness of the park. If it was safe to talk anywhere in London, it was here.

'We're worried about you, Seán,' I began. 'We don't like to think of you alone in that bed-sit. Besides, the police could issue your picture at any time. We think you should move into Pat's flat with George.'

We walked in silence for a few yards, while Seán considered this.

'For the time being I'm safe enough,' he said. 'And maybe they won't issue my picture after all.'

I could not understand his reluctance to make the move, as he had been very unhappy when we had first had to part him and George. Perhaps he liked his new independence.

'Even if your picture isn't published,' I said, 'the police may well have been issued with it.'

'Oh, I take that for granted, my friend,' he said. 'But it doesn't mean very much. A policeman on the beat in the middle of a busy London street is not going to recognize me.'

I tried a different tack.

'What do you do when the landlady comes in to clean?'

'There's no problem. I keep busy at the typewriter until she and her assistant leave the house.'

'All the same, we'd be happier if you and George were under the one roof.'

We walked again for a minute or two in silence.

'If you think I should join George at Pat's place', he said at length, 'I will. But I can assure you I am perfectly safe where I am.'

An odd thing happened as we walked along. A man cycled past on the road, braked hard just a few yards in front of us, and got off his bike. Startled, Seán and I stopped abruptly. But the man carried on walking away from us without glancing in our direction.

'Jesus! What was he up to?' Seán exclaimed.

'I don't know, but for a moment there I thought the police had caught up with us!'

Seán laughed.

'When they do,' he said, 'it won't be a man on a bicycle they'll be sending after us!'

It was a measure of how jittery we were that we should have both jumped to the conclusion that the man on the bicycle was tailing us. Still, it was an odd thing for him to have done, especially as the road is fairly level. Perhaps he just got tired of pedalling and decided to get off and walk.

Seán and I walked to practically opposite Gloucester Gate, and then turned back towards the tube station. Once he'd agreed to move in with Pat and George, it only remained to settle when. According to his own account, he did not make the move until the following Monday, 7 November; Pat and I think it was more likely to have been the next day. There was, after all, no reason to delay once the decision had been taken. We agreed he would leave a note for his landlady to say that he had an assignment that took him out of London, and that we would send the rent to her each week by post.

Whichever day it was, that evening Anne and I joined the others for supper, having arranged for one of the neighbours to babysit for us. It was the first time all five of us had been together since the Sunday evening after the break. Once again there was an atmosphere of celebration, but now we were not on the edge of our seats, half expecting the police to burst in on us at any moment. The fare too was not so frugal. Pat had made a large and tasty fish-and-potato pie, and we had a couple of bottles of red wine to wash it down with.

We talked through the events of the previous couple of weeks, laughing at some of the absurd and unnerving incidents. We were also intrigued over the story in the *Evening Standard* of Friday 28 October, which purported to give precise details of George's flight to Eastern Europe.

'That can only work to our advantage,' George remarked. 'The stronger the rumours that I am in Eastern Europe the less intense the hunt in this country is likely to be.'

'Provided, of course,' Pat added, 'the police believe them as well.'

We derived considerable satisfaction at the discomfiture of the Conservatives in their attempt to exploit the escape, and the fact that the Home Secretary Roy Jenkins had emerged so well from the debates. The numerous cartoons that had appeared in the Press were also a source of much amusement.

After the meal we talked yet again about the problem of money and of getting George out of the country. The two problems were linked in the sense that once we had a firm plan that could be costed and assessed I would be in a position to ask Bridget for her help. We questioned George again about how he felt about the plan to turn him black.

'I think,' he said, 'I could be rather more convincing as an Arab.'

Picking up a towel lying nearby, he wrapped it round his face and head and gave the traditional Arab greeting:

'*Salaam Alekum*', he said, bowing gravely and touching successively his forehead, lips and chest with his right hand as he did so.

Applauding the performance, we decided there and then that after the meladinin treatment had sufficiently darkened his complexion it was as the citizen of an Arab country that he would go through Immigration Control. However, he still wanted to delay a little longer embarking on the treatment.

I came up a day or two later and set up a crude studio in the flat to photograph both Seán and George. I used a single photoflood lamp in a reflector placed directly in front of the subject. I was interested in photography, and regularly turned the tiny downstairs toilet at Torriano Cottages into a darkroom to develop and print my own pictures. This was a practice run for producing eventual passport-style photographs. George, obviously, would have to be photo-graphed again when his transformation into an Arab had been completed.

But the harsh frontal lighting produced far from flattering results. There were gales of laughter when I brought the prints round to the flat a day or two later. Seán cupped his picture in his hand, held it at arm's-length, and with his head tilted on one side, commented:

'Well, Michael, let me give you a piece of advice. If you have any ambitions to set up as a photographer, forget them!'

The verdict on George's picture was that the appalling prison mug shot that had appeared in every newspaper did him rather more justice.

George never did start the course of meladinin. He remained nervous about the side-effects of the drug, and we think had never been wholly convinced that the plan was a viable one. The crucial factor, however, was that it soon became clear that Seán had no idea at all how to get hold of illicit passports. When we pressed him he became more and more vague about who it was that he had expected to provide him with them, talking instead about making inquiries among some ex-convicts that he knew.

Even if such contacts existed, the last thing we wanted was to have him touting round the underworld at such a time. Any of his ex-prisoner friends would certainly have realized that he was the Irishman the police wanted to interview in connection with Blake's escape, and would guess at once who the passport was for. It would take only one unreliable person for the police to get word of what was going on, and perhaps from that to trace Seán's – and George's – whereabouts. It was difficult, in fact, to imagine anything that would have put the whole venture in greater jeopardy.

In retrospect it is easy to see that the idea of Seán getting passports from underworld contacts was always a major weakness in the plan. We had not questioned it at the outset, perhaps because we had assumed that the police would not be looking for Seán. But of course even in those circumstances for Seán to have started asking around about false passports after the spectacular news of George's escape would have been looking for trouble. Nor could the passports have been obtained prior to the escape. Even if a passport-type photo could have been taken in prison and smuggled out it would show George as he was before we could change his colour or provide him with any other convincing disguise.

Before finally abandoning the idea of turning George black, and of him and Seán travelling on forged passports, we went through all sorts of alternative possibilities. One idea was to cross the Channel in a small sailing-craft and land him somewhere on the French coast. (Several papers in the immediate aftermath of the escape speculated that he might have crossed to the Continent in this way.) George would still be a long way from a safe haven, and would have several frontiers to cross before he found one; however, assuming we could supply him with a passport, he would not have had to cross the one frontier where police and customs officials would be most keenly on the look-out.

I went as far as making inquiries of a friend who had some sailing experience. Crossing the Channel, he said, presented no great problem in itself, though we would certainly need somone with a basic knowledge of sailing and navigation to accompany us. He himself would be willing to help, and if we used a small craft the whole operation need not be too expensive. But it would be a matter of luck whether or not we succeeded in evading coastguards and landing without being spotted.

We never pursued this idea seriously. Perhaps if any of us had had sailing experience we might have done so. In any case, once it became clear that we would not be able to provide George with a passport there was little to be gained by smuggling him across the Channel.

By now we had come to the conclusion that the only alternative was for us to conceal George in a container or secret compartment and drive him ourselves to a safe country.

George liked the idea – not least, we suspect, because it scotched once and for all the plan for him to take a course of meladinin.

'If it can be done', he said, 'I think it would be far preferable to my going openly through Customs, however cleverly disguised. Besides, it would be too dangerous at this stage for Seán to contact his friends about getting a passport.'

He really meant that he no longer believed such friends existed. But he was ever the diplomat, and wished to avoid offending Seán.

Although George joined in the discussions of how to effect his escape from the country, he had few if any suggestions of his own as to how this might be done. His role was rather to evaluate the proposals we put to him.

We had earlier rejected as impracticable the idea of building a false compartment in the boot of a car. Now we began to think about the possibilities of concealment in a larger vehicle, like a camper van. I started looking at Bedford Dormobiles, Transits and other models in showrooms. Some had a bench seat in the back, running along one side, with cupboards underneath for storage. The bench seat was hinged, and folded outward to make a bed, supported by the open cupboard doors. This seemed to offer possibilities. But if the vehicle was inspected by Customs officials, the storage space under the bed would be the first place they would look. And building a hidden compartment within the storage space seemed hardly more practicable than building one inside the boot of a car.

I was travelling into town on the bus one morning to take my class at Princeton College, when a possible solution struck me. Supposing the fold-down bed were supported not by cupboard doors which swung open – thereby revealing whatever was in the storage space underneath – but by drawers? If they remained open all the time, George could hide in the space behind them. Only if Customs officials had reason to be suspicious would they try to push them closed, or try to pull them right out, for the storage space under the bench seat was being accounted for by drawers which could be full of clothes and other items.

The more I thought about the idea, the more confident I was that it would work. I even began to toy with more elaborate (and in fact totally impracticable) ideas about building the drawers with some kind of collapsible sides and a back positioned on runners so that the drawer would collapse into itself as you pushed it in. After the teaching session I called round to Pat's printing works to discuss the idea with him, and later on went to see Matthew, who had some knowledge of woodwork.

Matthew dismissed at once the elaborate 'James Bond' version of the plan. But building drawers to replace existing cupboards, he said, was perfectly feasible. He would be quite prepared to work on such a conversion if we decided this was how we should proceed.

Having had to insist on George being moved from the house, he was now more than willing to help in some other way.

George and Seán also liked the idea. Before we took any further practical steps, however, we needed to consider who would drive the vehicle, if it could be adapted, and where it should be driven to.

On the first question we really had no choice. Pat didn't have a licence at the time, and Seán, who did, was out of the running. He would need not only a convincing disguise and a false passport, but a forged driving licence and green card to boot. If we could have secured all these for him we could equally well have provided them for George, and there would have been no need to smuggle him out in a concealed compartment in the first place. It was clear I would have to do the driving. Anne (who had no licence either) volunteered to come with me, and we also agreed that if the plan went ahead we would take the children with us. That way there would be considerably less risk of arousing suspicion.

George was not a man to display emotion, but he was visibly affected when Anne and I told him of our decision.

'If you go as a family this obviously greatly reduces the likelihood of discovery. But are you really sure you are prepared to undertake such a risk?'

'We have talked it over,' I said, 'and made our decision. Anne would much rather be with me than have me go on my own. Besides, we can treat it as a family holiday.'

There was a pause.

'Don't think', George said quietly, 'that I am unaware of what this decision entails, or that I will ever forget what you and Anne have undertaken.'

The route and destination were trickier questions. George had always favoured trying to reach a neutral country – preferably Egypt, which he knew, and where he still had relatives. (As mentioned earlier, his father was Egyptian, and he himself had spent several years at school in Egypt as a boy.) But we felt the idea of travelling by road and boat all the way to Egypt was a nightmare; on that long journey something might easily go wrong and George could well be discovered. What we were looking for was the shortest possible route to safe territory. It was us, not George, who suggested dropping him somewhere in Eastern Europe. (Commentators who have suggested that George hoodwinked Seán into thinking that he wanted to go to a neutral Third World country, and then once he was out of Wormwood Scrubs insisted on being taken to Russia, are quite mistaken.)

Once Eastern Europe had been settled upon he argued strongly for taking the Berlin autobahn and dropping him off close to the East German checkpoint on the outskirts of the city. We spread a map of central Europe out on the table and traced out a route. George had been posted in Berlin for about six years, and knew the city and the approaches to it well.

'You cross the frontier from West Germany into East Germany at Helmstedt,' he said, pointing to the place on the map. 'As citizens of one of the four occupying powers you cannot be refused a transit visa to enable you to travel to West Berlin which is about a hundred miles farther on. Once you've dropped me you will have to go on into West Berlin – you could stay there a few days if you wish.'

It seemed an excellent plan, and was quickly agreed. George's knowledge of the area increased our confidence in his proposal.

There remained the question of what to do about Seán once George was safely out of the country. One possibility was to make a second journey with the van to Eastern Europe. Seán, however, favoured travelling to Ireland and fighting any extradition proceedings the British authorities might set in motion. For the time being we could afford to leave the matter undecided.

Matthew came with me to a showroom in South London to look at vehicles. We picked out a van with suitable fittings. I forget the exact price, but I know we reckoned that with the materials for the internal conversion work, the ferry tickets, petrol and various sundries we would need £1,000. I met Bridget shortly afterwards and she agreed at once to put up the money.

We met again a day or two later and she wrote me out the cheque. As she did so she laughed nervously.

'This is the big one,' she said. 'I've never written out a cheque for this amount in my life before.'

'And I've never paid in a cheque of this size into our account.'

As an inveterate hoarder I kept that particular bank paying-in book and came across it when I was having a clear-out in spring 1988. It shows that the cheque for £1,000 was paid into the account on 10 November 1966. The following day was George's forty-fourth birthday, and the five of us met again for supper and a party at Pat's flat – would it be fish pie again, Anne wondered.

When we got there the table was laid and there was a familiar fishy smell coming from the kitchen. Anne shot me a resigned glance. I tried to keep a straight face and put our bottle of white wine besides the red wine that was already open on the table. The others had started drinking and the mood was jolly.

I remember we all joked about George's appearance, for George, probably the most fashion-conscious of the men present, had to make do with the rather ill-fitting clothes we had provided for him. He was a slightly built man, and we had over-estimated his size. The blue jeans we had bought him were too long in the leg, and were turned up a few too many times at the bottom. On top he wore a brown sports jacket but its shoulders drooped over his own, and the sleeves were too long. He was wearing one of Pat's shirts, open at the neck; Pat never wore a tie, and there were none in the flat. Thus through no fault of his own George looked very different from the dapper figure that some of the papers had recently published of him, dating from just after his release in North Korea. Pat remarked once jokingly to me that dressed in the outfit we had provided he should have no difficulty fitting in with Soviet society.

Anne handed him a parcel done up in fancy paper and wished him a happy birthday. He opened it to find a large and beautifully produced copy of the *Koran*. We had gone to some trouble finding it, and choosing an attractive edition.

'It's beautiful,' he said, running his hand over the cover. 'I expect to spend many happy hours reading it. But really it's much more than I expected; you should not have gone to so much trouble.'

Fish pie, red cabbage and salad was followed by a dessert of apple dumplings and whipped cream. Pat used to buy the apple dumplings from Rumbold's bakery in South End Green. There was plenty of wine, and when we had all drunk enough to overcome our embarrassment we sang *Happy Birthday* to George.

'Thanks to all your efforts,' he said, 'it's been the best birthday I've had for many years.'

Things had developed rapidly in the ten days since George had moved to Willow Buildings. We had settled on a firm plan for getting him out of the country, and had the money and know-how to carry it out.

What, in retrospect, we all find surprising is that we accepted Bridget's contribution in the form of a cheque, and that it was put through Anne's and my account. Remembering the extreme precautions we took with the first donation of £200, this now seems extraordinary. As mentioned in Chapter 4, not only was that initial £200 paid in cash, but as an added insurance I changed the original notes in a succession of London banks before handing the money over to Seán.

The decision to accept a cheque may have reflected the fact that we were much more centrally involved in the operation than I had been the previous July, when we had been handing over cash to Seán. Now I was buying the van, and was committed to driving George out of the country.

It was the custom of banks at that time to return used cheques to their customers with the monthly statement. Moreover, bank statements showed only the amounts paid into the account, or drawn on it, giving no information about the third parties involved in the transactions in either direction. So we probably assumed that by the time the van had been adapted and we were ready to set out on the journey the cheque would be back in Bridget's hands, and that even if things went wrong, our bank would not be able to trace the origin of the cheque. If the worst came to the worst, and the cheque was traced back to Bridget, we would maintain that it was a contribution to our general political work and that she knew nothing about the real purpose for which it was intended.

Assuming that we had to allow several days for the cheque to be cleared, we were probably not in a position to buy the van until about the 17th or 18th November. On the day in question I went by tube to the showroom in South London. The vehicle we had chosen was not, as Seán states, a Dormobile but a similar type of camper-van made by Commer. Unlike the Bedford Dormobile, however, which has sliding doors at the side, the Commer had double doors at the back – slightly better for our purposes, since it would make access to the proposed hiding-place at the back of the driver's seat that bit more awkward for any Customs officer to reach. More importantly, the fittings on the Commer could be more easily adapted than on any of the others we looked at.

The vehicle was two-toned; it had a light green body with a cream-coloured roof and upper side panels. The photograph in the plate section shows clearly the lay-out of the interior after we had made the adaptations. In the front there were three seats, with the engine and petrol tank underneath them. The vehicle had no exterior bonnet which meant that the driver and passengers were sitting right up over the road – a feature I particularly liked.

In the back, immediately behind the driver's seat and the left-hand passenger seats, were two single seats facing forward. (Only one of these, at the back of the driver's seat, is visible in the photograph.) Behind them, on the off-side of the vehicle, was the bench seat immediately underneath the side windows. To the rear on the near side (though not visible in the photograph) was a sink unit and stove. A foldaway table could also be set up in the back for eating meals and so forth when the bench seat was not folded down. The table-top can be seen in the photograph slotted inside the rear door. The roof also had a hard-top canopy with orange canvas sides which could be extended when the vehicle was stationary to give added headroom. When the canopy was up the canvas sides lit up the whole interior with a cheerful orange glow.

I was due at Princeton College at 11a.m. to take a class on the morning I picked up the vehicle, and thought I had allowed plenty of time to get there. But the formalities of buying the van took longer than I had anticipated, and I then ran into solid traffic jams driving northward towards the Holborn area. At one point, in my anxiety to get ahead I pulled across too sharply from one lane into another and clipped the tail of a van in front of me.

The van driver jumped out and said furiously:

'What the hell do you think you're doing?'

I was mortified, but also very anxious. The last thing I wanted was any kind of legal complication involving the vehicle. So I apologized profusely and explained I had only just bought the van and wasn't yet used to it.

I have rarely seen a man change his demeanour more quickly. From being flushed with anger he became positively sympathetic. He looked at his van and found that I had done no more damage than to bend the back bumper slightly.

'It's nothing at all,' he said. Then he added with a grin – 'anyway, it's the firm's van!'

After that I drove with added caution. I was half an hour late for my class, and found the head of English as a Foreign Language division had taken over pending my arrival. Fortunately he made light of it.

That evening I drove the van to Matthew and Rachel's house and we started stripping the fittings and furnishings on the off side where the modifications had to be made. Matthew had a large garage/workshop some distance from the house, and it was here that we worked and stored the necessary materials. Once the fittings were completely stripped, Matthew measured up and drew detailed plans. (I kept these for many years, but eventually burnt them along with all the other photographs and papers that we decided might incriminate us.)

By the weekend we were in a position to order materials. We decided we should stick closely to the original materials and colour patterns so that there would be as little clash as possible between the new fixtures and those we were not replacing. There were, for instance, formica facings and edgings on the existing furniture in a simple black and white design – we would do our best to match these.

At the timber merchants we were served by an attractive young woman with a lilting Scottish accent whom I felt I had met somewhere but couldn't place. I was surprised how easily she was able to match the formica sample we had brought with us, and we ordered a quantity of this and suitable wood for the drawers and other fittings. As she was making out the bill she looked at me quizzically and said:

'Don't I know you? Are you by any chance Michael Randle who used to be with the Committee of 100?'

I was taken aback.

'That's right. I thought somehow I knew you.'

'Elizabeth Brewood – I used to be active with the Scottish Committee of 100. I believe we met at the Holy Loch demonstration back in 1961.'

Elizabeth was married to Pat's partner in the printing firm, Douglas Brewood. She had, of course, no idea what we wanted the wood for.

We didn't get much further that weekend with the conversion. But once again I almost got into trouble with the van. I had parked it on a busy main road immediately outside a café where Matthew and I had gone to get a cup of tea. We had only been in there a few minutes when an irate policeman burst in demanding to know who owned the vehicle parked outside. He threatened to book me as I came out to move it. I think if he had not been so busy trying to keep the rest of the traffic moving he would have done so.

The conversion was in fact a far bigger job than I had ever imagined. I thought it would have been a relatively simple matter to replace cupboards with drawers, and had not anticipated that we would have to strip everything and that Matthew would have to redesign and rebuild the infrastructure from scratch. Fortunately he was a woodwork enthusiast, and his garage/workshop was well stocked with saws, hammers, chisels and other equipment. Most evenings after he had finished work I would drive down there. We rarely finished before midnight, and sometimes it was much later. Sometimes we would have a break half-way through the evening, adjourning to the local pub.

We worked intently, almost feverishly, with a radio in the workshop tuned to a pirate radio station playing non-stop pop music. There was still a sufficient sense of urgency to keep the adrenalin flowing, for we knew that neither George nor the rest of us would be out of danger as long as he remained in the country. Matthew, nevertheless, was not prepared to cut any corners, and maintained the highest standards of workmanship. I helped where I could, working under his direction.

At that time the seventy-year-old yachtsman Francis Chichester was attempting his singlehanded voyage across the Pacific in his yacht *Gipsy Moth II*. In early December, as he neared the Australian coastline, news of his progress frequently featured in the hourly news reports on the radio. Once, I remember, as our work was nearing completion we stopped to listen to the report, which said he was encountering difficulties within a few days' sailing-time of Sydney. I remember Matthew remarking on what an extraordinary feat it was, and how much he admired the man. By the time he made his triumphal entry into Sydney harbour on 13 December we had completed our task.

Although Matthew and I were kept extremely busy, the work itself acted as a therapy, relieving the constant tension and the nagging worry about whether we would be able to bring this venture to a successful conclusion. We could also see at the end of each evening how the work was progressing. The real strain was on the others. Anne and Rachel especially, alone most evenings until the early hours, found it an anxious and frustrating time. Sometimes – when for instance we were working on the drawers – the van itself would look no different at the end of a long evening than at the beginning.

Seán and George were feeling the strain as well. George could probably have coped quite well on his own – as he had appeared to do in prison. He had his yoga exercises, his studies, and his books. Seán too read a lot, but he got bored and restless. I think he also felt it was unnecessary for him to have to stay indoors the whole time, and that it would be perfectly safe for him to go out. We assumed that while George was with him he wouldn't do that, though Pat suspected that occasionally Seán did venture out.

Seán also refused to accept another precaution that we had all agreed upon – namely, always to address and refer to George as 'David'. George told us on several occasions that he hated the name George, and heartily wished he had been called anything but that. His father had been a great Anglophile, and had named his son after King George V; whether it was this royal association that put George off the name, I don't know. Seán, however, not only continued to call him George, but, following the custom in some parts of Ireland of using Christian name and surname, would address him directly as 'George Blake'. Even in the privacy of the flat this made us nervous. Perhaps it was a small gesture of defiance on Seán's part, signalling to us that he thought we were being absurdly cautious. But perhaps there were deeper reasons too, a need to keep a grip on reality in a disorienting situation by calling things and people by their real names.

Narrated by Pat Pottle
I still had a business to run while George and Seán were staying with me. The printing machinery had all been bought on hire purchase, and with the continual struggle to keep up with the payments, I could not afford to take time off. Every morning I would leave at 8 o'clock by underground to Warren Street station, and not return until 6 o'clock in the evening.

It is surprising how quickly one adjusts to new circumstances. After a short time I hardly gave a thought to my guests while I was at work, except when Michael called in. However, the minute I left for home a knot would form in my stomach.

It was an odd sensation. I felt tense, apprehensive, sometimes downright scared. But I was also on a kind of high. The constant flow of adrenalin acted like a drug.

One Monday evening – 21 November – travelling home on the underground I opened my *Evening Standard* to see a picture of George staring out at me from the front page. The headline in two inch block capitals read: 'The Getaway – In Detail' and the subheading above it was 'George Blake's escape cost £5000 – planned like a military operation.'[3]

The report claimed that Blake had flown to Frankfurt on the evening of the escape and had reached Prague a few days later; he was now living in East Berlin. I was so completely thrown that just for a moment I thought: 'But he can't be. He was at home with me this morning!' Then I looked up and began to think that everyone in the carriage was staring at me. I quickly folded the paper and put it in my shopping bag.

When I got home that evening we had a chance to study the report in more detail. It was based on an article that had appeared in the German magazine *Der Spiegel*, written by a British journalist of Czech origin called – believe it or not – Michael Rand! The similarity to Michael's name was a disconcerting coincidence. The report gave precise details of George's alleged flight to Eastern Europe, even naming the head of the East German espionage service, Marcus Wolf, as one of the principal organizers of the flight. The national dailies carried the report of the *Spiegel* article the following day, when police also interviewed Mr Rand. They apparently concluded that his story was based entirely on speculation and invention.

Sometimes I felt irrational urges to shout out the truth. I speculated what effect it would have. Probably people would take me for a nut and edge away!

The butterflies in my stomach were most active as I neared Willow Buildings from Gayton Crescent and looked up at the window of the flat to see if George had given the danger signal of drawing the net curtains. I would then have to decide whether to walk or run! Of course, if the police had been there the game was up anyhow, but at least I might have the chance of contacting Michael.

The flat was cramped with three of us living there. Bathing was a particular problem. All we had was the kitchen sink, which was one of the large, old-fashioned white enamel variety with a cold tap feeding it. Our only source of hot water was a small Ascot heater.

When I was on my own I managed all right – I could always nip round to my mother's flat every now and again for a proper bath. At Willow Buildings I would fill the sink, undress and wash myself down. The awkward part was raising one's leg over the edge of the sink. George was particularly embarrassed at being seen like this and we therefore agreed that anyone deciding to take a bath should give due warning to the other two.

Relations between Seán and myself became strained as time went by; we didn't quarrel but the atmosphere was often tense. I suspect

Seán secretly resented his changed role. In the early stage it was he who had made the major decisions and taken the lead. Now he was having to sit around all day, restrained from even setting foot outside the door.

Every evening when I came home, Seán and George would jump up expectantly, and inquire eagerly about progress on the van. But generally there was little to report. Michael came to see me regularly at the printing works to bring me up to date with developments. But though the work progressed steadily there were no spectacular breakthroughs of the kind that Seán and George wanted to hear.

After the evening meal, we would talk or read or watch television. Sometimes George would retire to his room and we could hear him moving about doing his yoga exercises. There was no central heating in the house and no fires in any of the rooms except the sitting-room. But we didn't use it (except occasionally to burn incriminating documents!) because the area had become a smokeless zone and the fireplace wasn't designed to burn coke or other smokeless fuel. Instead we had an electric fan heater which kept the room reasonably comfortable, and even warmed up Seán's and George's tiny bedrooms of an evening if they left their doors open. My own bedroom and the kitchen and toilet were always cold in the winter, so we usually wore jackets at all times.

At one time I started to have terrible trouble with one of my teeth. George and Seán kept urging me to go to the dentist, but I always put off doing so.

'How can you sleep at night with a raging toothache?' George demanded.

'That isn't a problem,' I answered. 'I just lie completely still and try to clear my mind of all thoughts until I go into a kind of trance and the pain disappears. Then I drop off to sleep.'

George became highly excited.

'But that's a very advanced stage in meditation,' he said. 'I've been practising yoga for several years now, and I have not reached that stage.'

'You mean to say that all those people who spend thousands of pounds travelling to India to visit their gurus could save themselves the trouble by simply not going to the dentist?'

He liked to spend time with me in the kitchen when I was preparing meals and passing on tips – such as putting a squeeze of lemon in the cream before whipping it.

'What shall we make tonight?' he asked me on one occasion when Anne and Michael were due round for supper.

I groaned.

'I suppose it's going to have to be bloody fish pie again.'

'Why do you always cook that when they come?'

'It's Michael,' I replied. 'He's a vegetarian. Fortunately, he's not too strict and will eat fish – so that's what they have to have. I don't know any proper vegetarian meals.'

As time went on there was evidence that both Seán and George were feeling the strain of their incarceration. One evening I came home to find them both looking pleased with themselves and obviously bursting to impart some news. It was George who spoke first.

'We had a visitor today,' he said, wanting to provoke a reaction.

'A visitor!' I said. 'For Christ's sake, you don't tell me you let someone in?'

'I answered the door myself,' George replied calmly. 'He was hammering so violently that I thought it might attract the attention of the neighbours.'

'You're behind with the rental on the television, Patrick,' Seán interjected. 'The shop had sent someone round to collect it.'

I continued to stare at them, angry and unsmiling. They were clearly disappointed.

'Anyhow, we paid him what was owing,' George said in a more serious tone. 'And then he left. I'm quite sure he suspected nothing.'

'Maybe not,' I replied, 'But he easily might have done. It was a silly and dangerous thing to do.'

By now they were both thoroughly crestfallen, and there was a strained silence as I went into the kitchen to make a cup of tea.

Afterwards George apologized.

'It was a piece of sheer bravado on my part,' he acknowledged. 'I promise you it won't happen again.'

There was a second incident a week or ten days later. The landlord was busy improving the flats with the aim of selling them off, and sent someone round to measure up the windows for replacement. Again the man had hammered on the door until Seán and George decided to let him in. This time they told me the story more diffidently, wary of my reaction. Seán had opened the door while George sat in his bedroom with the door shut. The man started by measuring the window in my bedroom while Seán took the opportunity to explain to George what was happening. They both then went to the sitting-room, passing pleasantries when the man came through.

'I can assure you,' George said, 'that the man was not in the least suspicious.'

I was not convinced. How many more occasions like this were there going to be?

As it happened, the major crisis took a different form. I came home to find George and Seán with their coats on, ready to leave.

'What on earth's going on?' I demanded.

George was at his most serious.

'I have decided,' he said, 'that I cannot go through with the plan to be smuggled out by Michael and Anne. It is putting them and their children at too great a risk. I have been responsible for the break-up of one family, and I do not want to have another on my conscience. Seán and I have talked the matter over and have decided on an alternative plan. We are going down to the docks, where we will attempt to board a Polish ship, or some other ship from an Eastern European country.'

I stared at him in disbelief. Then Seán chipped in:

'It's worse here than doing solitary in the nick.'

My astonishment turned to anger. The jibe about the nick was more than I could take. I came very close to landing him one.

George's concern, I felt, was genuine. He'd always been uneasy about the risk that Anne and Michael were running on his behalf, and had been brooding about this during the long hours of waiting. But I was also sure that Seán, frustrated at the whole situation, had been working on George, and had talked him into this harebrained scheme.

I restrained myself with great difficulty and persuaded them to sit down and talk the matter over. Their plan, I urged, was quite unrealistic. The dockland area was always well policed, and immediately after George's escape the Press had reported that a special watch was being kept on ships from Eastern Europe that were docked in London. Even if the surveillance was less intense by now, it was asking for trouble for two wanted men with no authorization to go wandering about in search of a suitable ship to board. After all the months of effort – after we had now worked out a feasible plan – were they really prepared to risk throwing everything away on a crazy scheme like this? And nothing, I added, would be more galling for us at this stage than for George and Seán to land themselves back in the nick. In the end they were persuaded, or at

155

any rate gave way. However, the episode did nothing to improve relations between Seán and me.

Our evenings continued to be spent in the same way – reading and watching television. I remember one conversation with George when I said to him that I thought spying was a seedy and dirty business, which had been given a romantic image by the Bond films and others. George replied:

'I can assure you that there's nothing romantic about walking around all day with a camera strapped between your legs!'

He also told me something of what had happened to him when he was arrested in 1961. After interrogation he was taken to a large house in the country and held there for several days. He said he was convinced that during that time his life hung in the balance, and the authorities were trying to make up their minds whether to accept the embarrassment of a trial and having to acknowledge publicly for the first time that Britain had an Intelligence Service spying on other countries, or quietly to get rid of him. He believed it was Macmillan personally who finally came down in favour of him standing trial.

After his conviction and sentence, George had suffered from delayed shock, and became deeply depressed. He remembered during this time having a conversation with a fellow-spy, Gordon Lonsdale (alias Conon Molody), who was in Wormword Scrubs at the time:

'You may be depressed now, but you and I will both be in Red Square to celebrate the fiftieth Anniversary of the Revolution'.

And as events turned out, he was right. Lonsdale was swapped in 1965 for the British businessman spy, Greville Wynne. George reached Moscow through his own efforts – and ours – in December 1966.

George told Michael and myself that he first became converted to communism in Korea in 1950, where he witnessed the corruption and repression of the Syngman Rhee government and the conditions ordinary people had to live under. He told the story of one particular night when he had left the home of an American in the diplomatic community there. Like most American houses, he said, it was overheated and its inhabitants lived in luxury. On the way home he passed a pauper shivering under a blanket in the street. This extreme contrast clinched for him the conviction that there was something fundamentally wrong and unjust about a system that could produce such disparity. Nor, he realized, was this just a feature of life in Korea; in Britain and the United States, and all capitalist countries, similar injustice and inequality was to be found.

I then questioned him about his period as a captive in the hands of the North Koreans from soon after the outbreak of war in June 1950 to his repatriation in 1953. He had taken part in a forced march to the northernmost part of North Korea with British, American and other prisoners; many had died on the journey. How, I asked him, did he square this with his new-found belief in communism? He replied that the North Korean guards walked just as far, and received exactly the same rations as the prisoners. It was hard, certainly, but it was hard for everyone.

During this period – from the time Seán joined George and me in Willow Buildings to the time he finally left the country – we would send the rent each week in the form of a £5 note to the landlady of the bed-sit in Highlever Road. I took elaborate precautions to prevent the possibility of the envelope or its enclosures being traced back to the Hampstead area, or having any give-away fingerprints or characteristics. Each week I would buy a new notepad and get Seán to write a letter to the landlady saying he was still away on business. I then burnt the rest of the notepad in the sitting-room grate to make sure the paper on which the letter was written could not be matched with any in the flat. After Seán had written the letter and addressed the envelope, I would don a pair of surgical gloves and wipe the £5 note, the letter and the envelope with a damp sponge to remove fingerprints. I used water, rather than spit, to stick down the envelope and attach the stamp, so that there would be no saliva on them which might be traceable. Finally, always handling the envelope with gloves, I would post it in Central London.

Were these precautions superfluous? Seán was convinced that they were. But we reasoned that if by chance the landlady became suspicious and took the envelope and its contents to the police they could well be subjected to forensic examination – and would certainly be so if the police took her suspicions seriously. However remote the risk, there was no point in running it when a few precautions would eliminate it altogether.

Narrated by Michael Randle
Matthew and I took the occasional night off and every so often Anne and I would spend the evening at Pat's, having a meal and talking over ideas and plans.

As work progressed on the van, the question of what to do about Seán became ever more pressing. He still favoured taking the mailboat to Dublin and making known his presence there. The Extradition Treaty between Britain and Eire specifically exempted people convicted of political offences, and he was convinced he could fight deportation on these grounds. He cited some IRA cases where the Irish courts had refused to allow extradition. Pat and I argued that these cases would be viewed very differently from one concerned with the escape of a convicted communist spy. Ireland was a Catholic country and anti-communist sentiment ran high; the Irish government would be under intense pressure to return Seán once he was arrested.

Seán would not be persuaded. He assured us, moreover, that even if he was deported and stood trial in England he would never name us to the authorities. Pat and I accepted this; Seán had a lot of courage and determination, and we were confident he would not deliberately shop us, even under pressure. But George said that if his interrogators injected him with a truth drug, with the best will in the world, he would not be able to hold anything back.

For Pat, Anne and I there was of course a further complication. If Seán stood trial, could we simply stand by and see him sentenced to a long term of imprisonment on his own? I think we all realized that that would be impossible, but it was a dilemma we would much prefer not to have to face.

Eventually, Seán agreed to follow George to the Soviet Union and stay there for six or twelve months to allow time for the excitement to die down and the clues to go cold. He was never happy about the decision, and we felt somewhat guilty about having pushed him into it. We did, however, impress on George his responsibility to take care of Seán during his stay there. Unlike George, he had no knowledge of the language, no friends or contacts in the Soviet Union, and little or no sympathy for the communist system. We also gave George the name of a friend through whom messages could be passed to us in an emergency.

It was one thing to decide that Seán should follow George to the Soviet Union, quite another to figure out how to arrange his exit. Making a second journey with the van was our first thought. But the more we considered it, the less we liked it. He might just manage to squeeze into the concealed compartment, despite being much bigger and stockier than George, but would he ever cope with being shut into a cramped dark space for perhaps eight or nine hours on end? We didn't think so.

But it was equally clear that he could not travel openly on a passport of his own, and that he had no safe method of obtaining a forged one. At last we decided to look into the possibility of forging papers ourselves. I took my own passport to Pat's printing works and we examined it together. It was obvious that we did not have the necessary skills to forge and print passports at his works. But pondering over the document, something else occurred to me. Seán's age and description was not so very different from the particulars given in my passport. If there was a way of substituting his photograph for mine, and reproducing the official embossment in one corner of it, we would have a solution.

In the days that followed I pondered different possible ways of producing a suitable mould. Then one day I tried an experiment with the bonding agent Plastic Padding – a product still on the market today. It comprises two tubes of chemical paste which you squeeze out into strips and mix thoroughly. Within five or ten minutes or so it sets very hard, not unlike plastic. Using this, I began to make impressions of coins, sprinkling the face of the coin with talcum powder so that it came away without difficulty when the mix had set. The results were promising.

The next stage was to see how well the Padding would take an impression from an embossed passport photograph. The photograph page of the passport, now as then, is embossed with an oval-shaped stamp bearing the familiar lion and unicorn motif at the centre and the words 'Foreign and Commonwealth Office' around the rim. The embossment is positioned in the passport so that it partly covers the bottom right-hand corner of the photograph and continues on to the page itself.

I found an out-of-date passport and steamed off the photograph from the page. It came off with surprising ease. I then mixed a new lot of Plastic Padding and waited until it had just begun to set and had lost its initial tackiness. Next I gave the face of the photograph a generous dose of talcum powder and placed the corner containing the embossment firmly in the mix. Half an hour later I was able to lift off the photograph, and found it had left a perfect impression of the embossment in the padding.

By now I felt we might be on to something. But how could the impression in the mould be transferred on to a new photograph? I wondered whether it would be possible to buy a small embossing machine, and to substitute the mould I had made for the original one, but soon decided that wouldn't be practicable. Had we reached the end of the line with this approach? Before finally abandoning the experiment I tried making a rubbing, placing a photograph face downward on the mould and scribbling on the back with a pencil. Soon a reverse image of the stamp appeared in the pencil marks, indented inward. When I turned the photograph over I was excited to find it bore a stamp in the corner with a very close resemblance to the original embossment.

In a little while I had perfected the technique. I found also that the edges of the passport photograph made a groove in the padding which could be used to give perfect registration on the photograph being doctored. This meant that when it was put into the passport the lines of the embossment would match perfectly with those on the page. I also placed a piece of tracing paper over the back of the photograph so that I wasn't scribbling directly on to it. Using a hard pencil, I found that the stamp on the front had a good clean edge to it.

After I had produced a result that Anne and I were reasonably satisfied with I put a doctored photograph back into the old passport and brought it round to Pat's works. He was elated. So too were Seán and George when we brought it for them to inspect a day or two later. As a Vice-Consul in South Korea, George was used to handling passports. He ran his fingers over the embossment and said he was sure we would have no difficulty. We decided that unless the police released Seán's photo to the Press, he would follow George out of the country not in the van but on a doctored passport.

During the late sixties and early seventies we were able to use this technique again, and to pass on the information about it to others to provide passports to US war resisters seeking sanctuary in Sweden. However, it is no longer feasible today. In Britain at least, passports have been modified so that the passport photograph is completely sheathed in a kind of transparent plastic envelope bonded to both sides of the page. It would be impossible to remove the plastic envelope without completely disfiguring the page underneath.

During the supper evenings at Pat's when we were not discussing practical plans we frequently talked politics. The debates could become heated when Pat and I challenged aspects of Soviet policy, such as the Stalinist purges in the 1930s, the persecution of anarchists by Stalinist agents during the Spanish civil war (as recorded by George Orwell in *Homage to Catalonia*) and the political repression in Eastern Europe after the Second World War. As far as any of us can recall, George never explicitly defended these policies, though I recall him once telling us of a conversation he had in a train at the end of the war with a Russian peasant woman whose eyes filled with tears as she recalled how Stalin had saved the nation in the dark days of the Nazi invasion.

Occasionally we would touch a raw nerve and George would make a speech passionately defending his belief in the Soviet communist system. He was convinced, he said on one occasion, that this system would triumph. Maybe not in his lifetime, maybe not even in his children's lifetime, but ultimately yes, it would do so.

'Freedom is also important,' Pat replied.

'Oh, yes,' George responded sarcastically, 'freedom is important. So are lots of other things. Washing machines are important. Television sets are important. Getting a man on the Moon is important.'

George was critical of the vagueness of our libertarian, quasi-anarchist beliefs and pressed us to say how we proposed to change the existing – and palpably unjust – social and economic order. We replied that it was the people themselves at the base who had to take power into their own hands through non-violent direct action. We and the organizations with whom we were associated had undertaken such action, and our hope was that it would spread as a means of effecting change.

'But that idea of "going to the people" has been tried and failed,' he replied. 'The *narodniks* tried it in Russia in the nineteenth century and it didn't work. I think there has to be action from above as well as from below if things are to change.'

George also argued strongly that whatever one might say about the Hitler–Stalin Pact, once it was involved in the war against Nazi Germany the Soviet Union played a decisive role in its defeat. He also argued that the existence of the Soviet Union exerted a crucial pressure on the Western colonial powers to dismantle their empires at the end of the Second World War.

Although Pat and I were passionately opposed to authoritarian and totalitarian regimes, there was some common ground between us and George. We were all unequivocally opposed to the American war in Vietnam – and George listened with interest to our accounts of the campaigns to persuade American troops stationed in various countries to refuse to serve in Vietnam and if necessary to desert. More generally, we were all opposed to the injustices and inequalities of capitalist society and committed to building a socialist alternative of some kind. (The crucial argument was, of course, over what kind of socialism, and how to go about building it.) We were of one mind also about the need to dismantle colonial empires and to resist further expansion.

Once, after a rather heated debate, it was George who emphasized that, despite our differences, we agreed on some fundamental issues. I was too caught up in the argument to leave it at that, and said that if one talked abstractly enough, and about ultimate goals, it was usually possible to agree; but one could still have a totally different view about how the goals were to be achieved, and what in a more precise sense those goals were.

Seán refused to become involved in the discussions, even though he certainly held definite views of his own. If he joined in at all it was to save George from embarrassment when we pressed home awkward points. Once, not long before his departure, George commented on how difficult it would be to explain to the East Germans and Russians the motivation of the people who had helped him.

'I shall have to explain to them that this is England, and that really what has happened could only happen here.'

I doubt if this was literally the case, though George may well have believed it to be so. Ironically, he was more Anglophile than any of us. On this particular occasion George went on to express his strong attachment to England and his hope that one day, somehow, it would be possible for him to visit the country again. He can hardly have been anticipating the revolution! – but perhaps he thought that East–West relations would improve to the point where he could return without risking arrest. I was puzzled, but hesitated before I put my next question to him.

'If you are so attached to this country,' I said finally, 'why did you spy against it for the Russians?'

'For Christ's sake!' Seán interjected, 'You can't ask questions like that!'

George was indeed nonplussed. He replied that he saw his actions as directed not against Britain but for the protection of the Soviet state, which was under threat from British and American activities.

Seán's unwillingness to enter into political discussions – indeed, his positive anxiety to protect George from our questions – contrasts dramatically with the political quarrels which, according to his own account, he had with George in Moscow. Perhaps during their time together in prison when they clearly had formed one of those close friendships which do spring up in such confined circumstances, and in the period in London after the escape, Seán simply did not want to confront the fact that they had very different political views. However, once the atmosphere between them began to sour he started raising deliberately provocative questions and bluntly stating views which could only end in acrimonious disputes.

There was one revealing incident around this time. Anne and I had come round for supper and we had all had wine to drink with the meal. Seán lay sprawled on an armchair, apparently fast asleep with his tie loosened and the top button of his shirt open, while the rest of us sat round the table talking. The discussion turned to what might happen when George and Seán reached Moscow.

'I can tell you one thing,' George said, lowering his voice to a murmur and leaning towards us, 'when we do get to Moscow, our friend here is going to have to learn some discipline.' He nodded his head in Seán's direction.

Seán's face broke into a grin. He cocked one eye open.

'I heard that!' He closed his eye again and appeared to go back to sleep. Pat, Anne and I broke out into great guffaws of laughter. George smiled too, but it was one of only two or three occasions that we saw him blush with embarrassment.

Notwithstanding our political differences with George none of us ever doubted that we had done the right thing in helping him. However, ideally we would have liked to have struck a simultaneous blow against injustice in the Soviet bloc. Thus, in a romantic and unrealistic way, we speculated on the possibility of picking up someone in East Berlin who wanted to go to the West and using the same secret compartment in the van to take him or her across the frontier. We discussed this openly in front of George, who said he thought it was an excellent idea, though perhaps recognizing that we were hardly likely to carry it off. To do so would have required contacts and careful advance planning, and clearly we had enough to think about getting George and Seán out of Britain without planning another difficult and dangerous operation for the return journey. (I am happy to say, however, that a few years later we did use other camper vans modified in the same way to smuggle books, pamphlets and duplicating machines to human rights activists in Eastern Europe.)

We also pressed George to use any influence he had in Moscow to secure the release of the two Soviet dissident writers Sinyavsky and Daniel. Both had been sentenced in September 1965 to terms of 'corrective labour' – Sinyavsky to seven years, Daniel to five. George promised to raise the matter, though without holding out any particular hope of success.

Some time round about the middle of the second week in December, perhaps the 8th or 9th, the conversion work on the van was complete. It was quite a transformation. There was one narrow drawer at the back, clearly visible in the picture, and two much wider ones in front of it. In the photograph the middle drawer has been removed to show the opening to the compartment where George was concealed. This secret compartment extended from behind the two larger drawers to the underneath of the forward-facing seat immediately behind the driver's seat. We placed a piece of foam rubber in the hiding-place so that George would not be too uncomfortable during the long hours he would be confined there.

As the work neared completion we fixed the departure date for Saturday 17 December; by then Princeton College would have broken up for the Christmas vacation. We bought a ticket for the midnight ferry crossing on that date from Dover to Ostend and obtained the necessary Green Card Insurance document and an international driving licence. The last wasn't strictly necessary, but we wanted to avoid any possible complications, especially at the border crossing into East Germany. I also bought two yellow plastic fittings to attach to the headlamps on the van once we had crossed the Channel. This both redirected the beam for driving on the right-hand side of the road, and turned it yellow – the standard colour for headlights in mainland Europe.

One thing, however, still troubled me about the provisions for George on the journey. He would be confined for perhaps eight or nine hours at a stretch; would he be able to go that long without wanting to pee? I raised the matter with George, who dismissed the problem, saying he was sure he could cope.

I was still doubtful, and decided to make some inquiries about fitments for invalids and incontinent people. I went to a specialist shop in Central London and explained to the assistant that I had an elderly incontinent relative and asked him if they had anything that could be of help.

'Certainly, sir,' he said, lowering his voice in the discreet, considerate manner of an undertaker. 'The device,' he continued 'fits onto the "member" and is positioned down the leg of the patient inside the trousers. Is your relative confined to a wheelchair?'

'He is,' I said.

'That's all right,' he went on. 'But, of course, we would have to have the member measured.' He lowered his voice still further. 'They do tend to shrivel, you know, as people get older.'

I told George about the results of my inquiries.

'They do have something we could fix you up with,' I said, 'if we want to be on the safe side.'

'I don't really see that it's necessary,' George replied.

I started to laugh, and had difficulty getting my words out.

'Only if we do decide you should have it, you'll have to measure your . . . er . . . whatsit.'

By now all the others were laughing too. Poor George went scarlet. He waved his hand in the air as if brushing aside an unwelcome thought.

'No, no!' he said hurriedly. 'There's absolutely no need.'

Later, however, and perhaps simply in deference to our concern, he agreed to take an empty hot water bottle with him in the compartment to use in an emergency.

The forthcoming journey preoccupied us most of our waking hours. As the time approached what began to bother me was not so much the journey to East Germany with George as the fact that when it was over there was still the further hazard of having Seán travel on my doctored passport. I mentioned this to Pat one day when I visited his printing works.

'Why doesn't he travel on my passport?' he said at once. 'It's the obvious solution. I can't imagine why we didn't think of it before.'

I was closer in age to Seán than Pat, and this was one reason we had not previously considered this alternative. We had simply taken it for granted that it was my passport that would be used.

There was another advantage in using Pat's passport. If Anne and I arrived safely in Berlin we could phone Pat at his work to let him know, and Seán could be on his way even before we returned to this country.

The van was ready a week or so before the departure date. I drove up to Pat's flat to take George out on a trial run. Pat and Seán came down with him to see him safely stowed away. Everyone was impressed. The standard of workmanship on the fittings was truly professional – even the most thorough examination would provide no clues that many of the original fixtures had been replaced.

George crawled into the compartment and positioned himself on the foam rubber.

'Is it OK?' I asked anxiously, leaning into the opening.

'It's fine,' he replied, settling down into the most comfortable position. His voice had that echoey quality you get in wooden sports pavilions. 'You can put the drawer back now if you wish.'

I did so. We had put a swivel catch at the back of the drawer which he could turn to prevent the drawer being pulled completely out, and he now did this to secure himself inside the compartment. As I drove away it was uncannily quiet inside the van. I found it difficult to believe that there was another human being in the back.

On an impulse I drove down to our house in Kentish Town. Anne and the children were there, and also Bridget. We avoided any formal introductions, though Bridget realized who George was. She was knitting, and carried on working while we chatted and drank tea. George and I didn't stay long for fear of worrying Pat and Seán. George said afterwards how attractive he found Bridget. This was not surprising, for not only was she a beautiful young woman but she had an open and generous nature that came across at once when you began talking to her.

On the way back, however, there was an unexpected crisis. I tried to do a U-turn on one of the narrow roads with a steep camber in the Hampstead area. Somehow, because of its length, the van got stuck on the crown of the road in a position where the back wheels couldn't get any purchase. I tried pushing it with the driver's door open and with one hand on the steering-wheel. It wouldn't budge.

I began to rage inwardly at the sheer stupidity of the situation and had visions of the whole operation coming to grief because of this ridiculous mishap. Fortunately at this point a man walking down the road offered to give me a push. A minute later I was on my way again. George, hidden away under the seating, was quite unaware that anything untoward had happened.

When we got back he was in confident mood.

'As soon as I got inside that space in the van,' he said, 'I could tell that everything was going to be fine. I am absolutely sure now that we are going to succeed.'

Postscript by Pat Pottle

The ordeal was nearing its end. George would leave tomorrow and if all went well, Seán would follow a few days later.

I had gone mad that day and for our last meal together bought some incredibly expensive fillet steak, a bottle of whisky and two large bottles of plonk. (George, I had learnt by now, was knowledgable about wine, but our finances simply could not run to a good vintage.)

We all enjoyed the dinner, reminiscing over the adventures of the previous few months, but none of us could forget that George was to leave the next day.

Seán, who had been drinking whisky steadily all evening, nodded off to sleep and we helped him to his room. I started to clear up the glasses, and George hung around as I started to wash up. He suggested a last drink before we retired. It was obvious he wanted to talk.

'Pat, I cannot express my feelings towards you all – you have risked everything to help me. Seán, you, and especially Michael, who is risking his whole family.'

I was slightly embarrassed and tried to joke.

'If it all goes well – and I'm sure it will – your days in hiding are nearly over. But if after you've been in Russia a while you begin to think that you have only swapped one prison for another, give us a ring.'

He laughed and said, 'I hope I will not have to ask for your assistance again!'

I reminded him of his promise to intercede for Sinyavsky and Daniel, and George promised to put their case as strongly as he could.

CHAPTER SEVEN

Exit in Pursuit of a Bear

Narrated by Michael Randle

D (for Departure) Day was Saturday 17 December. We booked the
midnight car ferry from Dover to Ostend. This would mean that the
children would be asleep in the double bed at the back as we passed
through British customs, and the chances of a search would be
minimized. We expected to arrive in Ostend around 4a.m., when
again it would be natural for the children to be resting. Finally, we
planned to drive straight through from Ostend to Berlin, crossing
the critical frontier between East and West Germany at Helmstedt
at around 7.30 or 8.00p.m. If everything went according to plan we
would reach Berlin by midnight.

It would be a gruelling twenty-eight hours of virtually non-stop
travel. Our instinct was to get George to Eastern Europe as quickly
as possible. But the danger of doing things this way was that I
would become exhausted, perhaps even fall asleep at the wheel.

Concerned about this risk, I went to see the doctor who had set
George's broken wrist and asked him if he could prescribe anything
that would help keep me alert.

'Yes', he said, 'I can give you some pills that should help. But the
body needs sleep – the pills can only do so much.'

He questioned me further about our plans for George and Seán,
but seemed singularly unimpressed with what I told him.

'They must both be crazy,' he said, 'if they think the KGB are
going to provide open house for any friends Blake may care to bring
along with him.'

Anne and I spent the last day or two sorting out what we would
need for the journey: footwear and clothing, bedding, books to
read. Anne, I remember brought along Laurie Lee's *Cider With
Rosie*; I chose an edition of the *Collected Poems* of Yeats together
with a *Daily Express* course on Conversational German which I
had made desultory efforts to work through over several years.

On Saturday morning we bought our provisions – bread, cheese,
tomatoes, tins of soup, and tea and coffee. We wanted to be

completely self-sufficient until we reached Berlin. I also bought a small briquette-shaped transistor radio. Placed against the van windscreen, it worked reasonably well if the signal was strong.

A story in the early editions of the *Evening News* caused us momentary alarm. It suggested that vehicles leaving Britain on the car ferries might face searches. A few weeks earlier, when the work on converting the van was already well underway, police had stopped a hearse travelling up the M1 and searched a coffin because they had had a tip-off that Blake was concealed inside it.

We took comfort from the skill with which Matthew had made the adaptations to the van. But in any case at this stage we were committed, whatever the risks might be.

Finally, there was always the possibility that my own movements in and out of the country were still being monitored, as I knew they had been even up to two years previously. (In 1964 when I was going through Customs at Dover on my way to a War Resisters International Council meeting at Mainz-Kastel in Germany, the plainclothes detective standing behind the passport desk in Dover greeted me by name and asked if I was off to attend another peace conference!)

Much of the afternoon was spent loading up the van with the enthusiastic help of our two children. We had told them nothing about bringing anyone else along with us. For them it was simply going to be a holiday in Germany – their first trip abroad.

At 6.30p.m. we drove up to Pat's flat for a final dinner. I suppose we had fish pie again – though I can't vouch for it! When we sat down to eat George proposed a toast to the success of the journey.

'I don't foresee any difficulty', George reassured us. 'It's unlikely there'll be any searches at all, and even if there are, it's most improbable the Custom's officials will insist on getting the children out of the bed, much less on searching behind the drawers.'

'Anyway,' Pat teased, 'who'd suspect Michael? He has such a respectable, middle-class look about him.'

George considered this, then, attempting to be diplomatic, added: 'Well, let's say "puritanical".'

We discussed what we might do after we had dropped George off in East Germany.

'Why don't you spend a few days at Goslar?' George suggested. 'It is a charming little town in the Harz mountains south of Brunswick and would only involve a small detour. I used to spend holidays there. It would be lovely for the children too, especially if there's snow – which you can usually rely upon having at this time of year.'

The ferry company recommended arriving at Dover an hour before embarkation. We thought half an hour would be ample time and planned to leave at 8 o'clock, thus allowing ourselves three and a half hours for the eighty-mile journey. But we delayed our departure, reluctant to leave the warmth and good cheer of the flat. At about 8.15p.m. Anne said:

'I really think we must be going.'

'Yes, yes!' George agreed. 'It would be ridiculous to miss the ferry.'

But Pat remembered one last task to be done that we had decided upon some weeks earlier, but kept forgetting about. We had agreed that George, Seán, Pat and I would sign a blank sheet of paper which would become the final page of an account of what had happened – but only in the event of one or more of us being arrested. The idea was that if any of us were not arrested we would write up the story and put the money it earned into a legal and welfare fund. This was principally to provide insurance for my family if I, or Anne and I, were sent to prison.

We signed the paper. Then Seán, Pat, George and I went down to the van parked in Willow Road; Anne stayed behind for a few minutes with the children so that they would not see George climbing into his hiding-place.

'Pat, Seán – goodbye. Believe me, I will never forget what you have done.'

'Goodbye, is it?' Seán replied in a tone of mock outrage. 'You'll not be getting rid of me so easy. I'll see you in a week's time.'

'Yes, indeed,' George said with a laugh. 'In your case it should be *au revoir*. And I very much hope, Pat, that one of these days we can also meet again.'

'Good luck!' Seán called out in the strong Limerick accent he adopted when raising his glass in a toast.

George climbed into the van.

'Don't forget this,' I urged, handing him the hot-water bottle.

He took it sheepishly, then, lying on the floor, wriggled himself into the far corner of the cavity.

'Remember, if there are any problems, bang as loud as you can on the side,' I instructed.

'Well, of course if it's necessary,' he said. 'But I really don't foresee any difficulties.' His voice sounded distant and muffled.

I put the middle drawer back into position and folded the bed down, just as Anne arrived with the children. We put them to bed, but they were too excited to think of sleeping.

Anne and I climbed in the front. The children's enthusiasm was infectious; I too felt a sense of excitement as I started up the engine.

'Bye, Seán! Bye, Pat! We'll be phoning you Monday morning.'

I said it not so much to confirm the arrangement as to reassure myself that everything would go according to plan.

It took us a long time to get out of London, although the rush-hour was well over. We crossed the river at Blackfriars Bridge, picking up the New Kent Road and the beginning of the A2 at the Elephant and Castle. But south-east London seemed to stretch on interminably.

After Dartford we finally left the built-up area and could move more freely. But we had already been travelling for the best part of an hour and were way behind schedule. This was the first time I had driven the van on an open road, and I found that even with the accelerator hard down it wouldn't go much more than fifty miles an hour on level ground. On a good downhill stretch it might reach sixty, but uphill it slowed right down again.

'I wish to God we'd set off a bit earlier,' Anne said. 'We're only just going to make it – if that.'

'We'll be OK,' I reassured her, 'provided there are no more hold-ups.'

By the time we by-passed Canterbury, I felt we were well on our way. But as the road crossed the North Downs the going became much slower. We were perhaps ten miles or so outside Dover when Anne turned to me in alarm.

'Listen,' she said. 'I think I can hear something. I think he's knocking.'

I strained my ears. With the engine directly underneath us at full revs it was difficult to hear anything. Besides, I couldn't bring myself to believe that we had already run into an emergency. Not so soon.

'No, I don't think so,' I answered. 'I can't hear anything.'

I drove on.

'There it is again!' Anne shouted. 'Michael, you've got to stop. It's definitely him knocking.'

And indeed this time there could be no mistake. The banging was loud and insistent. I slowed down and pulled into the side of the road, still finding it hard to believe that things had gone wrong so quickly. Perhaps there was not enough air in that confined space for someone to be kept there for more than a very short period of time. If there was a serious problem we would have to cancel the whole trip before even reaching the South Coast.

By this time the children were asleep, but we had to wake them.

'Come on – Seán, Gavin – wake up!'

They opened their eyes, dazed and heavy with sleep, unsure of where they were or what was happening.

'Are we going on the boat now?' Seán asked.

'Not quite yet. Come in the front with Mummy and she'll wrap you up.'

When they were both in the front, Anne enveloped them in a blanket, making a kind of tent over their heads so that they could not see what was going on in the back. She also switched on the transistor radio and turned it up loud. I pulled out the drawer.

'George – what's wrong?'

He didn't answer at once, but crawled out of the cavity, and stood up. He was pale and retching, holding the hot-water bottle away from him at arm's-length.

'I need some air,' he said.

He stumbled to the back of the van and once outside began taking deep breaths. From time to time he bent double and straightened himself up again. We had stopped on a high, lonely stretch of road, and there was a cold breeze blowing. By now the children had started to complain and whimper. They were cold and sleepy. I didn't want to hurry George, but I was terrified that we were going to miss the ferry.

After five or ten minutes some of the colour began to return to George's face.

'I'll be all right in a minute,' he said. 'It was that hot-water bottle – it gives off a smell like gas and was making me feel sick.'

Eventually he was ready to go back into his compartment, and I put the drawer into position. Some minutes later we set off again.

Although George had been certain that it was the hot-water bottle that had brought on the nausea, Anne and I were by no means convinced that it was the whole story. Lack of proper ventilation, we suspected, was the root problem. How then would George survive the confinement that lay ahead?

For the rest of the drive we listened intently for any sounds from George's hideout. But there was no further incident. We reached Dover about ten minutes before the ferry was due to sail, terrified the officials would say that we were too late. In fact there were one or two vehicles immediately ahead of us and soon several behind us.

The passport check was perfunctory, and we followed the cars ahead of us to Customs clearance. My nerves were taut, but I did not feel frightened. I glanced at Anne. She had swung the driving mirror in her direction and was applying eye make-up as if totally unconcerned. She told me afterwards that this was not deliberate, just something she decided she needed to do at that moment. But what with that and the sleeping children we must have looked the model bourgeois family.

There was no check of any kind at Customs. An official, hardly stopping to glance in our direction, waved us through on to the ferry. We parked it as directed, leaving the doors unlocked as the notices ordered, and carried the two boys, still half asleep, up the steps to the lounge above.

After all our panic, the ferry did not leave for about another twenty minutes or so. Seán puts the delay at two hours, but it was nothing like as long as that. We managed to get the children back to sleep; Anne and I, still extremely tense, drank coffee and fretted about George.

Some time into the journey there was an announcement on the ship's tannoy. Would the owner of vehicle number so and so please report to a certain office? I looked across at Anne.

'Can you remember the number of the van?'

'I can't, I'm afraid – you're the one that's been working on it for the last six weeks.'

The message on the tannoy was repeated.

'Somehow, I don't think that was it,' Anne said. 'In any case, the best thing is for us to sit tight.'

At about 4.30a.m. British time – 5.30a.m. local time – the ferry docked and we hurried down to the van. We had half expected it to be surrounded by officials waiting to challenge us about our stowaway, but there was no one there. The inside of the van seemed eerily silent.

Because we were among the last of the vehicles boarding the ferry, we were now faced with a delay getting off. I considered putting the yellow plastic attachments on to the headlamps while we were waiting in order to conform with Belgian traffic law, but thought better of it. I didn't want to be half-way through the job when our turn came to move.

The metal gangplanks clanked as we drove over them and on to the quayside, and the morning air was chill as I wound down the windscreen next to the Customs official.

'Your green card, sir, please,' he said in English as we drove level. He peered in through the side windows. The children had already settled down and the scene could not have looked more normal. Handing me back the card, he waved us on.

There was still no sound from the back. Anne moved close to me and whispered:

'I don't like it; it's all too quiet. I have this terrible feeling that he's dead – suffocated. Oh, Michael, what are we going to do if he is dead?'

'I'm sure he's all right.' I replied, trying to convince myself as much as Anne. 'I'll pull up once we're away from the docks and let him out.'

'No, no, I think we should drive clear of the town. If he is all right we don't want to risk him being spotted.'

We drove on for about another half hour along the main road to Brussels. Those few miles were the longest in the whole journey.

It was still completely dark when we pulled up. Aside from the short break between Canterbury and Dover when he was feeling sick, George had been confined in the hideout for eight and a half hours.

The stretch of road where we had stopped was deserted at that hour of the morning, and a strong cold wind blew across the flat countryside. A hundred yards or so to our left a single electric-light bulb shone out from a farm building.

We repeated the routine with the children that we had performed earlier on the road to Dover, while I removed the drawer.

'George! Are you OK?'

There was a shuffling sound from inside the cavity.

'I'm fine,' he whispered back. 'A bit stiff, that's all.'

'My God, am I glad to see you!' I said as he got out. 'Anne and I were giving you up for dead.'

'No, no – I was fine once I had got rid of the hot water bottle.'

He stood by the side of the road and had a long pee.

'So far so good,' he said. 'I'm sure we are going to make it.' There was excitement as well as relief in his voice. It was getting past Dover and landing safely on the Continent that had always worried him most.

Once he was out of the van Anne removed the blanket from around herself and the children. They showed no surprise when we let George into the van and seemed more interested in getting back to bed. They must have recognized him from the previous night but didn't question how he had suddenly turned up again in Belgium!

I put the yellow plastic attachments on to the headlamps and we set off, George sitting on one of the forward-facing seats in the back.

It was the happiest part of our journey. We sensed success and were not yet too exhausted to savour it. 'Did you sleep at all?' Anne asked.

'No, but I was quite comfortable on the foam rubber.'

'What did you think of during all those hours?'

'Well, I've had some experience of being on my own in a confined space! It was a chance to do some meditation.'

In Wormwood Scrubs, I remember George having won a certain renown for standing on his head for fifteen minutes morning and evening as part of his yoga exercises.

Dawn broke as we drove towards Brussels, but the sky was dull and overcast. I could feel the wind tugging at the sides of the van as we went along. Anne started to nod off after her sleepless night, and conversation with George dried up. It was difficult in any case to hold a proper conversation with George because of the engine noise. The van warmed up and became fuggy. Quite suddenly as we were approaching the outskirts of the town I had an overwhelming desire to sleep. The rear lights of the cars in front began to dance in a zig-zag across the road.

'I'm going to have to stop a minute,' I announced. 'Otherwise I'll fall asleep.'

I got out, and took some deep breaths of the chill morning air. I felt somewhat less drowsy when I got back into the van, but nevertheless took two of the doctor's pills before setting off again. Within a few minutes I had that euphoric sense of being one step removed from the scene around me; at the same time I lost the sensation of sleepiness.

'I'm impressed with the pills the doctor gave me,' I told Anne and George. 'Suddenly I feel wide awake again.'

'That's quite extraordinary!' George commented. 'If you have any to spare I'd be much obliged if you could let me have a couple before you drop me. I've probably got another long night ahead of me.'

We got lost in the centre of Brussels and couldn't find the directions for Aachen. It was light now, and about 8.30 in the morning; the streets were starting to fill with people, and the traffic was getting heavier.

I stopped and wound down the windscreen to ask a young woman the way. But George leaned past me and addressed her in Flemish. She was able to put us on our route, but Anne was perturbed that George had shown himself in this way.

'He isn't doing what he said he would do!' she whispered when we stopped for petrol a few miles farther on, 'He was meant to keep out of sight the whole journey, but now he's even talking to strangers in the street.'

Soon after leaving Brussels we pulled into a lay-by to have breakfast. We folded away the bed, set up the table in the centre space, and used the calor-gas cooker for the first time. We had tea and toast, and the children had cereal as well. They loved the novelty of sitting round a table to eat in a van with its own cooker; it was the first time they'd been in a vehicle where such a thing was possible.

We reached the border at Aachen around 11a.m. A few miles before the checkpoint, we hid George again. What the boys made of this strange ritual of being shielded in the front of the van while George alternately disappeared and reappeared, we never knew. But if they were at all puzzled, it certainly didn't bother them, and they seemed to accept the situation without question. Given another year or two, it would have been a different story.

It was raining when we crossed the frontier. Neither the Belgian nor German officials showed any interest in the van. The latter didn't even examine our passports but waved us on as soon as they saw we were British.

From Aachen we took the autobahn northward in the direction of Düsseldorf and Essen. The rain beat down heavily, making driving difficult. Lorries thundering past sent clouds of spray across the autobahn, and there were frequent warning signs about the cross-winds.

At around 12.30p.m. we stopped again and prepared a lunch of tinned tomato soup and cheese sandwiches. We felt protected as the rain drummed noisily on the metal roof of the camper. But by now we had been on the road for about six and a half hours, and the novelty had begun to wear off for the children. They became quarrelsome, and we had to distract them with sweets and drinks, and games of 'I spy.' George joined in the games, doing his best to keep them entertained.

After Essen, the autobahn continues north-westward, passing south of Bielefeld and Buckeburg, and circling Hanover and Braunschweig (Brunswick) before reaching the border at Helmstedt. By the late afternoon, the rain was beating down so fast that it was difficult to see properly. To cheer ourselves up we put the radio on, and tuned into some music, even though the motor driving the windscreen wipers cut into the reception.

Suddenly the interference stopped. It took me a second to realize what had happened – the wipers were no longer working. I slowed right down, leaning forward to peer out of the windscreen, which was awash with rain. It was like looking out of a lower-deck porthole in a heavy sea.

We limped to a garage. George speaks fluent German, and on this occasion Anne and I were more than happy for him to do the negotiating. A couple of mechanics, complaining about all the unnecessary and inaccessible screws English designers used in everything they built, took apart the electric motor that powered the wiper blades. (This was situated at the bottom centre inside the windscreen, and was set in motion by pulling out a small lever from the housing it clipped into when the motor was switched off.) I couldn't understand what the mechanics were saying, though it clearly wasn't complimentary. George translated afterwards for our benefit, adding with feeling that however many screws the English used, and however bad their designs, he would give one Englishman for ten Germans any time. He remained a firm Anglophile to the end.

When the mechanics had finished taking apart this wretched product of English engineering they announced to us (via George) that it was beyond repair and that we would have to find a garage that stocked the right spares. But on a Sunday afternoon, they added, we were unlikely to do so. In the meantime all they could do was to put back the motor so that the small lever could be rotated backward and forward by hand to operate the blades and keep the windscreen clear.

For several hours, in the continual pouring rain, Anne and George took turns in operating the wipers – the task of keeping them going was much too tiring for one person. At last, towards nightfall, the rain eased off and finally stopped.

We by-passed Hanover at around 6p.m.

Once again, however, I was overcome by an overwhelming desire to sleep. I bit my lip and concentrated all my energies on fighting the drowsiness, but still the car lights in front seemed to sway and I could feel my eyelids drooping.

Anne said she would make tea and told me to stop at the next lay-by. Unfortunately I didn't see it until the last minute and pulled up abruptly. Everyone and everything lurched forward, some of the mugs crashing to the floor and the tea slopping over the table.

'What did you do that for?' Anne said in some frustration.

'I'm sorry. I've missed several lay-bys and didn't want to miss another.'

The tea was good – though having stopped I felt extremely reluctant to get moving again. I had two more pills and gave two to George, and the three of us discussed the procedure we would follow after crossing into East Germany.

'It would be a mistake', George said, 'for me to reveal myself to the East German guards at Helmstedt – the van will still be under observation from the West German side. If they see an extra person getting out you will be in difficulties later on. They might even recognize me. I should remain in hiding until we are close to the East German checkpoint on the outskirts of Berlin. If we were stopped by a patrol car it would be difficult to explain why there was one passenger without papers; it's much better I should do that kind of explanation on my own at the Berlin checkpoint. As you near Berlin you will come to a large bridge; once you have crossed it you can let me out.'

Soon after we had resumed our journey, George commented:

'I must say, these pills have a quite remarkable effect.'

'Beats meditation, does it?' I asked.

He laughed.

'Complements it, at least.'

As we approached Helmstedt, there was a curious incident. I mentioned earlier that the noise of the engine made it difficult for the driver to hold conversations with anyone in the back. This meant that I would often simply nod or say yes when George was speaking without really being sure what he had said. Suddenly, however, there was a note of urgency in his voice, and now I heard him say distinctly:

'I really think you must stop and that we should put up somewhere for the night.'

I was stupefied. Now that we were approaching the journey's end, had he suddenly lost his nerve? Had he had second thoughts about the whole idea of going to the Soviet bloc?

'But why?' I said.

'If the van isn't going right you shouldn't attempt this last part of the journey tonight.'

'What's wrong with the van?'

'Didn't you say there was something the matter with the engine?'

I breathed a sigh of relief and told him that as far as I knew the engine was fine. I can only surmise that earlier, when I hadn't caught what he had said and had politely nodded in response, he had in fact been expressing a worry about the engine. From then on we must have talked at cross-purposes until he told me to stop.

At around 8.30p.m. we stopped a few miles from Helmstedt to hide George away for the last time.

'This is the big one, George,' I said. 'If we get through this frontier you're out of danger.'

'I think we've as good as done it,' he said, sounding both tense and excited. 'I don't anticipate any further problems at this stage.'

'What about at the East German checkpoint? Mightn't the examination be more rigorous there?'

'I don't think so – not when you're travelling on a transit visa to West Berlin.'

I hid him away for the last time, and we put the two boys back into bed. I squeezed Anne's hand:

'The worst will soon be over. It's going to be all right!'

Leaving West Germany was simple, the merest formality. Crossing into the GDR was another matter – at least psychologically. The border was sealed off with a fence topped with barbed wire. On the far side of the road was a high observation tower manned by guards with machine-guns. Searchlights on the tower played on the fence below and the approaches to the crossing. The observation tower, the high fences, the armed guards brought back all those sinister images from wartime feature films and newsreels about POW camps and concentration camps. It confirmed all our worst imaginings about Soviet-controlled Eastern Europe.

I stopped the van at a signal from a guard who directed me into the customs and immigration shed. The application forms for the transit visa were in German, and there seemed to be two places at the bottom for signature. I signed in both places and then handed

179

back the form to the uniformed official behind the counter. He looked at it quizzically.

'So you are the officer of the German Democratic Republic in charge of the Helmstedt frontier post, are you?'

He pointed to the form.

'That's where I sign, not you', he went on. Now, however, I thought I detected the trace of a smile. 'Come on, then,' he continued, 'we need to see your vehicle.'

It was the first time during the journey that anyone had made a move to examine it, and we were extremely tense.

'Open up,' the guard commanded, nodding at the doors.

The children were in bed at the back, though not asleep – as they had only recently been disturbed when we hid George. The guard glanced around, but didn't bother lifting the bed to examine the contents of the drawers. He nodded again, and the examination was over. That was the nearest we came to having the van checked during the whole trip, either on the outward or the return journey.

After the immaculate autobahns of West Germany, the long, dark road that connects Helmstedt to West Berlin was grim. The road itself was in poor condition with potholes in places and no hard shoulder at the side; it is argued that this is partly because the East German authorities have little interest in maintaining a road chiefly used by Western military traffic. However, from the moment we had crossed the heavily guarded checkpoint there was a tangible sense of having entered an alien and hostile territory.

After thirty-six hours without sleep and twelve hours of almost continuous driving, I was by now almost fainting with exhaustion. I wanted us to stop but I wasn't sure if this was allowed, and kept going. At least it was the last leg of the journey.

I had a sense of anti-climax, Anne too was tense rather than elated, and had been shaken by the appearance of the frontier post and the dark, poorly maintained road. I could not shake off either a nagging sense of guilt that we had exploited our apparent normality as a family group to deceive the frontier officials.

And now another thought began to trouble me. The plan had succeeded, yes, as far as rescuing George was concerned. But was it really possible that one of the most wanted men in Western Europe could be dropped off at a frontier post without the news leaking out? Indeed, might not George's arrival be observed from the Allied checkpoint close by? When I had suggested to George back in late October the idea of scrambling over the wall of the Russian

Embassy he had insisted that the British secret service would know about it within a matter of hours. Even if George's arrival at the East German checkpoint had not been observed at the Allied post, wasn't it possible the Western secret services would quickly discover what had happened? The truth might emerge even before we left Berlin, and we could find ourselves detained and interrogated on the way out of the city.

The mistake, I think, was keeping George in hiding for almost the whole of this long final leg. We should have stopped soon after we had crossed the frontier post and taken time to celebrate. If it was indeed the case that vehicles were meant to keep moving on this stretch of road, we would have run the risk of being challenged by a passing police patrol. But after all the risks we had taken it would have been reasonable to have put up with this small additional one to savour the moment of our success.

At last we crossed the bridge and I released George from his hiding-place.

'Well,' he said triumphantly when he had emerged, 'we made it!'

'Yes,' I said, but a little flatly, wondering if that was as true for Anne and myself as it was for him.

I took the foam rubber on which George had been resting and walked with it a hundred yards or so into the wood at the side of the road, finally throwing it as far away from me as I could. It was pitch-black in the wood and squelchy underfoot from all the rain. The water rose over the rim of my shoes and soaked my feet.

When I got back to the van the children were back in bed, and George was sitting on the forward-facing seat immediately behind me.

'It's been a long and difficult time for both of you,' he said. 'I can't begin to tell you how much I appreciate what you've done and the risks you've taken.'

'We're only happy that it's worked out in the end,' Anne replied simply.

However, as we drove on I voiced some of our fears. George did his best to reassure us.

'I think you will be perfectly safe. My arrival will remain a secret – for ever.'

'But what about the guards at the Western post? Mightn't they see you arrive?'

'That's highly unlikely. It's a quite different situation to what would have obtained if I'd been discovered at the East German

181

checkpoint at Helmstedt after the van had just gone through the West German post.'

I wanted to believe him, but I was still feeling disconcerted by the stark image of an authoritarian state which had confronted us at the Helmstedt checkpoint.

'It was a bit like being thrust into a movie scene from the last war,' I said to George. High barbed-wire fences, observation towers, guards with machine guns, the lot. It seems like a pretty grim place if you have to have all that at the frontier – hardly a good advertisement for the Soviet bloc.'

'That's more to do with the fact that they are Germans than that they are communist. West Germans or East Germans – it doesn't make much difference.'

For the second time that day, George's anti-German feeling had surfaced. But I don't know how fixed was the attitude he expressed.

I also reminded him again about making a plea on our behalf for the imprisoned Russian writers Sinyavsky and Daniel when he reached Moscow.

Although George confirmed that he would do so, he sounded more doubtful about getting any results than he had done before. One interpretation of this is that he had simply been humouring us earlier; but it is also possible that as the time to carry out this undertaking approached, he began to weigh the prospects of success more soberly and realistically.

We also talked about what he would do when he reached the East German checkpoint on the outskirts of Berlin.

'I'm not looking forward to the first half-hour or so when I turn up without any papers and tell them who I am. They may take some convincing! They'll find the story I have to tell them pretty incredible too. But, of course, once they are convinced things should be different. The hardest thing of all will be to explain to them the motives of you and the other friends who helped me.'

George, always meticulous about his appearance, also dwelt on personal matters. He was thinking, he told us, of growing a beard.

'Tell me frankly, now,' he said, 'what do you think? Would I look better with a beard or without one?'

In the circumstances the question seemed almost comic.

'I think you should grow one,' I said. 'Pat can do the same now you're no longer staying with him.'

We stopped when the lights of the checkpoint were visible in the distance, perhaps another mile or two farther on. George swallowed down two more of the doctor's pills and said goodbye to us.

'It's fantastic, what you two have done,' he said earnestly. 'Believe me, I will never forget it or do anything that could put you and your family at risk.' He was to be as good as his word.

He had climbed over into the middle passenger seat as the two boys were now fast asleep in the back. I stepped out into the road with him. George stood there a little awkwardly, wearing the trilby hat and the long overcoat we had bought for him. Now he would no longer need to pull the hat down over his eyes as he had when we were moving him around London in the back of Bernard's car.

'Michael, once again thank you. We should be celebrating in champagne. One day I hope we may be able to do so.'

'Good luck, George.'

We shook hands for the last time and I got back into the van. I caught a last glimpse of him in the driving mirror, faintly illuminated by the rear lights of the van. He waved – and almost at once was lost in the darkness.

It was a relief, once we had got through the passport and customs formalities at the two checkpoints, to come to the cheerful lights of the city. We found the Kurfürstendamm without difficulty, and were able to book in at the hotel George had recommended. It was spacious but unremarkable; I recall brown marble and brown wallpaper, but little else. Our room was large with two double beds; one that the children shared, one for Anne and myself. We were all exhausted and went to bed at once, sleeping until late the next morning.

We awoke in high spirits, for the first time fully savouring the success of our mission. After breakfast I booked a call through to Pat's works. He answered the phone himself:

'Stanhope Press here.' The line was clear. It could have been a local call.

'Pat, it's Michael. I'm phoning from Berlin.'

'Mike! – How did it go?

'Perfectly. The task is successfully completed.'

'That is just fantastic! I can hardly believe it. We've been thinking about you and Anne ever since you left. How's Anne?'

'She's fine – tired, but fine. We're making some trips today. I'll give you another ring in the morning.'

We did some sightseeing and shopping during the rest of the morning, buying Gavin the anorak he is seen wearing in the photograph taken in the Harz mountains. We also managed to get a new motor for the windscreen wipers and had that fixed.

In the afternoon we drove as planned through Checkpoint Charlie to East Berlin to get an idea of the procedures involved. As the barrier on the Western side was about to lift we were startled by a bright flash – the van had been photographed. We discovered later that this was standard procedure for all vehicles going through the checkpoint. But it meant that if the news of George's arrival ever did leak out there would be a photographic record of our presence in Berlin at this time. Whether it still exists more than twenty years later is anyone's guess.

We spent just long enough in East Berlin to use up our East German marks on tea and cakes at a large restaurant and tea-room.

Back in West Berlin we spent a second night at the hotel, phoning Pat in the morning to say we had made the trip as planned. We looked round the shops again trying to decide whether or not to take George's advice and spend a couple of days in Goslar.

Then in the afternoon a newspaper report sent us hurrying out of the city post-haste. The hoardings spoke of the arrest of a woman in Berlin who had assisted a spy – when I bought the paper I spotted Blake's name in the text. The woman who had been arrested was a certain Frau Baumgarten.

My first thought was that Blake's flight to the East-German checkpoint had been discovered. However, with the help of a pocket German–English dictionary I made out that this wasn't the story. It appeared rather that Frau Baumgarten was suspected of being an accomplice in Blake's escape from Wormwood Scrubs. This in some ways was still more frightening. Suppose some entirely innocent person was picked up and charged with assisting Blake?

The Times first carried the Baumgarten story and the speculation of her involvement in the Blake escape on 23 December 1966, so clearly the news had broken at that time, although she had actually been arrested the previous October.[2] E. H. Cookridge in his book on Blake gives a more detailed account of what happened. She and two Arab accomplices were arrested in October 1966 charged with obtaining passports and false identity cards and in November they were interviewed in Moabit Prison, West Berlin, by MI5 officers investigating a possible link-up with the Blake escape.[3]

At the time, however, to discover a newspaper story that linked Blake to a woman under arrest in West Berlin only two days after we had dropped him off on the outskirts of the city was terrifying. It might have been less so if I could have worked out exactly what the report was saying – but my pocket dictionary didn't get me very far. Suddenly we felt trapped in the city. We wanted to get away.

We checked out of the hotel and set off back along the autobahn to Helmstedt. On the way, I remember, we picked up a performance of a cello concerto by Haydn on the radio. It is a particular favourite of mine and brought a strange reassurance. All at once I was confident again that things were going to work out.

We slept that night in the van, and the next day, 21 December, drove to Goslar as George had recommended, booking in at a pension built in the style of a Swiss chalet. The town was every bit as charming as he had promised – lots of timber-framed houses with steeply pitching roofs, and churches with open campaniles. As Anne and I strolled through it that night church bells were ringing and it started to snow. By morning there had been a heavy fall. We drove up into the mountains and made a giant snowman; photographs we took show Seán and Gavin running through the snow with the van clearly visible in the background. We also still have a postcard sent by Anne to her family dated 22 December and describing the exhilarating day we had just spent.

Next day before setting out on our return journey we went back into the mountains and dug up a small Christmas tree to take back home with us. This time we didn't rush the journey but camped again in the van that night and took a daytime ferry from Ostend the next day.

At Dover the Customs official asked me if we had brought back anything from our trip.

'Only a Christmas tree,' I said.

'I'm afraid, sir, we are going to have to confiscate it. No trees or plants are allowed to be brought into the country except under controlled conditions because of the danger of introducing diseases.'

I had to sign a form acknowledging that Customs had seized the tree, and giving them permission to burn it. Anne was extremely distressed and for the time being the incident quite overshadowed everything else!

We spent Christmas Day and Boxing Day with my parents in Sussex and drove back to London on 27 December, calling round to see Pat in the afternoon. To our surprise we found Seán was still there, though the plan had been for him to set off a day or two after I had phoned through from Berlin.

They greeted us with hugs of welcome and with demands to tell them all about the trip. Pat opened a bottle of wine.

'Not much to tell, really,' Anne said. 'Nobody even looked inside the van except the Customs man in East Germany – and of course that bastard at Dover who pinched our lovely Christmas tree. We'd have got away with it, only Michael had to go and declare it!'

We filled in some of the other details – George's bout of nausea on the way to Dover; our fears when we pulled out the drawer outside Ostend that he might have suffocated; the broken motor for the windscreen wipers.

'But what about things this end? Have you made any progress with the passport?'

'Hang on a minute,' Pat said, pulling it out from his jacket.

I opened it up. Seán's face stared out at me, the embossment clear and sharp. The registration too was exact.

'It looks terrific!'

'That's all I've been waiting to hear,' he said. 'We can now book Seán's departure.'

Pat now takes up the story of what happened at their end after Anne, I and the children had left with George for Berlin.

Narrated by Pat Pottle

After George had left and Seán was on his own in the flat, he started creating all sorts of problems. On the Monday when I returned home from work I discovered a newspaper and several other items that I knew had not been there in the morning.

'Christ, Seán – you haven't been out?'

'Why wouldn't I?' he said with sullen defiance. 'I've spent five years locked up. Isn't that enough?'

'But you could be recognized?'

'By whom? The public haven't seen my photograph; and the ordinary bobby on the beat won't recognize me.'

'But why take the risk? It's only for a few more days.'

Each morning after that I would plead with him before setting off to work to stay inside. He would readily agree – but it was clear to both of us that he had no intention of keeping his word.

One evening I said I would go with him to a photo-booth in a railway station for the passport photos.

'Unnecessary, Patrick!' From his pocket he produced a packet of photographs. He had been to a portrait photographer in Hampstead High Street and had them taken.

I went mad.

'For God's sake, Seán, are you trying to get us all arrested? You must have had to leave a name and address and you must have had to return a few days later to pick them up!'

'I wasn't so naive as to give my own name and address – what do you take me for? Anyway, you've gone security-mad. If there'd been any problem I wouldn't be here now with the photographs.'

Next day while cleaning up the flat I found a duplicated letter signed by Seán complaining bitterly about the conduct of a certain doctor at Wormwood Scrubs. I seem to remember he described him as a 'butcher'. When I questioned Seán about the letter he said he had given his word to fellow-prisoners that on his release from prison he would send a letter to the Home Office and the national newspapers on their behalf complaining about the doctor's treatment of prisoners and questioning his competence. This he had now done.

Where and when he had the letter duplicated, I don't know; it would not in the least surprise me if he had enclosed a photograph with the letters. No doubt he also posted them at the nearest postbox in Hampstead.

This time we had a serious row.

'Listen, Seán, I've no wish to be arrested, even if you have. I sometimes think you'd like nothing better than to be arrested and walk back into D Hall as a hero. – "The man who broke Blake out. Good old Seán, true to his word." '

'I don't intend to go back into D Hall, Patrick, or any other kind of bloody hall. I refuse to get paranoiac about security, that's all.'

Infuriated, I accused him of having ruined all our plans: I listed his lying about selling the Humber car; the episode of the car keys; promising to get passports when he had no means of doing so; his telling us he had found a self-contained flat, which turned out to be a bed-sit – with a landlady coming once a week to clean out. And now, the final straw, leaving the flat regularly and having photographs taken; and even sending out duplicated letters to the Home Office and the Press in his own name!

The list would have been longer if I'd known then what we learnt when his book was published in 1970; including that he'd phoned the police about the getaway car three days after the break.

Seán replied calmly. 'Whatever you say, we're all still free. You worry far too much about all these things, Patrick. To tell you the truth I stopped today outside the police notice-board at the station in Haverstock Hill, and not a single policeman passing in and out paid the slightest attention to me!'

However, when not arguing over his misdemeanours, I got on extremely well with Seán. In fact, in a way I quite admired him for his confidence and complete disregard for precautions. If there was any worrying to be done, then I could do it for the two of us. It was in this atmosphere that I set about forging the passport for him.

I followed the procedure Michael described earlier. When the passport was finished I was excited. It looked good. Seán thought so too.

Next day I took it to work to show it to my partner, Doug Brewood. He took one look at the passport and said:

'It's terrible! You can spot it a mile off! You'll never get away with it!'

I was deflated. I'd only shown Doug the passport in the expectation of getting a boost to my morale. Now as I looked at it more closely I saw it through his eyes. You could after all see that the embossment had been made through the 'brass-rubbing' technique and that it lacked the sharply defined edges produced by a proper embossing stamp.

That same day, Matthew came in to see if there was any news of Michael and Anne. I showed him the passport; his reaction was the same as Doug's. 'It's an obvious forgery. It would be suicide to send your friend to a Customs post with a document like that.'

By now I was completely demoralized. I kicked myself for having taken the passport to work. But having done so, I decided there was nothing for it but to wait for Michael's return.

Seán and I spent a strange Christmas together. On the one hand we were elated at the success of George's flight; on the other we were apprehensive about Seán's forthcoming journey.

Michael called in after Christmas. He'd no sooner looked at the passport and said how good it looked than my doubts disappeared. Now, once again, it took on the appearance of a professional job.

Narrated by Michael Randle
That week we made the final preparations for Seán's departure. We booked him on the overnight train and boat service from London to Paris which left Victoria Station at 8.30p.m. on Saturday 31

December, New Year's Eve. The advantage of this service was that the carriages were loaded directly on to the ferry and the passport and customs control took place at Victoria station itself. Thus we would be able to accompany Seán to the station and satisfy ourselves that he had overcome the first and most testing hurdle. From Paris we had booked him on a direct flight to Tempelhof Airport in West Berlin. We felt confident that if the passport survived the scrutiny of British officials, it was not likely to be challenged in Paris or Berlin.

Early on Saturday evening the members of the 'escape committee' assembled together at Pat's flat for the last time and had supper together. We went over the practical arrangements. Seán had been practising Pat's signature for the last couple of weeks and could now do quite a passable imitation – he would need to forge it on landing cards in France and probably West Berlin. We agreed also that he would phone me from Paris the next morning to let me know he had arrived safely.

But there was one issue we couldn't agree about. Pat and I were intent on going back to Highlever Road as soon as Seán was safely out of the country in order to remove all his possessions, including the walkie-talkie sets that had been used for the escape, and anything else that might have been left there.

'Why do you want to do that? You're always on to me about not taking risks; this one is completely unnecessary. The only person who could possibly be incriminated by anything in Highlever Road is me. And none of us has been back there since early November. For all we know the police have it under observation.'

'Yes, but it's also quite possible the police have not discovered it,' Pat responded. 'We don't know for sure what clues they might pick up from the things you've left there. If we manage to clear the flat, no one will ever know what it was used for.'

'Well, I can assure you, Patrick, that there is absolutely nothing – absolutely nothing – that could possibly incriminate you.'

Pat and I continued to press him, and in the end he reluctantly handed over the keys.

We drank several toasts that night to the success of the escape. The mood was jubilant, but with an underlying tension. Seán had never wanted to join George in the Soviet Union and was understandably apprehensive; he would have been much happier taking the boat train to Dublin and taking his chances on extradition.

189

'Mind you,' he said, 'I have no intention of staying in Russia. After six months or so when you have had a chance to cover your tracks, I'll return to Limerick.'

We drove to Victoria Station in the camper-van and waited in the Golden Arrow Bar for passengers to be allowed on the train. Seán drank several whiskies, and, after the wine he'd had earlier, became quite tipsy. At one point, returning with some drinks he sat down heavily and lost his balance, spilling some of his drink over Anne. He was profusely apologetic. He then proposed a toast to Scotland Yard and we drank to that. Then he and I together sang the chorus in Gaelic of *Amhrán na bhFiann*, the Irish national anthem (which I learnt in my childhood in Dublin).

The announcement that passengers were now boarding came over the tannoy. Seán kissed Anne.

'Anne, you're a wonderful woman. Michael doesn't know how lucky he is.'

He embraced Pat and me in turn.

'I'll ring you tomorrow from Paris to let you know everything's all right. Good luck, now.'

'Good luck, Seán.'

We went out into the station with him and watched him as he walked unsteadily to the barrier, his pork pie hat set at a jaunty angle. The ticket collector smiled as he presented his ticket. We watched him go into the Passport Control and Customs building at the side of the platform, and waited anxiously for him to emerge. When he did so he turned towards us with a large grin and gave a farewell wave before boarding the train.

'I hope he's going to be all right,' Pat said. 'He drives you mad at times, but it's impossible not to like him.'

All of us felt a mixture of relief and guilt; relief that Seán would soon be out of reach of the British authorities and that we wouldn't have to worry what he was about to get up to next; guilt because we knew that it was pressure from us that was causing him to board the train and undertake a journey that he would much rather not make.

Next morning around ten o'clock he phoned me from Paris.

'Everything is going fine,' he told me; 'I've had no problems. But I do have one very important piece of information for you and Pat. Do not on any account go back to the flat. I phoned through, and I can tell you now for certain that the police are there watching it. Be sure to tell Pat. It would be suicide for either of you to go back.'

What were we to make of this? How could Seán possibly know that the police were at the flat, even if he had talked to the landlady (who didn't in any case live in the building) or one of the other residents? By now we knew from experience that Seán was quite capable of inventing stories. But then again, maybe he had managed to find out something.

I went to see Pat and we weighed the pros and cons. According to what Seán had said on previous occasions, there was nothing that could incriminate either of us at Highlever Road. But could one be sure of this, even if Seán honestly believed it to be true? We would feel more secure if we personally removed everything that had belonged to him. But was it worth the immediate risk for the sake of this reassurance? We debated the points over and over again. Pat was inclined to leave things as they were, while I thought we should clear the flat. In the end we decided to do so and to drive down there together that afternoon in the camper-van.

I picked Pat up after lunch and we set off, both still unsure if we were doing the right thing.

'Mike,' Pat said when we were on our way, 'I have a suggestion. Why don't we phone through to Highlever Road? If someone answers the phone straight away it's likely to be the police. If not we are probably fairly safe.'

We looked out for phone-boxes. We tried two but they were both vandalized. By now we were in the North Kensington area and we decided to take the risk and go to the flat anyway.

We parked the van in Oxford Gardens, perhaps forty or fifty yards from 28 Highlever Road, and both put on gloves. We walked down the small front garden and let ourselves in with Seán's Yale key. Everything was quiet and there was no one about as we went down the long, narrow passage to Seán's room facing us at the far end. But we could see a light shining through the frosted panel above the bathroom door on our left and through the gap underneath the door. We held our breath and nodded to each other as we crept quietly past. Clearly there was someone in there. Was it one of the other tenants or could it be a detective keeping watch on the room?

Once inside Seán's room, we locked the door and felt that bit safer. We opened the case Seán had left behind and began systematically emptying the drawers. There was a wallet of black-and-white photos, a bundle of letters, assorted papers – plus the items we knew were there, such as his typewriter and the walkie-talkie sets. We worked frantically, bundling everything into the case without speaking. The five or ten minutes we spent there were among the most fraught of the whole venture. But finally, after a last-minute search to check we hadn't missed anything, we were ready to leave. Pat carried the case and Seán's portable typewriter; I took the television. As we opened the door and went down the passage the light was still on in the bathroom. But we left the house unchallenged.

It was with a sense of enormous relief that we closed the door on 28 Highlever Road for the last time. A few houses down two women talking by the garden gate looked up as we went past, fell silent, and eyed us curiously. Pat remarked when they were out of earshot:

'They must have us down as one of two things. Either we are a couple of sneak thieves, or we are from a rental firm come to repossess the telly.'

As soon as we reached the van we dumped everything into it and drove off. Not until we were well clear of the area, however, and certain we had not been followed, could we breathe again.

The items we had collected were photographs dated from the period when Seán was planning the escape. One of them, taken with the aid of a time exposure, showed him in silhouette standing by the window in his room in the prison hostel with the walkie-talkie held close to his mouth, its aerial extended. The towers of D Hall were clearly visible through the window. In another the walkie-talkies, and various other items used in the escape were laid out neatly on the bed. There was also another set of photos taken inside the prison on a tiny camera Seán had smuggled into George.

But the most interesting and incriminating part of the haul was the bundle of letters we had found in the drawer. These proved to be all the letters George had written to Seán before they had established radio contact. In several of them George urged him to contact me as he had a strong feeling that I would be willing and able to help. He did not, of course, mention me by name but referred to me as 'our mutual friend', and said he had received Christmas cards regularly from me since I had left prison.

There is no doubt that these letters, if they had fallen into the hands of the police, would have given them a valuable lead. The police would only have needed to check the record of who George had received letters or cards from to narrow down the field to a handful of people – perhaps to no more than two or three. Seán's confidence, therefore, that there was nothing that could possibly incriminate any of us was quite mistaken.

It was not until some four years later when Seán's book was published that we were to learn the full extent of the risks to which he had exposed us over the return to Highlever Road. In it he says that on Friday 30 December, the day before leaving for Paris, he sent a photograph of himself to a Fleet Street newspaper with a note on the back saying simply – 'Seán Bourke – 28 Highlever Road, W.10.[4] His intention, he says, was to make sure the discovery of the flat would occur, and be widely publicized, before Pat had a chance to return there. According to his account, Seán pretended to be a foreigner and got a child from the street to write the note and address the envelope so that it would look as though it had come not from him but from someone else, perhaps someone who bore him a grudge and had decided to betray him.

Seán states in his account that he felt it necessary to take this step to forestall a perverse determination on Pat's part to go back to Highlever Road. Pat, he alleges, had once said that he wouldn't mind having the opportunity of standing in the dock at the Old Bailey and telling the authorities exactly what he thought about sending a man to prison for forty-two years. 'It was this apparent indifference to arrest and imprisonment,' Seán writes, 'which worried me. If Pat was determined to go back to Highlever Road, I was equally determined that he should not.'[5]

In fact Pat had expressed rather more doubts than me about returning to Highlever Road. If Seán had wanted to make quite sure we could not do so, he had only to ditch the Highlever Road keys in the nearest drain. That, however, would have meant confronting us directly on the issue.

Seán acknowledges that Pat might not believe that the police had the flat under observation, 'or would not *want* us to believe it', and that if the police kept quiet for some time he might once more start insisting on going back there. Seán claims, however, that his strategy took care of the problem; by sending the note to a newspaper rather than directly to the police, he had ensured that the latter would be under constant pressure to allow the story to be printed. But he had not considered the possibility that publication could be delayed, for say twenty-four or forty-eight hours – long enough for Pat and myself, had we decided to ignore his enigmatic warning from Paris, to have walked straight into a trap. In fact it seems likely that the newspaper never passed on the message to the police, or did so only after another fuse that Seán had lit before his departure detonated with an explosion that was to shatter our confidence in him and our own peace of mind.

For almost two weeks after Seán's departure all was quiet. Speculation about Blake and how he had escaped disappeared from the newspapers and we had begun to settle down to our normal routine. I divided my time between teaching at Princeton College and working at University College on an M.Phil thesis. One Friday morning, however – Friday 13 January — I had lunch with John Morris, one of the lecturers at the university who had been active in the Committee of 100, who had encouraged me with my studies while I was in Wormwood Scrubs but who knew nothing about my involvement in the Blake escape. We were having coffee in the Common Room when I caught sight of a headline in an early edition of the *Evening Standard* that someone was reading. 'Blake Hunt Murder Threat' it said in large letters.[6] John saw me looking at it and said with a smile that he thought it was probably a bit late to be hunting for Blake. But my heart was pounding. I simply could not imagine what it was that the headline referred to. As soon as possible I excused myself and left to buy a paper.

The sub-heading read: 'All-out search by Yard men after "I'll kill you" note to detective', and the account said that a letter threatening death had been sent to a detective in Crawley, Sussex, Detective Sergeant Michael Sheldon, who had had a home-made bomb sent to him through the post five years previously. The letter *bearing a Hampstead postmark*, had been posted on New Year's Day but had been kept a closely guarded secret. The report went on to say that the Yard have been searching for the sender of the letter 'in case he might be able to help enquiries into the escape of master spy George Blake from Wormwood Scrubs.' Scotland Yard was 'considering whether to release the name and picture of a man they think might help their enquiries into the death threat letter this weekend'. His name and description had already been circulated to Interpol and every police station in the country. A warrant for his arrest had been issued by the Director of Public Prosecutions in connection with the sending of the letter.

Pat, Anne and I were shattered. In all the time we had been seeing him during 1966 Seán had never given us the slightest indication that he still bore a grudge against Sheldon or had sought in any way to excuse his action in sending him a letter bomb in 1961. We could scarcely believe that he had sent such a letter – and posted it in the

Hampstead area – on the very day he was leaving the country for good.

The following day, *The Times* carried a short piece on its front page headed 'Letter Threat to Kill P.C.' It was accompanied by a photo of Seán – the first to have been published since Blake's escape. The report gave Seán's full name – Seán Alphonsus Bourke – and said he was aged thirty-two, was born in Limerick city and sometimes used the name O'Grady.[7] Again this was the first time Seán's name had been released. But curiously there was no mention in the *Times* report of any connection with Blake. A peculiar thing about the press handling of the case was that the *Evening Standard* of 13 January emphasized the connection between Bourke and the Blake escape but did not publish his name or photograph, or give any description of him, whereas *The Times* published the name, photograph and a description, but omitted any mention of Blake.

The publication of Seán's picture in *The Times* almost certainly led to the discovery of Highlever Road. On Friday 20 January, exactly one week after the *Evening Standard* report of the bomb threat, Seán and Blake were back in the headlines. The *Evening Standard* for that day carried a banner headline: 'Blake Hunt – Dramatic Moves in London' beside a full-length picture of Seán. The story said that Seán had rented a 'two-roomed flatlet' in Highlever Road in October and moved out only ten days previously, taking with him a typewriter, television and radio equipment. Close secrecy about the address had been kept by Scotland Yard 'while detectives had made enquiries which they hoped would lead them to tracing Bourke.' The Yard were appealing to landladies and hotel proprietors in West or North West London to contact the police if they thought Bourke had lodged or sought lodgings at their houses; he might be using the names O'Grady, O'Riordan or Sigsworth.[8]

Next day the story figured prominently in most of the national newspapers. 'Blake believed to be still hiding in Britain' was the *Guardian* headline, accompanied by pictures of both George and Seán.[9] But the most intriguing article was that in the *Daily Mail*. This reported that the landlady at Highlever Road, a Mrs Lottie Heveningham, had been to the police after seeing Seán's picture in the paper the previous week – presumably the one published in *The Times*. Still more startling was her claim that 'from the very start' she had been suspicious of Seán, whom she had seen with a beard, moustache and glasses – and also without them. 'I phoned the police', she is reported as saying [i.e. in October 1966 when he first rented the bedsit] *'but they didn't take any notice.'*[10]

Seán makes no mention of the threat to kill Sheldon in his book. His motives in making the threat are hard to fathom. Perhaps it was a final gesture of defiance aimed at terrifying a man he had never been able to forgive; perhaps it was a flirtation with the danger of discovery before joining George in Moscow, a step about which he clearly retained misgivings.

One puzzling thing is why the police waited for two weeks after they had received the threatening letter before releasing his name and photograph to the Press. Still more surprising is the fact that they waited yet another week before letting the Press know that the Seán Alphonsus Bourke wanted in connection with a death threat to a Sussex policeman was the same 32-year-old Irishman they had been hunting for since late October in connection with the Blake escape.

But they made two other and more important mistakes. The first was to ignore the phone-call from Mrs Heveningham, the landlady at 28 Highlever Road, informing them that she had a suspicious lodger. The second – the really crucial – misjudgment was the decision not to release Seán's name and photograph as soon as the Humber car was discovered on 25 October 1966. Had they done that Mrs Heveningham would certainly have gone to the police, as she did when his picture was eventually published in January 1967, and we would have been hard-pushed indeed to have kept Blake free.

CHAPTER EIGHT

The Exile's Return

Narrated by Michael Randle

The publicity about Seán Bourke's involvement in the escape alerted a few friends and relatives to the possibility that I too might be involved. Indeed, on the day the *Guardian* piece appeared – 21 January – one couple arrived in some alarm to see if everything was all right. I took them into the front room and showed them 'the hottest TV set in the country' – the set I had carried off three weeks before from the bed-sit in Highlever Road.

After this unexpected burst of publicity things went very quiet. The Mountbatten Report had been published on 22 December while we were still in Germany, and given extensive press coverage; but by the time we returned it had dropped out of the news.

After the excitement of recent months it was hard for any of us to settle down. Pat and I even fantasized about trying to repeat the success of the Blake escape – perhaps we could find a way of making contact with the Krogers and freeing them as well!

Soon, however, we directed our energies into campaigning against the war in Vietnam, in particular the campaign to persuade US servicemen not to participate, and young Americans of draft age to refuse to be conscripted. Pat, I and Ken Weller – another activist from the Committee of 100 in the early 1960s – formed a Vietnam Information Group to publish and arrange for the dissemination of material about the war. Working with War Resisters International and other organizations, we arranged for this to be distributed at US bases in Britain and Europe and other areas where young Americans congregated. These war resisters including young men who had left the army ('deserters' in the eyes of the American authorities) as well as those wanting to avoid the draft, the so-called 'draft dodgers'.

During 1967 the media began to publicize these efforts. The *Observer* even carried a feature article about the Group, with a picture of Pat printing the leaflets at his works. Soon, questions were being raised in the Commons about the Group. On 19 June

1967 the Conservative MP Mr Peter Blaker, asked the Attorney General, Sir Elwyn Jones, in a written question if he would 'refer to the Director of Public Prosecutions the activities of the Vietnam Information Group with a view to prosecuting them for incitement to disaffection by publishing from an address in Britain pamphlets for distribution to United States servicemen, urging them to desert.' The Attorney General replied that these activities had been referred to the DPP.[1]

But the political event that was to have the most profound effect on our personal lives was the occupation of the Greek Embassy in late April, just a week after the Colonels' Coup. Briefly, what happened is that about fifty activists took over the Greek Embassy in London on the evening of Friday 28 April with the intention of sending telex messages to all other Greek embassies throughout the world, urging them to declare themselves against the fascist military regime. That particular weekend was a public holiday in Greece, and we hoped our action would help stimulate mass resistance at this early stage.

The demonstrators were mainly members (or former members) of the Committee of 100, or students from the London School of Economics.

Pat and I, together with two young Greek women students from LSE, Maria and Felitia, were part of an advance party approaching the Embassy. To symbolize our peaceful intent we all carried bunches of daffodils. As the door was opened, a goods van packed with demonstrators pulled up, and they rushed out and raced to the open door, pushing past the caretaker into the building.

We had expected only the caretaker and his wife to be there and had calculated that by preventing them from leaving we could postpone the arrival of the police. This would give us time to send our telex messages. But in fact there were several other Embassy officials around, one of whom escaped by a basement door and alerted a policeman outside the US Embassy just down the road. Within a few minutes there were police everywhere smashing windows and breaking down doors to gain admission.

All the demonstrators were arrested. On the way to West End Central police station, however, Pat noticed that the door of the police van carrying him and his fellow-demonstrators had not been properly secured. When the van pulled up at traffic lights he kicked the door open and shouted 'Everybody Out!' Within seconds the van had emptied and all but a couple of people got away. Unfortunately, I was not in that particular van and spent the weekend in police custody. George Brown, the Foreign Secretary, made a statement describing the demonstration as 'an outrage'. We were soon charged, initially under Section 1 of the Public Order Act of 1936, though later further charges were brought including Affray and Conspiracy to Trespass.

The committal stage dragged on throughout the summer, and the case did not reach the Old Bailey until October. Meanwhile, at Whitsun (while I was out on bail), Anne, and I and our family spent the weekend with Pat and other friends at Walberswick on the Essex coast. Among the party was Sue Abrahams, then Secretary of the Committee of 100. Later that summer Pat and Sue married and moved together into Pat's flat in Willow Buildings. Soon afterwards they found themselves harbouring yet another fugitive, this time an American draft-resister. Using the same technique as we had done for Seán, we were able to provide him with a forged passport and send him to safety in Sweden.

After the Whitsun break I got temporary work at the office of the International Confederation for Disarmament and Peace (ICDP) typing background papers for an international conference on the Vietnam war. It was, I think, an important milestone in the efforts of the Vietnamese to make their voice heard in the wider world.

The Blake escape, meanwhile, had largely disappeared from the Press, though extracts from a book about him by the writer E. H. Cookridge were serialized in the *Daily Express* in the summer of 1967. In September, however, the story came back with a vengeance – and in a way that none of us ever for one moment anticipated. Seán Bourke, the media announced, had visited the British Embassy in Moscow and asked to return to Britain!

Seán's visit took place on 4 September, though it was not reported to the Press until 21 September. A statement by the Foreign Office was printed in full in both *The Times* and the *Guardian* the following day. The text was as follows:

> On September 4 a man claiming to be Seán Bourke, and a citizen of the Irish Republic, called at the embassy in Moscow without papers and made inquiries about means of returning to the United Kingdom.
>
> He claimed to be staying with Blake in Moscow and to have arranged Blake's escape from this country. He had no immediate proof of his identity.

The embassy explained that they would have to establish his identity and he would have to obtain an exit visa. Authority also had to be sought from the Government of the Irish Republic. Accordingly he was asked to call again.

He has not so far done so. It has been confirmed by photographs that the man was indeed Bourke for whose arrest there is a warrant in the United Kingdom. The embassy were given the necessary instructions to enable them to contact us if Bourke called again. The Government have been in touch with the Irish Government throughout.[2]

The *Times* report went on to say that British Embassy officials had been told to make arrangements for Bourke's return if he called again. The *Guardian* was still more explicit on this point. British and Irish governments, it reported, had 'agreed on a course of action' and Seán would be 'issued with the documents necessary for his return'.

This was an alarming prospect for us all. Our arrangement with Seán was for him to return after six months or a year, not to Britain but to Ireland. There he would have a fighting chance of defeating any attempt to extradite him. But if he came back to Britain he would face certain arrest and trial. Even if he maintained a complete silence about our role we felt we would still have to decide whether or not to come forward and identify ourselves as the people who had assisted him. To add to the complication, I now had the threat of a prison sentence hanging over me on account of the Greek Embassy demonstration. Pat, however, was convinced that once Seán had left the Embassy the Russians would make doubly sure he would never return. We even wondered if he was still alive.

The next day *The Times* gave further details of Seán's visit to the Embassy, quoting the First Secretary, Mr Peter Maxey, who described Seán as looking 'rather scruffy, like a man coming in straight off work'.[3] There was clearly a mutual antipathy between Seán and the people he met at the Embassy – four of them in all, according to his own account. 'With the exception of the Consul,' he told the Russian who had been assigned to look after him, 'they were a load of snotty nosed bastards'.[4]

Some commentators have suggested that by making public the fact that Seán had come to the Embassy the Foreign Office saved him from execution. But this is pure speculation; there is no evidence that the Soviet authorities ever considered repaying Seán for the role he played in Blake's escape by executing him. Moreover, if the British government's intention was to forestall the possibility of Seán being executed, they took their time about taking any action. Seán could have been dead and buried in the two and a half weeks between his visit to the Embassy and the Foreign Office statement if the Russians had really been out for his blood.

Seán's own explanation seems more plausible. The British authorities had made the statement as a tit-for-tat for the embarrassing loss of face they had suffered the previous weekend when police boarded a Moscow-bound plane and took off a young Russian student, Vladimir Kachenko, claiming that he was being forced to return against his will. As soon as Kachenko was allowed to speak for himself he denied this, and three days later flew back to Moscow. It appears from Seán's account of the discussions he had with Blake about the case that both MI6 and the KGB had been trying to recruit Kachenko, who had suffered a nervous breakdown as a result.[5]

Two weeks or so after the story of Seán's visit to the British Embassy had appeared in the Press, I was back in prison. At the Old Bailey on 3 October all the twenty-three LSE students involved in the case were given two-year conditional discharges; the following day the other defendants were fined apart from three of us with previous convictions, who were sent to prison. Terry Chandler – one of the Committee of 100 defendants in the 1962 Wethersfield trial – was sentenced to fifteen months; Del Foley, a younger activist, to six months; myself to twelve months.

I found this sentence much harder to take than the previous one, partly because we had never expected the Embassy demonstration to result in anyone going to prison for an extended period, but more importantly because of the separation from Anne and our children.

I spent the first three or four months of my sentence in Pentonville preparing my case for the Appeal Court. After the Appeal was turned down (by Lord Parker) I was moved to the small and relatively relaxed atmosphere of Lewes prison in Sussex.

But it was while I was still in Pentonville (and I think only a matter of a few weeks into the sentence) that I experienced one of the blackest days of my life. I was called up before the Governor one morning and informed that two Scotland Yard officers wished to interview me; it was up to me whether or not to see them. The sensible thing would have been for me to say that I would only see them when my lawyer could be present. But I knew this would mean a delay of days or perhaps weeks, and I was desperate to know the worst, whatever that might be. I agreed to see them, but returned to my work – once again in the tailor's shop – in a state of shock.

I was convinced that the interview would be about the Blake escape, and that the police had somehow uncovered our role in it; indeed, I could think of no other reason why Scotland Yard would want to question me. The recent publicity about Seán in Moscow only served to reinforce this impression.

My task at that period was to count out the piles of garment sleeves that the other prisoners on the machines had made, and separate them into right-hand and left-hand ones. It was a task of crushing tedium that left me feeling literally sick with boredom. But at least I could hold on to the thought that in eight months or so it would all be over.

Now the day of release seemed to be indefinitely postponed. I looked around the workshop trying to imagine possible ways of escape. But I knew only too well how much planning and organization had gone into Blake's escape, and that this was not something that could be achieved overnight. Besides, security at all British prisons had been stepped up, so that escape would be more difficult than ever. There was no getting away from it; I was trapped.

When the Special Branch arrived later that afternoon I asked the screw who accompanied me to the interview room to sit in on the discussion. One of the officers placed a hard-cover briefcase on his lap, opened it and took out some papers.

'We want to ask you some questions', he said, 'about the distribution of leaflets on the US Air Force base at Wethersfield in August of last year.'

I wanted to laugh aloud. It was even on the tip of my tongue to say, 'Is that all?' But I contained myself, and, doing my best not to smile, answered:

'Yes, I took part in that action.'

'And are you a member of the Vietnam Information Group?'

'I am, yes.'

I was so relieved – and so confident of the political embarrassment we could cause if we were prosecuted for urging young Americans not to fight in Vietnam – that I had no hesitation in answering the questions they put.

Pat's printing works, I found out later, was raided by Special Branch round about the same time. They entered the premises unannounced, and Pat demanded at once to see their search warrant. As soon as he saw it he realized a mistake had been made in drawing it up. His premises spread over two houses, and the search warrant was made out for the house number where he stored paper and spares.

'Right, everyone out of this building! This warrant is for next door – you're not allowed in here!'

Special Branch returned in due course with a new warrant. They found nothing.

In early December Mr Blaker again raised the issue in the House, this time in the form of an oral question. The Attorney General, while confirming that it was an offence under the Army Act to encourage desertion among members of the American armed forces, said that the DPP had come to the conclusion in this case that 'the public interest would not be served by a prosecution'.[6]

I was released from Lewes prison in early July. In August I went to Vienna for the Council Meeting of War Resisters International and took part in a delegation to Bratislava at the invitation of the Slovak Peace Committee. It was a tense and exhilarating moment in Czech history, indeed in the history of East and Central Europe in the period after the Second World War. Perhaps I was projecting my own feelings on the situation, but I had a sense that the people strolling with such evident ease in the streets were savouring a new and welcome experience. The Peace Committee people too were more open than any I had previously encountered. Normally they echoed faithfully the current government and Moscow line. The Slovak Peace Committee, however, was willing to talk about their hopes and fears. When we expressed concern at the recent military manoeuvres of Soviet forces on Czechoslovakia's borders, one of them said:

'They are still going on. We don't yet know what will happen.'

Four days later Soviet and Warsaw Pact forces invaded. I had returned to Britain by then and heard the news with disbelief. I went at once to the WRI Headquarters in London and in conjunction with the General Secretary, Devi Prasad, composed a statement condemning the invasion. We sent it to the various press and news agencies. Part of WRI's own press statement, sent to all the Peace Committees in various Soviet-bloc countries, read as follows:

We have learnt today with grief and horror of the invasion of Czechoslovakia by Russian and other Warsaw Pact troops.

At the Council Meeting in Vienna on August 17, 1978, The War Resisters International welcomed the moves towards greater freedom in Czechoslovakia and condemned the threatening military manoeuvres by Warsaw Pact forces. On the same day a delegation from WRI including the Chairman and General Secretary were welcomed to Bratislava by the Slovak Peace Committee and had the opportunity of learning at first hand of the overwhelming desire for greater freedom . . . Two of our members are still in Czechoslovakia. Our contact with our Czechoslovak comrades is therefore intimate and personal. We feel at one with them in this hour of tragedy . . .

The invasion once again underlines the reactionary and repressive role played by the two military alliances, the Warsaw Pact and NATO. Warsaw Pact forces are directly involved in repression. NATO is powerless to help and its very existence poses a threat to security in Europe which hampers and restricts progressive development in the countries of Eastern Europe.

The invasion also strengthens the hand of right wing and reactionary forces in the west whose blanket condemnations of socialist and progressive movements will now carry more weight. It will be easier for instance for these forces to present the American aggression against Vietnam as part of a crusade against totalitarian communism. The invasion therefore is a betrayal not only of the Czechoslovak people but hardly less of the Vietnamese people and others struggling for peace.

The War Resisters International fully supports the dignified resistance of the Czechoslovak people which has included sitdowns in front of Soviet tanks, strikes and non-cooperation. We express our hope, even in this dark hour, that peaceful yet uncompromising resistance may eventually secure the withdrawal of invading forces and the continued progress of Czechoslovakia towards true socialism under conditions of freedom.[7]

For the next four or five weeks I worked full-time for War Resisters International as joint co-ordinator of an international protest against the invasion. On 24 September teams of people from seven Western countries staged simultaneous demonstrations in Moscow, Budapest, Sofia and Warsaw, distributing leaflets in the language of the country and unfurling banners in a public square with the slogans: End NATO; End the American War in Vietnam; End the Occupation of Czechoslovakia.' All were arrested, held for varying lengths of time according to which country they were in, and finally deported.

I co-ordinated the publicity at the London end, issuing a press release at 4p.m., when the demonstrations began, and holding a press conference at 7p.m. that evening. Pat and Sue Pottle were also involved, acting as the British phone contact for the five Danes who demonstrated in Warsaw. While four of them displayed the banner and distributed leaflets, the fifth phoned through to Pat and Sue an account of what was happening. The latter recorded the conversation and brought the tape along to the press conference in the evening.

The demonstration received considerable media coverage in various countries, and was the lead item on ITN's news bulletin that night. It is worth quoting the following from *Izvestia's* report of the demonstrations:

> What we have here is a trick that was planned in advance and carefully prepared. It is not difficult to guess who needed it and why. No one will be deceived by A. Papworth's and V. Rovere's protestations that they supposedly acted out of 'strictly pacifist motives'. We are concerned with something else now – with the fact that the intelligence services of the Western countries, in their subversive activity against the forces of socialism, have recently been making more and more frequent attempts to use, and, from all indications, not without success, politically myopic people, people who, frequently without being aware of it, become pawns on the chessboards of the imperialist intelligence services and bourgeois propaganda.[8]

Not long after the 'Support Czechoslovakia' demonstration, Pat and I received a tip-off that Seán Bourke would shortly be returning to Ireland. The message came via a mutual friend, who had occasion to visit the Soviet Union from time to time, and whose name Pat had given Blake shortly before he left Britain. Sure enough, on 15 October *The Times* reported that Seán was to return to Ireland. The Irish government had already at his request issued him with travel documents, and he had telephoned his family the previous day to say that the Russians had assured him that no obstacle would be placed in his way. He expected to fly to Ireland 'in the next few weeks'.[9]

Seán returned a week later, on Tuesday 22 October. Television news that night carried pictures of him on the flight from Amsterdam and at Shannon Airport, talking flamboyantly about his role in

Blake's escape. I was staying with a friend in Bradford at the time, while I worked on a two-week teaching project at the Regional College of Art. I watched the news with mixed feelings.

Next day the Press carried reports and pictures. 'It is just two years to the day since I helped Blake to get out of gaol, but it's marvellous to be back on Irish soil,' *The Times* reported him as saying. He added:

> Of course I sprang Blake. He asked me to. He was just another human being languishing in prison to a slow lingering death with forty-two years ahead of him. He said when I was leaving: 'Will you get me out of here?' And I did. I sprang him all right. It was only a few minutes by car to Highlever Road, where we stayed in a flat together for two months.[10]

Seán, according to the report, had gone on to say that he and George had flown together on forged passports to Paris from London airport, and from there to Berlin, where a Russian colonel had given them a champagne reception. After that they went to Moscow, where for the first six months he had shared a flat with Blake, and where they had wined and dined together in the fashionable bars and restaurants. *The Times* report ended by saying that the Home Office had refused to comment on whether or not the British government would be seeking Bourke's extradition.

The following evening Seán gave a lengthy interview on Granada Television's *World in Action* programme. On this occasion he mentioned for the first time the fact that a two-way radio was used in planning the escape and that Blake had escaped hidden in a secret compartment in a van. However, he claimed that he had bought and adapted the van himself and driven Blake via Belgium and West Germany to a point in East Germany a few miles from Berlin. He had then driven on to West Berlin and spent a few days there before returning to Britain. Later, he said, he had travelled on a false passport to Paris and West Berlin, crossing over to East Berlin at Checkpoint Charlie.

Next day *The Times* carried a full report of the interview:

> When the interviewer said that he did not believe that the KGB would have allowed him to leave Moscow unless they were certain he would not damage their interests, Mr Bourke said that he had no intention of damaging anybody's interest.
>
> 'Let me get one thing straight. I am not on anybody's side. I do not give a damn what point KGB scores over MI6 or the CIA, and I do not

give a damn what point the CIA scores over the KGB. It does not interest me. I am 100 per cent amateur in this business.'[11]

This was Seán at his best, confident and apparently carefree, charming and intriguing the journalists who had been bombarding him with questions since his return. Even *The Times* correspondent was clearly captivated, describing him in one report as a 'colourful Irishman'. In Ireland itself, by all accounts, he became something of a local hero. But in Britain we were hanging on his every reported word wondering what he might next reveal.

On 31 October Seán was arrested by Irish police on a Scotland Yard warrant, and a district justice ordered that he should be handed over to the British police in fifteen days. His lawyer appealed at once against the order, and on 4 November he was freed on a £2,000 bail. *The Times*, reporting this development, noted that it was the beginning of what was expected to be a 'long legal wrangle' over the extradition warrant.[12]

Seán was no sooner out on bail than he began making phone calls to my home in Torriano Cottages. The first time I picked up the phone and heard his voice at the other end of the line, I froze.

'Hello, Michael, this is Seán here,' he said in the most casual way. 'How are you keeping?'

He was phoning about the tapes he had left with me. He now needed them urgently; could I put them in the post to him care of his solicitor?

I tried to cut the conversation short and said I did not think it was a good idea to post them. He maintained that there was no problem, and phoned again a day or two later, insisting that he must have them.

Not many days afterwards a journalist from RTE arrived on the doorstep, saying he had been sent by Seán to collect the tapes.

'He says that if you want proof that I have really come from him to say to you "Who fears to speak of '98?" ' (This was a reference to Pat M's joke in Wormwood Scrubs when first Bertrand Russell and then Vanessa Redgrave resigned from the Committee of 100.)

I made a copy of the tapes for my own files, and handed over the originals. He assured me that if ever I wanted a good-quality copy for myself he could make me one, using proper up-to-date equipment. He also assured us that he had given Seán a solemn undertaking not to make our identity public, and could give us the same promise. It was the one and only time we met him, and although we have long since forgotten his name, we have often thought about him. We would like to pay tribute to his integrity in sticking by his promise when many another journalist would have succumbed to the temptation to make a name for himself by breaking it.

Seán's appeal in the Irish High Court began on Monday 20 January and lasted a week. It was widely reported in the British press. *The Times* report of 21 January was headed 'Seán Bourke raised £1,000 to free spy', and began:

> Three friends of Seán Bourke put up the money required to organize the escape of the Russian spy George Blake, it was stated in the High Court in Dublin today. Between them they raised £800 which it was stated was used by Mr Bourke who had £200 to 'spring' Mr Blake from Wormwood Scrubs where he was serving a 42-year sentence for espionage.
>
> The existence of these three men was mentioned for the first time today . . . Mr Declan Costello, SC, for Mr Bourke said his client returned to Ireland from Moscow in October last year and 'was anxious to ensure that the friends who had assisted him in the escape of Mr Blake would not be apprehended. He took the view that sufficient time having elapsed, this would not happen. He believed that by returning to Ireland under Irish law he would not be extradited to England. That belief is to be tested in this court.[13]

The *Guardian* report of the same day quotes Mr Costello as saying that Seán 'approached three friends of his whom he knew were sympathetic to Blake's political views and they agreed to help him and they raised about £800'. Both reports indicated that in other respects Seán was sticking closely to the version of events he had given to the *World in Action* programme the previous October.

But on the fourth day of the hearing, giving evidence on his own behalf, Seán elaborated the story of how Blake was smuggled out of Britain:

> I bought a large van fitted with a small kitchen unit and a bed in the back. Under the bed was a large drawer. I cut off the back half of the drawer, making a cavity and this was sufficient for Blake to lie in. I pushed the drawer in after him and a friend drove the van to Dover and crossed to Ostend in the ferry. This was then driven to East Germany.[14]

Here Seán had dropped the claim made in the *World in Action* programme that he himself had driven the van to East Germany.

From our point of view, the more Seán elaborated his story, the nearer he came to identifying us and our role.

Legally, however, Seán had a strong case in fighting the extradition warrant – stronger, certainly, than any of us had initially appreciated. Irish law on extradition had been amended three years previously, so that those exempted from extradition included not only persons charged directly with a political offence but those charged with 'an offence connected with a political offence'. On Monday 3 February the High Court judge, Mr Justice O'Keefe, ruled in Seán's favour and ordered his release. He could not, he said:

> regard Mr Bourke's reasons for helping Mr Blake as being sufficient to make what would otherwise not be a political offence into an offence of a political character. But Mr Blake's offences were clearly political offences. He was a political prisoner in the sense that he was in prison convicted of committing a political offence . . . I think the offence of helping him to escape can be classed as an offence connected with a political offence . . .'[15]

Once again Seán's charm and flamboyance had clearly captivated the paper's reporter:

> Mr Bourke walked out of the court room and said as he stood on the bank of the Liffey in the sunshine that he was 'extremely happy'. He said the first thing he planned to do was to walk down the Liffey and have a pint of stout to celebrate. 'What better way of celebrating a victory in Dublin?'
>
> He also planned to send a telegram to tell George Blake the result. He went on: 'I am sure he already knows. There must have been a KGB man . . . in court. I did not see him, but there must have been one'.
>
> He said he would certainly go back to Russia for a holiday but he did not intend to go to Britain. He said: 'I do not think I am very popular in London this morning. But if the Attorney General were to give a guarantee that he will not charge me with anything at all, and for good measure throw in an OBE, I think I would consider going.[16]

Even the *Times* leader writer on the same day took a surprisingly relaxed view of the result.

> The merit of the Irish decision is that it grants asylum for someone charged with a crime which has not seriously damaged the interests of the state, which did not involve violence, but which has caused the political authorities embarrassment and humiliation, as it was intended

among other things to do. When the right of political asylum is in danger of general erosion it is no bad thing to have it secured in a case of such a kind.[17]

In February the *News of the World* published extracts from the tape recordings Seán had made of his conversations with Blake on the two-way radio. 'Amazing Spy Tape Recordings' was the frontpage headline in two-inch high letters in the issue of 9 February 1969, with a photograph underneath of the eastern perimeter wall which Blake had scaled to make his escape. There were further extracts in the following issue, 16 February. It emerged subsequently that the paper had sponsored a trip to Moscow by Seán's brother Kevin in August 1968, shortly before Seán's own return to Ireland.

What surprised me reading the 9 February issue was that none of the transcribed tapes were familiar. The conversations had occurred before Pat or I were aware that Seán had been making recordings. As noted in an earlier chapter, he must have left these tapes with friends or relatives, perhaps during his visit to Ireland the week before the escape, and never told us of their existence. It was only in the second instalment of the *News of the World* story on 16 February that extracts from the tapes I had sent on to him via an RTE journalist were published.

There was one item in the 9 February issue that caused us acute alarm. After a reference on the tape to 'friends' who might be able to help with fund-raising, Seán is quoted by the paper as explaining: 'Those friends . . . were a university graduate and his wife. Blake didn't know them personally, but I did and they were very eager to help us in any way they could.' Seán had spoken earlier of three friends who had helped him, but this was the first mention of a university graduate.

The Irish Attorney General appealed to the Supreme Court against the High Court judgement, but on 30 July the decision to refuse extradition was upheld. Meanwhile, however, on 3 July Seán was charged with the illegal possession of a firearm and a quantity of ammunition. He claimed in court that he had obtained them in self-defence because of threats he had received, and he was given a conditional discharge.

Seán stopped phoning me after I sent on the tapes to him, and in 1969 I moved up with my family to Bradford, where I had obtained a full-time teaching post in Complementary (General) Studies at the Regional College of Art, a department run by my old friend and colleague Albert Hunt. With the Irish Supreme Court decision, it seemed that the whole Blake episode was finally behind us.

Not so. In the spring of 1970 I received a telephone call from a journalist friend of mine to say he had just received an advance copy of a book called *The Springing of George Blake* by Seán Bourke. He thought I ought to see it as there were unmistakable references in it to Anne and me and another friend.

He put a copy of it in the post, and I agreed to consider reviewing it for one of the weeklies. I read it with great consternation. In it Anne and I were given the pseudonyms of 'Anne Reynolds' and Michael Reynolds', and Pat Pottle that of 'Pat Porter'. There were personal descriptions of us, and information about which area of London we lived in, our family background, religious upbringing and political beliefs. Thus, describing the meeting with me at my house in 1966, Seán writes:

> I got out at Camden Town and walked for about twenty minutes . . . It was a modest house for a man with a modest income . . . He would never himself be materially well off, for he was a socialist at heart. But he was not a Communist, any more than I was, and I wondered whether this would influence his decision. His background was Irish Catholic, though he himself was only half Irish, his mother being a Dublin woman and his father a Londoner.
>
> I rang the bell and almost immediately the door opened. Michael shook my hand vigorously. 'Come in Seán, come in.' . . .
>
> 'This is my wife Anne,' he said introducing me to an attractive girl of about twenty-five . . .
>
> 'These are ours', Michael said, 'nodding at the two small children playing on the floor. 'One is four and the other is two and a half.'[18]

All the details were accurate, even down to the ages of Anne and the two children, and the approximate time it would take to walk from Camden Town station to the house. The vital clue that Seán had deliberately missed out, and whose inclusion would have positively identified us, was that Pat and I were Committee of 100 members who had been in prison at the same time as him and Blake in 1962. Seán also muddied the waters somewhat by claiming that Blake met the two of us for the first time after the escape. This, however, would hardly be enough to throw any diligent investigator off the scent.

When the book was published in June 1970 it was on the whole favourably reviewed. The *Times Literary Supplement* reviewer made some telling points:

Escape from prison is of perennial interest. Everyone is to some extent a prisoner and for those who break out (even if they have previously broken in) there is something of the fellow feeling that awakens the instinctive desire to shelter the hunted. If the present book is to be believed, it affords a striking example of this.

Seán Bourke, nearing the end of his term of imprisonment at Wormwood Scrubs – the very name inspires sympathy for the inmates – met the Russian agent George Blake, and for motives which appear to have been purely humane decided to engineer the latter's escape from the prospect of some thirty years more of incarceration. When Blake's relatives failed to provide the working capital for the enterprise, a young married couple with children, friends of Bourke, undertook to raise the money and also to harbour Blake. Another friend came into the scheme. When Blake was injured coming over the wall a doctor came to attend him, asked no questions and took no fee. The ready cooperation of these disinterested and apparently otherwise law-abiding people was one of the major factors in the success of the escape.[19]

The reviewer paid a glowing tribute to Sean's writing style and also thought that the story had about it 'the ring of truth, allowance being made for reconstituted dialogue.' But other reviewers were more sceptical about his story, some suggesting that his Anglo-Irish friends in particular might be figments of his imagination, invented to disguise the identity of those who had really master-minded the escape.

In fact there was evidence in the book that this was not the case – though as far as we are aware no reviewer spotted this at the time. It was provided by the history of the original manuscript, as described on the book's fly-leaf, and the photographs of several pages from it which were included among the illustrations. The manuscript had been confiscated by the Soviet authorities in August 1968 when Seán's brother Kevin tried to smuggle it out of the Soviet Union. However, in spring 1969, after repeated requests from Seán addressed to the KGB headquarters in Moscow, it was sent to him in Dublin, though with the entire final section dealing with Seán's life in the Soviet Union removed, and the rest heavily censored – apparently in Blake's own hand.

The photographs show pages with passages blocked out, presumably by Blake, together in some instances with Seán's notes restoring the original text. Here then was unmistakable evidence of what Blake and the KGB thought was sensitive material and ought to be omitted. One photograph includes most of the passage quoted above but with Anne's and my name excised, plus the phrase stating that Anne was about twenty-five years old and the reference to the children and their ages. Seán had obligingly provided notes showing exactly what had been cut out to save the reader the trouble of cross-checking against the printed text. The obvious inference – which could hardly be overlooked by any trained security officer – was that not only were the alleged helpers real people but that their names and family details provided important clues to their identity.

At least one writer, Phillip Knightley, has subsequently questioned the authenticity of the history of the manuscript as described in the book. He argues that it would have been pointless for the Soviet authorities to have confiscated and censored the manuscript, if they were then going to send the censored version to Seán in Ireland, since 'there was nothing to stop [him] from reinstating the censored material and ignoring the amendments – as he says this is exactly what he did.'[20] In Knightley's view 'the only story which fits the facts is that the escape was organized by the Russians who contracted out some work to the IRA'. Bourke, he suggests 'was a minion hired because he knew Blake and was about to be released under the hostel system which allowed him free access between the outside world where he spent the days, and the prison where he slept at night.'[21]

Obviously this is not 'the only story which fits the facts', and Knightley's conclusions show how even such a well-informed and generally perspicacious commentator on the world of espionage can build up a theory on the basis of the slenderest evidence and convince himself that it is the only plausible explanation of the known facts. Of course, it is true that Seán could – and did – restore the censored passages in his manuscript, and the KGB, and Blake himself, would have known he could do this. Presumably the object of the exercise, from the point of view of the Soviet authorities, was to give the strongest possible indication to Seán of what they thought he ought not to include. It was a final plea, when they could no longer control what he did, to show some sense of responsibility towards those who had assisted him. It didn't work, but it was an eminently reasonable thing to have attempted.

Blake and the Soviet authorities, in fact, come out rather more creditably from this particular incident than does Seán himself. (We take it for granted that George was involved in the operation because aside from the claim that corrections were in his hand, he was the person uniquely placed to judge what details it might be risky to include in the account.) Neither Blake nor the KGB stood to gain anything from the removal of our names, or details about us, and our judgment is that George was genuinely concerned to prevent us being arrested and imprisoned because of our efforts on his behalf.

Pat and I felt that an intelligent boy-scout could have worked out from the book who we were – and one other friend who read it used this very expression. Thus for several weeks we lived on our nerves, wondering how soon we would be called in for an interview by Special Branch.

As the months elapsed and there was still no visit from the police, we breathed more freely. It seemed inconceivable that Scotland Yard were still unaware of who we were, but we assumed that a decision had been made at a high level not to prosecute us. Whether we were right about this, or whether the police simply never suspected us, must remain an open question.

Why might the authorities have made such a decision? Firstly, four years after the event it would have been difficult to obtain evidence that would stand up in a court of law. Secondly, even if the evidence was forthcoming, a prosecution at that stage would have done little to enhance the prestige of the security services, given that the principal actors in the drama were safely out of reach, and that an escape widely believed to have been a high-powered operation costing thousands of pounds and masterminded by the KGB would have been shown to be the work of amateurs working on a shoestring budget. We had little doubt however, that if the authorities could have got hold of Seán, or if he had decided to return to England and give himself up – as he later threatened to do on several occasions – we would then have been hauled in for questioning and very likely have faced prosecution.

What is surprising is not so much that we were not prosecuted after Seán's book was published in 1970 but that we were not even questioned. Perhaps the authorities wanted to avoid embarking on a course of action which might have forced them to prosecute. Another possibility was that despite all the clues, they really did not know who we were.

But we were not taking any chances. We still had the letters and photographs which Pat and I had collected from Highlever Road after Seán's departure on New Year's Day 1967. These included letters from George to Seán discussing the escape before they had established the two-way radio link-up, and photographs showing

Seán standing close to the window in Wormwood Scrubs Hostel using the walkie-talkie, with the turrets of one of the wings clearly visible in the background. I had also kept the rather grim photos of Seán and George that I had taken in Pat's flat after the escape, the plans for the conversion of the Commer van which Matthew had drawn up, and a set of photos showing the hiding-place in the van which I took early in 1967 after our return from Germany. Now, reluctantly, I burnt them all – or so I believed. In fact one of the negatives showing the secret compartment in the van was tucked away on its own in a negatives envelope and avoided the fire. It is reproduced in the present book. The only thing I deliberately retained was an account in about 40,000 words of the escape and our involvement in it which I had written early in 1967. This I lodged with various friends for several years before I repossessed it when the danger of discovery appeared to be over. The walkie-talkies we had disposed of much earlier, in October 1967.

Aside from the passages in the book which threatened to expose our identities its fascination for us was the revelation of some of the steps Seán had taken in the weeks and months after the escape, and the extraordinary account of his period in Moscow. It was at this point we first learned that Blake's mother had been visited by the police an hour after the break and given them Sean's name; three days after the escape, on Tuesday 25 October 1966, Sean had phoned them and informed them of the registration number and whereabouts of the getaway Humber car; and that just prior to his own departure he had sent a picture of himself to a national newspaper with his name and the Highlever Road address on the back.

Seán's period in Moscow is the stuff of the spy-adventure novel. He and Blake had become completely estranged within a short time of their moving into a flat together, and Seán claims to have overheard a conversation between Blake and a KGB man in which George appeared to be suggesting that Seán should be murdered. Seán was also told that he ought to remain in the Soviet Union for at least five years.

At this point Seán decided to take the future into his own hands. On 4 September he walked into the British Embassy in Moscow, told them he was wanted in Britain for helping George Blake to escape from Wormwood Scrubs, and that he had come to give himself up. The outcome of that visit has been narrated earlier; he was informed that the Embassy could do nothing straight away but that he should come back a week later.

Seán decided to try to live rough for the period in order to avoid going back to Blake's flat. He persuaded the Russian guard outside the Embassy that he was a tourist whose passport was in his hotel, and took a bus and taxi to the outskirts of the city. For two days and nights he lay low in a forest and park, until he ran out of food and money. He then returned to Blake's flat, resigned to the possibility that he would be arrested and shot.

Instead he received an assurance from 'Stan', the KGB man assigned to look after him, that arrangements would be made for him to get an Irish passport and return home; meanwhile he would be taken on a conducted tour of the Soviet Union. However, when this process seemed to be taking too long, he decided to phone his brother Kevin in Scotland, arranging for him to come out and see him in the summer. Finally, he became attached to a young Russian woman, Larissa – to whom, incidentally, his book is dedicated.

The only parts of this story that can be independently corroborated are Seán's visit to the British Embassy in September 1967, and his phone call to his brother Kevin, who did fly out to Moscow in August 1968 to see him. However, the story of his adventures is entirely plausible, and shows Seán acting with characteristic courage, resourcefulness – and total unpredictability. He must have been an almighty headache for his Soviet hosts, who could never be sure what he would get up to next.

As for his account of George's betrayal of him, we feel we must suspend judgment until the latter has told his side of the story. The extent of Seán's disillusionment is summed up in his comment to his brother Kevin when he visited him in Moscow in the summer of 1968:

> . . . he [Blake] is a born traitor. Blake does not betray for ideals; he betrays because he *needs* to betray. If Blake had been born a Russian he would have betrayed the KGB to the British. That's how he's made.[22]

This sounds like the judgment of a deeply embittered man. Obviously, if Blake really did try to have Seán murdered he had every reason to be bitter. But Seán doesn't allow for the possibility that George might have been genuinely concerned about the risk to Pat and me from his early return to Ireland. That George was concerned on our account we have no reason to doubt; he had shown this already when he was in hiding in Britain, and there is further evidence of it in the efforts he made to persuade Seán to change our first names and the descriptions of us in his book.

Moreover, George had nothing to gain personally from having Seán stay with him in Moscow, and no doubt was mightily relieved at a personal level when he finally left the country.

Seán dismisses George's fears on our account rather too easily. He reports his comment to George: 'Michael and Pat are at this moment free men, living and working in their own country among their own friends. They are in no danger from me or from anyone else.'[23] Later, when the question is raised by his KGB companion, Stan, Seán assures him that the police would get no information about us from him and that they would have to 'kill me first'. Stan accepts Seán's sincerity but points out that British Intelligence could give him drugs, which would make him talk without realizing it and says that one of their own men who had been subjected to such treatment by the British had become a nervous invalid and was now on a state pension. Seán then treats this as a crude attempt by Stan to intimidate him, and ignores his crucial point – namely, that however sincere Seán might be, if he fell into the hands of British Intelligence he could be induced to reveal our names – against his will, and without his even being aware of it – by the use of drugs.[24]

The specific allegation that Blake tried to have Seán murdered arises from a conversation which Seán says he overheard between Blake and Stan:

> 'As I see it, Stan,' he [Blake] said slowly, 'you are faced with only two alternatives. You can go out there now and tell him that he must stay in this country for at least five years whether he likes it or not – and if you like I will tell him for you. Or you can . . .'[25]

The sentence, Seán states, remained unfinished, but he believes its implications are clear; if Seán refuses to accept an enforced exile in the Soviet Union he should be eliminated.

Pat and I are sceptical about the story on two levels. Firstly, we wonder if the conversation ever took place: for why would George and Stan talk in English, not Russian? George was a fluent Russian-speaker, and indeed on another occasion Seán has him making an announcement in Russian for the benefit of the two cleaning ladies in the flat and then translating into English for Seán.[26] If he was plotting the elimination of the person to whom he owed his liberty, and whom he knew was in the same flat, why did he conduct the conversation in English?

Secondly, if the conversation did take place as Seán records it, did he misinterpret it? The strains on both Seán and George during this period must have been very great, pitchforked into a strange country with no clear role and an uncertain future. It was clear when I met Seán again in Ireland that he had periods of doubt and guilt about what he had done. And George himself in an interview on Moscow television in April 1988 recorded the difficulties he experienced during his early period in Moscow:

> It is always difficult for a man who's been in prison for a long time to readjust to normal life. And here it was a different country for me, with different traditions, and a different society.[27]

Given, in addition, the enormous differences in the backgrounds and temperaments of the two men, it is not surprising that they quickly became estranged, or if each began to blame the other for frustrations and tensions. It was also a situation where misinterpretation of motives and intentions can easily occur.

It was somewhat later in 1970 that I went to Ireland to visit friends and relatives and look up Seán. I stayed with friends in the Donneybrook area of Dublin and tracked down Seán's whereabouts quite easily, getting his address in the Sandymount area from newspaper reports of the extradition proceedings, and then locating him in the phone book.

I phoned him from a callbox.

'It's Michael here,' I said, without giving my surname. There was silence for a few seconds as if he was unsure who it was.

'Michael! I see, how are you? Where are you ringing from?'

'I'm here in Dublin, in O'Connell Street. Can I come over and see you?'

'You can, of course!' – and he went on to explain how to get to him.

Seán was living in a modern low-rise block of flats called Leahy House which I found without difficulty. It had one of those security systems where you have to identify yourself through a speaker to the person in the flat, who then releases the lock on the exterior door. Sean lived on an upper floor, I think the first or second. I pressed the doorbell and waited, wondering how he would look more than four years after we had sung the *Amhrán na bhFiann* together in the bar at Victoria Station, and how he would react to me.

When Seán opened the door he was holding a revolver in his hand. However, in the dim light of the passageway where he was standing I did not notice this.

'Michael! – it *is* you! Good. Come in!'

He led me to a sparsely furnished room at the far end of the flat and put the gun down on the table.

'Sorry about the dramatics,' he said, nodding in the direction of the revolver. I think he was a little disappointed that I had not noticed it earlier – it rather spoiled the dramatic effect!

'Some students from Queen University in Belfast', he went on, 'were threatening to kidnap me and take me over the border to the North. I've had to take certain precautions.'

I now had a chance to have a proper look at him. He had always been on the stocky side, but he had filled out in the last four years and was distinctly overweight.

'It's the easy living,' he said, noticing my glance – 'that and the lack of exercise.'

There was no food in the flat, so we took the bus back to the centre of Dublin where he treated me to an expensive meal at the Gresham Hotel. I had lobster salad, and between us we drank a bottle of wine. Seán seemed very much at home there, ordering the dishes with aplomb.

'So, what did you think of the book, Michael?'

'Well,' I said evasively, 'I certainly found it very interesting.'

'Do I sense some reservations?'

'No, no!' I protested – though he had guessed aright. In due course I expressed some of them. I trod delicately, however, all the time conscious of how he and George had fallen out in Moscow. I wanted desperately to avoid the whole venture ending in bitterness and recrimination.

I told him that I thought some of the dialogue was not accurate, pointing to several passages in particular – to which he retorted that I ought to be aware that he had a photographic memory. My chief complaint, however, was that he had sailed so close to the wind in describing Pat, Anne and myself.

'Tell me one thing, Seán. Why on earth did you use our actual Christian names, and give us the surnames Reynolds and Porter, which are so close to our real surnames?'

He reflected for a minute or two.

'It only goes to show,' he said at length, 'that I'm not the simple, uncomplicated Irishman people sometimes take me for.'

It was no answer, of course, but I did not press him further. I now regret this, and the fact that I did not raise other questions with him, such as why he had informed the police about the Humber car, why he had sent a note to a newspaper about the Highlever Road flat, and above all why he had sent another threatening letter to Michael Sheldon on the very day he was leaving England.

We went on to discuss Seán's allegations about Blake.

'Obviously I'm not in a position to judge the situation,' I said. 'You say you believe he was trying to get you killed, but you never actually heard him saying so explicitly.'

'No,' he said, looking at me sharply, 'and I was careful in the book not to claim that I had.'

I sensed, however, that he wanted me to come out wholeheartedly on his side and was unhappy that I was not prepared to do so.

As regards his own plans, he said he had decided after the success of his book to become a full-time writer, and was currently engaged on another book. Some of the critics, he told me, had compared his style to that of Brendan Behan.

'Wouldn't it give a chap great encouragement?' he said.

However, as we rose from the table, he sighed:

'I'm afraid, Michael, all the excitement and thrills are over. Life is very humdrum and ordinary these days.' It did not strike me at the time, but in retrospect I think it was an indication of how restless he was feeling.

Next day I was out taking a stroll along Sandymount strand when I saw Seán's familiar stocky figure coming towards me with a dog on the lead.

'Michael! I didn't expect to see you again so soon.'

'Me neither. Whose is the dog?'

'It belongs to one of the neighbours; I usually take it with me when I go for a walk.'

I changed direction to stroll with him as far as the Martello tower that figures in Joyce's *Ulysses*. It was a bright morning with the sea air crisp and clean. The tide was far, far out, and there were no breakers, only tiny ripples breaking silently on the distant short-line. As we turned back towards Sandymount the sun was warm in our faces.

'Who would have thought four years ago,' Sean said, 'that the two of us would be strolling here together one day on Sandymount strand?'

We met again in Limerick – I think it would have been May or June of the following year. Seán had told me that if ever I wanted to contact him in Limerick to get in touch with the Munster Fair Tavern, and it was there, later that evening, that I met him. He booked me in as his guest to the hotel where he was then living. However, I was taken off-guard when I was asked to sign my name, and on the spur of the moment I signed myself Michael Reynolds – the pseudonym he had given me in his book. Seán was highly tickled at this, though I soon realized it was a mistake. It was evidence, if the whole story ever came to light, that Reynolds and Randle were one and the same person.

It was not a happy visit. Seán was drinking heavily and by the second evening had become morose and quarrelsome. We'd had a large meal with drinks, and then adjourned until late to the Munster Fair Tavern. On the way home Seán stopped to buy pig's trotters. Back at the hotel he ordered brandies and ham sandwiches to be brought up to my room and sat on the bed next to me while he ate and drank. Then the accusations started.

'You betrayed your country, Michael Randle. Blake was a spy and a traitor and you and Pat helped him to escape to Russia. That makes you traitors as well.'

'That's bloody nonsense! We helped him because of the vicious sentence he'd received. By the time he escaped he wasn't in a position to betray any secrets. That's what you said yourself when you first asked for our help.'

Seán's accusations suggest that there were moments when he felt deeply ashamed at having helped Blake escape. I may well have reminded him that it was he who had approached us in the first place, though I can now only remember snatches of what became an increasingly angry exchange. I do recall that at one point he said that the whole operation would not have taken place without our help. He referred also to the occasion when I was about to move George from Highlever Road and asked him on behalf of the people who would be sheltering him for an assurance that he would not return to espionage work if he ended up in the Soviet Union.

'That was sheer bloody hypocrisy. You knew what he would say – that there was only one thing he could say. There was no point in asking him that question, apart from having me hear you asking it.'

'The point was to make quite clear what our attitude was. You were never willing to ask the awkward questions.'

Suddenly in the middle of the argument he keeled over on the bed. His eyes were wide open and staring and he was breathing heavily. I tried to rouse him, but for a minute or two could get no response. He was a dead weight on the bed and I could do nothing with him. By now we were into the early hours of the morning, and the trip was turning into a nightmare.

He came round slowly, and to my relief said he thought he should get to bed.

'It's not the first time, I've passed out,' he said. 'I'm going to have to cut down on the booze. The doctor told me recently that if I didn't I'd be a dead man within twelve months.'

Next day he saw me off to the station. His mood was subdued.

'You got very heated last night.'

'I had good reason to be,' I replied, still feeling stung at the things he had said.

We walked some little way in silence.

'Does it not occur to you,' he said at last, 'that a chap might be testing you out?'

One story Seán told me was that he had phoned Scotland Yard on a number of occasions and spoken to the man who had been in charge of the inquiry into Blake's escape. The detective had assured him that Scotland Yard knew the identity of the people who had helped him but that they decided not to bring a prosecution against us. This tallies with what we were later to hear from the Dublin journalist Kevin O'Connor.

I saw him only once more after that visit – when we were touring with the children in that part of Ireland. He was living by then in a cottage outside the city itself next door to a Polish exile with a curious hybrid accent, part Polish, part Irish. We had a drink together in the Munster Fair Tavern, but didn't linger. He told us he was still working on his second book and hoped it would be published shortly.

From time to time he wrote to me in Bradford. The last time was in early 1977 as we were about to move to Staffordshire. In it he said his life had come to a standstill and that he had made a decision to come back to Britain and give himself up to the authorities. This was a terrifying prospect, but I did not think it advisable to write back to try to dissuade him, and wasn't in a position to make a trip to Ireland to see him. After that we lost touch. He died on 26 January 1982 after collapsing in the street in Kilkee, a seaside resort in County Clare where he had gone to live in a caravan. The cause of death was certified as 'acute pulmonary oedema, left ventricle failure, and coronary thrombosis.'[28] By all accounts he was destitute.

How do we evaluate Seán's motives or explain some of the irrational and irresponsible things he did before and after the escape? Why did he fail to sell the Humber car registered in his name as we had agreed and to replace it with one that could not be traced to him? Why, four days after the escape did he – by his own admission – phone the police and tell them of its whereabouts and registration? Why having done that did he allow me to go looking for it, given the risk that I might have been caught if the police were keeping it under observation? Why was he so anxious that Pat and I should not go back to Highlever Road and empty the bedsit – to the extent again of sending a message to the Press which he assumed would be passed to the police, also sending a threatening letter to the Sussex detective, Michael Sheldon, just before leaving the country on 31 December 1966? Why finally did he sail so close to the wind in the names and descriptions of Anne, Pat and me in the book he published in 1970?

There isn't one single explanation for all these things, though we can suggest a possible common motive. Seán, we think, was entirely genuine in his response to George's plea to assist him escape. He was singleminded in his efforts to organize it, and courageous in the way he carried it out.

But in real life, no one's motives are entirely straightforward or one-dimensional; there are always subsidiary considerations, some of which one may be reluctant to acknowledge even to oneself. Seán we think realized at a certain point that the escape had all the makings of a first-class story and set about making a careful record that he could later draw upon – whether the escape itself succeeded or failed. This would explain the photographs taken on the self-timer in Wormwood Scrubs Hostel showing him talking into the walkie-talkie with D Hall towers visible in the background, and the fact that from the outset he recorded the conversations with Blake over the two-way radios.

Seán's difficulty, however, was that his story might not be believed. This problem would be largely overcome if he was publicly named as the person the police wanted to interview in connection with the escape. Many of his apparently irrational actions can be explained in terms of an effort to bring this about. It explains why he used a car registered in his name, why he personally informed the police afterwards of its whereabouts, and why he sent information to a newspaper about Highlever Road the day before he finally left Britain. It may even partly explain – though it can in no sense excuse – his threatening letter to the Sussex detective, Michael Sheldon. Seán may have calculated that the receipt of that letter would push the authorities into naming him in connection both with that offence and with the escape of Blake. Whether intended or not, that was certainly the consequence of sending the threatening letter.

What this theory does not explain is why he allowed me to risk discovery and arrest by setting out to find the Humber car with the intention of driving it away. Nor does it explain why he did not make it impossible for Pat and me to clear out Highlever Road after his departure by simply throwing away the keys. In both instances he did try hard to warn us off; but when the crunch came, he allowed us to go ahead with our plan. We believe he was not prepared for an outright confrontation with us by telling us the truth – it was psychologically impossible for him to tell me not to go looking for the car because he had already informed the police about it; at the same time he found it impossible under pressure to maintain the fiction that he had thrown away the car keys.

It is much harder to fathom why in his book he gave us pseudonyms which were so close to our real names – Pat Porter, and Michael and Anne Reynolds and why he put in lots of circumstantial details about us. We are convinced that he had no intention of 'shopping' us. Seán could be erratic and foolhardy, but he was no 'grass'.

Perhaps it was because Seán was so blasé about security matters that he saw no particular danger for us in what he wrote. Perhaps too he found it easier to relate to the characters in the book by giving us pseudonyms close to our real names than if he had given us entirely fictitious names. It was an irresponsible thing to have done, but we do not believe it was done maliciously.

We all liked Seán. He was impulsive and generous, and had a great deal of charm and style. He could drive you mad at times, and he was not a good person to have around when discretion and self-control were called for. But he planned Blake's escape and had the courage and initiative to carry it out. Without that, none of the events described in this book would have happened. And George Blake would, at the time we are writing, still be in prison.

CHAPTER NINE

A Time to Speak

Narrated by Michael Randle

With Seán's death, we all thought our role in the Blake escape was over, and that we had nothing further to worry about on that score. Occasionally Pat and I speculated what we would do if some journalist looking into the case latched on to the connection between Reynolds and Randle and Porter and Pottle, and publicly accused us of being involved. But this possibility seemed remote so long after the event.

Anne and I had moved back to Bradford in late 1980, and at about the same time Pat and Sue moved from Wales to London, where they set up an antique shop. As my work involved visits to London every six weeks or so we saw each other regularly. More often than not I would stay with Pat and Sue overnight, sometimes on my own, sometimes accompanied by Anne.

The first hint of trouble came with the publication in the *Observer* of 23 November 1986 of an extract from Phillip Knightley's book *The Second Oldest Profession*.[1] Though Knightley himself tended to discount Seán's account, the piece provoked several letters in the following week's *Observer*. One was from Kevin O'Connor, a Radio Telefis Eireann (RTE) journalist, who strongly defended Bourke against Knightley's criticisms; another was from the author H. Montgomery Hyde stating that he was working on a biography of Blake which would show that the escape was financed not by the Russians or the IRA but from another source. He had, he claimed, obtained the details from a fellow-inmate of the prison at the time.[2]

In spring 1987 I received a phonecall from someone who had seen a publisher's blurb about Hyde's book. He told me it claimed the book (published by Constable) would reveal that the Committee of 100 had been involved in Blake's escape. This was enough to set me worrying about the account of the escape I had written in early 1967 and still had in the house. It was the one remaining piece of concrete evidence. I dreaded the thought that I might be responsible for Pat and others going to prison, as well as myself,

225

because of my account, and reluctantly, I decided that the time had come to destroy it. I brought it down to the living-room and skimmed through it for the last time before throwing it on the open fire. Then, quite irrationally, I pulled out our copy of Seán's book and burnt that as well.

In August the matter took a new turn. A journalist friend phoned me again to say he had received a review copy of Hyde's book. He read me the most damaging passage:

> In addition there were two other prisoners [in Wormwood Scrubs in 1962] with an Irish background – Michael Reynolds and Pat Porter (these were not their real surnames). They both belonged to the Committee of 100, the nuclear disarmament group formed by Bertrand Russell, the philosopher and social reformer, who was the first President of the Campaign for Nuclear Disarmament. In 1960 he had split the CND to form the more militant Committee of 100 dedicated to civil disobedience in pursuit of its aims. Michael Reynolds and Pat Porter had helped to organize the civil disobedience demonstration at Wethersfield RAF base in December 1961, for which they were imprisoned from 1961 to 1963.[3]

This was no mere hint, but positive identification. Only five people had been imprisoned in Wormwood Scrubs in 1962 for organizing the Wethersfield demonstration, and Pat and I were the only ones with the appropriate first names.

'Should we be talking about this over the phone?' I said nervously.

'Well, perhaps we shouldn't, but the fact is that unless you take some action immediately, like serving an injunction, this thing will be in the public domain within a matter of weeks.'

He drew my attention to an acknowledgment to Nicholas Walter, a Committee of 100 member. Nicholas had guessed the identity of 'Porter' and 'Reynolds' when Bourke's book was published in 1970, and discussed the Blake escape with Hyde in December 1986. Whether anything he told Hyde materially assisted the latter in identifying us remains unclear.

My friend promised to send me his copy and I said I'd consider reviewing the book for *The Guardian*. I phoned Pat and we arranged to meet the following week, by which time I would have had a chance to read the book and work on the review.

When I received the review copy I discovered that much of it was drawn from Seán's account. Whole passages of narrative and dialogue had been taken from it with minimal changes – such as replacing the 'I' of the original with 'Seán' – and there were no footnotes by the borrowed passages to show that they had come from another book. Nor was there any acknowledgement in the Introduction of the debt the book owed to Seán's work, simply a statement of fact that Seán had written a detailed account of the escape, and of his time in Moscow, which was published in 1970. Finally, the Introduction concluded with the statement:

> I ought to add that I have not improvised any of the conversations which had been recorded in the following pages. Their sources have all been authenticated.[4]

The book incensed me, as it did Pat when he read it. Hyde never presented the evidence for his allegations but simply asserted that Pat Porter and Michael Reynolds were two Committee of 100 members imprisoned in Wormwood Scrubs for their part in organizing the Wethersfield demonstration of December 1961. And to our knowledge he did not try to contact us and question us directly.

Hyde stated in a subsequent letter to the *Guardian* that he witheld our real surnames at the request of one of his informants 'so as to spare them possible embarrassment and trouble with the authorities'.[5] But he had gone so far already that there was little point in withholding our names.

His book identified us yet produced no evidence that would stand up in a court of law to support the allegations. Could we have sued or taken out an injunction? The police decision after the book's publication not to prosecute indicated to us that if they did not have evidence to prosecute, neither did anyone else have evidence to defend themselves against a libel action, if we had decided to take them to court. However, a libel action would have meant publicly denying our involvement in the escape.

But though we wouldn't sue, we decided to fight back. We would use the review to attack the whole business of international espionage and the hypocrisy of George's 42-year sentence, and make it quite clear – short of legally incriminating ourselves – that we were happy he had escaped and would see nothing to be ashamed of in having helped him to do so. Moreover, if it came to a prosecution we would fight the case – as we had done in the Wethersfield trial in 1962 – squarely on the humanitarian and political issues.

I worked on a draft review which Pat and I agreed should appear under both our names. We undertook to get the review to them in time for it to appear on the book's publication day, 28 September.

The six weeks between receiving the review copy and its official publication were extremely tense. I brooded about the likely consequences. Prison seemed a real possibility, despite the lapse of time and the dearth of hard evidence likely to stand up in a court of law.

In early September Anne and I went on holiday to a friend's cottage in the Dordogne. I had arranged to send the review to the *Guardian* before we left, and had it all sealed and ready to post. But at the last minute I had second thoughts and decided instead to take it with us on holiday and mull over it for another ten days.

When we got back Pat was having similar doubts. He questioned whether anyone would take Hyde's book seriously. By reviewing it on the day of publication we would be drawing attention to it, and to the allegations about us. If we held back, we could always publish the review later if the media picked up on the story in a big way. We would then also have the satisfaction of knowing that we had not brought the trouble on ourselves by precipitate action.

On publication day there was nothing – either in the *Guardian* or anywhere else. However, just as we were beginning to think that the book would pass unnoticed Richard Norton-Taylor, a journalist on the *Guardian*, phoned to say that his piece would be appearing the following day.

It proved to be a discreet news item of about five hundred words headed 'Nuclear disarmers freed spy Blake, author says.'[6] It pointed out that five members of the Committee of 100 were in Wormwood Scrubs with Blake after the Wethersfield demonstration in 1961, and said that two of them were 'given thinly disguised aliases' in the book. The *Guardian*, it continued, had contacted former members of the Committee of 100 who were seeking legal advice – a clear indication that the writer knew who the people concerned were and had been in touch with them.

Unknown to us, there had already been an article about the book in the Irish press. On 23 September, as we later discovered, the *Irish Independent* ran a long review by Kieran Fagan saying that Hyde's book provided new evidence about the identity of the people who had assisted Seán Bourke, including the fact that they were members of the Committee of 100. He hinted at a much wider conspiracy surrounding the Blake escape involving both the KGB and British Intelligence, and concluded that when we knew, 'as we must soon, the identity of Bourke's Irish CND friends' we would have an important clue 'to why Seán Bourke took on the establishment and won'.[7]

On Thursday 1 October I received the first of many calls from Barrie Penrose, a reporter for *The Sunday Times*.

'You may remember me,' he said. 'I used to be called Barrie Sturt-Penrose – I was a foot-soldier in the Committee of 100 in the early 1960s. I was always one of your admirers and I'm phoning you as a friend to warn you that a book is about to be published by a man called Montgomery Hyde which as good as accuses you of helping the spy George Blake to escape from prison. It hasn't yet been published, but I have seen a review copy.'

'It has been published,' I said, 'and was commented on in Tuesday's *Guardian*.'

'Yes, I saw the *Guardian* piece,' he said, dropping the pretence that the book had not been published. 'It isn't true, is it, that you helped Blake to escape?

Taken off guard by the question, I did what we had determined not to do and said no. It was only then that Penrose revealed that he was now a journalist working for *The Sunday Times* and author of a number of books about espionage.

I said I had no further comment to make, and as soon as he was off the line I telephoned Pat. Before long Penrose phoned him too, and it became apparent that he was preparing a major piece for the paper that weekend.

On Friday morning at about eight o'clock, I looked out of the window to see an unfamiliar car parked in front of the house. A suspicious-looking man was sitting inside it reading a newspaper. I thought it odd, but told myself not to be paranoid. Two hours later the car was still there. When I opened the door to fetch in the milk, the man in the car swung round and aimed a camera with a long-focus lens in my direction.

I beat a hasty retreat, and phoned Pat at once. He had the same story to tell; a car had been parked outside the house all morning – he didn't know if it was the Press or the police.

When Penrose phoned Pat later that morning Pat challenged him about the photographers.

'If you wanted a photograph, why didn't you just ring up and ask me?'

Penrose assured him categorically that the photographers were nothing to do with *The Sunday Times*.

'They could perhaps be from RTE in Dublin,' he suggested – 'I happen to know they are very interested in the story. Anyway, since you mention that you have no objection to us having a picture of you, would it be all right to send someone round right away?'

Pat was hoist with his own petard. What could he say but yes?

When Penrose phoned me again that Friday afternoon he confirmed that his paper would be running a story. He was also convinced, he said, that Pat and I had been involved in the escape. This time I made no denial.

'That's something you will have to make your own judgement about.'

On Saturday afternoon Anne and I drove up to Bentham in the Yorkshire Dales for a camping week-end with some friends. We had our own tent, but spent the evening in their caravan on the same site, drinking and playing games. We tried not to let the thought of what the next day might bring spoil the occasion. In the morning I got up just before eight o'clock and listened to the news and the review of the Sunday papers on the car radio.

'Nothing at all on the radio,' I reported back to Anne, fifteen minutes later, looking inside the tent. 'I'm going to walk down to the village now to get the papers.'

It was about half a mile's walk to the paper shop in the village and that morning there was a gentle but refreshing drizzle, more like mist than rain. By now I was feeling more optimistic and decided that either the story was not in at all or that it was buried somewhere on an inside page.

I was quite mistaken. As soon as I stepped inside the shop I saw the front-page headline in *The Sunday Times*. It was 'Soviet Spy was sprung by CND men.' Underneath, to the right was a profile shot of a young George, bearded and wearing a collar and tie. I bought a copy, glancing at the story as I left the shop but then putting the paper away until Anne and I could look at it together. She had made tea on the gas primus stove when I got back and was about to pour it out.

'Well?' she said.

'It's the lead front-page story.'

We read it together in shocked silence, warming our hands over our mugs of tea. In addition to the front-page story, the 'News in Focus' section was taken up with an article entitled 'The "Blake

Escape Committee".' It had prominent photographs of Pat and myself taken in the late 1950s–early 1960s as well as the pictures the *Sunday Times* photographers had obtained two days previously; there were also shots of George and Seán. The piece concluded that there was no doubt Pat and I were the Pat Porter and the Michael Reynolds of Seán's book:

> The descriptions of Reynolds and Porter by Bourke and Hyde match Randle and Pottle in almost every detail – religion, parentage, wives, mortgage, addresses, qualifications and political sympathies. Indeed Randle and Pottle expected MI5 to call when Bourke's book was published in 1970.[8]

For a while we sat in the tent thinking of the effect the story would have on our lives – and especially how friends and acquaintances would react. Anne's situation at work was more difficult than mine. I at least was working in surroundings where political issues were constantly debated, and controversial views held, and where something of my background was known. Anne, in an NHS hospital among people with a very wide range of political views, had no idea what to expect. But I knew that in my case the publicity was bound to create difficulties for the School of Peace Studies. I therefore decided I should see Professor James O'Connell the following day and offer him my resignation.

We arrived home that evening half expecting the Press – if not the police – on our doorstep. There was nobody there. Instead we found a note from one of our closest friends wishing us luck and saying we could come and stay with him if we wanted to lie low for a few days. This was a welcome encouragement. Several other friends made similar offers over the following few days.

We had hardly got inside the house, however, before the phone started ringing. The first call was from the local *Telegraph & Argus*, and it was followed by calls from several other newspapers – the 'first wave' had begun.

Next morning I went to see Professor James O'Connell. He pointed out that he was faced simply with allegations – and allegations that related to events said to have taken place more than twenty years previously, long before the School of Peace Studies had been set up. He therefore refused my offer of resignation.

Pat arrived later in the morning to discuss the situation.

Oddly, there had been little reaction from the media – to *The Sunday Times* story – of the morning papers only the *Daily Mirror* had run a piece about it.[9] However, at two o'clock Anne rang from the hospital with the cryptic message that she thought I ought to get a *Telegraph & Argus*.

I went down to our local newsagents where the young woman behind the counter exclaimed:

'Oh, I see you have become a celebrity!'

The headline in large letters read: 'We Are Couple in Red Spy Mystery'. That's what they had made of my saying yes, I was the person mentioned in the *Sunday Times* report! There were prominent pictures of George Blake, Anne and me.

By Wednesday we had finished our statement and review and on Friday our review took up most of the 'Agenda' page of the *Guardian* – it had been given the title 'Blood on the Spy Trails.'[10] The statement we had made was not published in full, but was quoted extensively in a report by Richard Norton Taylor entitled 'Two Admit Account of Blake Escape could identify them.'[11]

Here for the record is the full text of the statement.

We do not intend to confirm or deny the allegation made obliquely by Mr H. Montgomery Hyde in his new book, and explicitly by a Sunday newspaper last weekend, that we assisted in the escape from Wormwood Scrubs, and subsequent flight to the Soviet bloc, of George Blake in 1966.

Mr Hyde relies almost entirely on a book published by Seán Bourke in 1970. If the events surrounding Blake's escape correspond with Bourke's account, no stigma in our judgement would be attached to any persons identified as his assistants.

Nevertheless neither Mr Hyde nor Barrie Penrose in his story in *The Sunday Times* of 4 October produce evidence of our involvement. *The Sunday Times* story also contains a number of inaccuracies. We were not founder members of CND. Michael Randle does not run Bradford University's Peace Studies department and he has a fellowship, not a lectureship, at the university. The story also falsely attributes to Mr Hyde the allegation that 'Reynolds and Porter were part of a wider conspiracy to free Blake which was based within a clique of 1960s peace campaigners' and that the plotters were 'figures in the then vocal CND movement and the breakaway group the Committee of 100'. Mr Hyde makes no such allegation.

We have no doubt that after Bourke's book was published the British Security Services were fully aware that we two matched the descriptions of Porter and Reynolds. If the police did not act then, and did not even question us, it was presumably because they realized there was no real evidence of our involvement. We are confident they will take the same view today. Nevertheless should Scotland Yard wish to interview us, we will be happy to meet them at any time – preferably over a glass of Irish whiskey in memory of Seán Bourke.

Neither of us in the course of a long association has ever had any dealings with the espionage services of any state. We have, however, opposed and campaigned against the nuclear war preparations of both East and West as well as interventionist and repressive policies by both sides. This has at times involved breaking the law, usually openly, as in the case of the Wethersfield demonstration, occasionally clandestinely, as when we played a (very modest) part in helping US war resisters find sanctuary in Sweden during the Vietnam war. We campaigned against that war, but we also opposed the Soviet invasion of Czechoslovakia in 1968, in that instance helping to organize simultaneous international protests in Moscow, Warsaw, Budapest and Sofia. Today we oppose the proxy US war against Nicaragua but also the Soviet intervention and continuing war in Afghanistan.

We do not condone Blake's role as a double agent, particularly if, as has been alleged, his activities led to the execution of western agents and double agents whom he named to the Soviet authorities. But Western Intelligence agencies also have blood on their hands. This has been dramatically underlined in a book just published by Bob Woodward on the CIA which establishes beyond reasonable doubt that the agency was responsible for a terrorist car bomb attack in Beirut in March 1985 in which over 70 people were killed and several hundred injured. The time indeed is long overdue for a reassessment by both East and West of their extensive espionage activities which ruin lives, poison international relations and contribute to an unhealthy public obsession with spies and spying.

The 42-year sentence on Blake reflects no credit on British justice. It was clearly influenced by the Cold War. As Blake's QC, Mr Jeremy Hutchinson said at the Appeal Court in 1961: 'This sentence is so inhuman that it is alien to all the principles on which a civilized country would treat its subjects.' His escape, as the then Prime Minister Wilson stated, posed no threat to British security. For our part we do not regret that he escaped instead of deteriorating slowing down the years in a succession of British jails.

If we were involved in Blake's escape we clearly could not say so publicly without pointlessly inviting prosecution. But we would have no apologies or regrets for an act of human solidarity that cut across political disagreements and across the lies, and murderous obsessions of superpower politics and the Cold War. If we were not involved we would not regard it as a slur on our character to be named as having been so. Thus on the basis of what has been said so far we will be issuing no writs and making no denials.

At the weekend *The Sunday Times* returned to the story. Pat obtained an early edition from Kings Cross station on Saturday evening and read it to me over the phone. It was headed 'Blake: CND Plot Probed by Yard' and the gist of it was that Scotland Yard's special branch had launched an inquiry into 'a CND-inspired plot' which had helped to free George Blake, and intended to interview Pat and me later in the month. It was a nastier piece than the previous week's in so far as there was a sustained effort to implicate CND. It was also more worrying for us personally if the story that Scotland Yard had reopened the case was correct.

There were other significant developments. Montgomery Hyde wrote a letter in the *Guardian* on 13 October, in which he strongly objected to 'the manifestly unfair statements' about his book, notably that he had 'plagiarised extensively "uncorroborated" details given by Seán Bourke.' He stated that he had paid a substantial fee to the representatives of Bourke's estate for permission to use and quote from Bourke's book and that he had acknowledged this in the introduction. Much of the corroboration had been obtained from confidential sources which he did not feel at liberty to disclose.[12]

I checked my copy of the book and confirmed that there was no such acknowledgement in the introduction. But as I sat down to compose a reply to Hyde a thought struck me: could the acknowledgement have been added at a later stage – ie. after the review copies had gone out? I phoned Pat, who had the book in its final hardback form, and sure enough he found that there was now an additional sentence thanking John Farquharson Ltd and the publishers, Cassell's for permission to quote from Bourke's book. Two day's later, on 15 October, *The Guardian* carried our reply.

Some days later, on 19 October, we received a simple letter of support from the critic and writer John Berger. It was dated 13 October and read:

Dear Patrick and Michael –
Just wanted to tell you how happy I was to read you (and about you)
in the *Guardian*. And to tell you how much you have my admiration –
and my best wishes.

John

John Berger had been a member of the Committee of 100, and he
was someone whose writings Pat and I had long admired. His letter,
coming at that time, gave our morale a tremendous and much-
needed boost.

During the period following *The Sunday Times* reports, Pat and I
had refused to give interviews, referring everyone to the *Guardian*
statement. But among the most persistent caller was the RTE
journalist Mr Kevin O'Connor. He had been one of the people who
had written to the *Observer* in 1966 following the publication of
extracts from Phillip Knightley's book, and someone whose help
Hyde had acknowledged in the introduction to his book. I assumed
because of his close interest in Bourke, and because he worked for
RTE, that he must be the journalist to whom I had handed over
Seán's tapes in 1968. Thus when he rang me early in the week
beginning 11 October and said that he had just flown over from
Dublin and was at Bradford University, I agreed to see him.

I soon discovered that he wasn't who I thought he was but a man
with a bee in his bonnet about a larger conspiracy. He was
convinced that the Labour MP Tom Driberg had masterminded the
escape, and he began to question me about whether I had ever had
any dealings with Driberg. I was in an awkward position. I'd only
ever met the man once in 1963, and then very briefly. But I could
not state definitely that he had nothing to do with the escape
without thereby confirming that I had myself been involved.
However, I told O'Connor I thought he was barking completely up
the wrong tree and left it at that. (Later, when the affair had blown
open, we learnt that Kevin O'Connor had claimed that Bourke
himself had stated that Tom Driberg (Lord Bradwell) helped him to
mount the escape at an early stage.[13]

Pat and I find it difficult to believe that Seán would have made
any such claim. We cannot, of course, *prove* that he did not
approach Driberg – that would be literally impossible to do. But we
do know that Seán at no stage had any money to put into the
project, that it was Pat and I who found George places to stay after
we discovered that Highlever Road was unsuitable, that it was we

235

who found a doctor to treat George's broken wrist, and that we finally organized the departure of both George and Seán from the country. What role, then, could Tom Driberg have possibly played? The reality, of course, is that he had about as much to do with the escape as Santa Claus.

O'Connor did, however, bring over some interesting material, including the tape of a radio programme about Seán that he had made a few years previously for RTE, and the page from the *Irish Independent* of 23 September with Kieran Fagan's review of Hyde's book. The radio programme included extracts from the tapes Seán had made of his conversations with Blake over the two-way radio. O'Connor had followed the Blake–Bourke story over a number of years and had got to know the Scotland Yard 'leg man' on the Blake escape case. This man had told him that Seán used to ring them up from Ireland and engage them in long telephone conversations; Scotland Yard, he said, had known the identities of his helpers in England for a long time but a decision had been taken not to prosecute them because they were not 'criminals' and were now leading useful lives in the community.

The long-awaited call from the police came the following week, on Tuesday 27 September; when the West Yorkshire Constabulary informed me that two officers from Scotland Yard wanted to come to Bradford the following day to interview me in connection with recent press reports; would I kindly ring a Detective Sergeant Lynch in London to confirm the arrangements. I rang Detective Lynch and said it would be more convenient for me to come to London where my solicitor Ben Birnberg could be present. He was agreeable to this.

'There's one other matter you may be able to help with with,' he said. 'I know from the press that you are in touch with Mr Pottle, and I wonder if you could give me his telephone number as I need to speak to him as well?'

It sounded like a joke. There were we convinced that our phones must be being tapped, and Scotland Yard was having to ask me for Pat's number!

The meeting with Lynch and another detective was finally arranged for 11a.m. on Friday 30 October at Holborn Police Station in Theobalds Road.

Pat and I arrived early – about 10.45p.m. – and waited outside. For both of us the events of the last few weeks – and in particular the fact that we were now facing a police interview more than twenty-one years after Blake's escape – had a surreal quality. It was hard to believe it was really happening.

When Ben still hadn't arrived by 11a.m. we went inside the police station to report our presence. The young policeman behind the desk asked us what it was in connection with. Pat and I looked at one another and hesitated. Then Pat said:

'It's in connection with newspaper stories about the escape of George Blake.'

The policeman looked none the wiser – he'd obviously never heard of George Blake! He checked his list and asked us if we would mind waiting a few minutes. When Ben arrived he told us, just to cheer us up, that he had known cases where clients who had come to the police station for an interview had not been allowed to leave! However, he didn't think that was likely to happen in our case.

Five minutes later a woman, smartly dressed in a skirt and blouse, and wearing a string of pearls, and a small, dapper man in a dark suit stepped into the waiting-room from an interior door. The man introduced himself as Sergeant Lynch, and his companion as Detective Inspector Crampton. All three of us – Pat, Ben and I – registered momentary surprise: we had all simply taken it for granted that the Inspector would be a man.

It was all very polite and civilized. We shook hands and the Inspector expressed sympathy for me on account of my heavy cold. Lynch had a way when he talked to you of moving his body from the waist rather than simply turning his head, and we wondered afterwards if this was the result of an illness. They led us downstairs to a tiny room with soundproofed walls. There they left us alone for a few minutes while they set up the equipment in the interview room next door.

'I should tell you', Ben informed the two detectives when they returned, 'that my clients do not intend to make any statement.'

Pat was first to go into the interviewing room with Ben. They must have been in there for ten minutes – a long time, I thought, in which to say nothing. But finally the door opened and Pat came out.

'Do you want me to send Mike through?' I heard him asking – but apparently they weren't quite ready to receive me. Instead Pat and Ben returned to the ante-room and the three of us were left together for perhaps five minutes while Pat told me exactly what questions the detectives had put to him.

'The questions may take an completely different form with you,' Ben said.

In fact they didn't. Once inside the interview room Lynch explained the procedure. The interview would be simultaneously recorded on two tapes; one, the master tape, would be sealed in my presence and only opened in court if there was a trial; the other they would use for reference purposes. He then formally cautioned me and the interview began.

The initial questions were harmless – name, date and place of birth, occupation, marital status, date of marriage (which I got wrong!). Then it was my father's date and place of birth, followed by my mother's. I was puzzled why they would want to know these, but I reflected afterwards that Seán had stated that Porter and Reynolds both had Irish mothers, and our answers established that this was true of us – Pat's mother came from Tipperary, mine from Dublin. But where, we wondered, did the detective sergeant's father or grandfather come from with a name like Lynch!

The next question came nearer the mark.

'Do you know Barrie Penrose?'

I remember how one of my uncles had answered such a question in a different context – 'Oh indeed I bloody well do!' But I said:

'I'm not prepared to answer that.'

'Do you wish then to terminate the interview?'

'Yes,' I said.

Lynch switched off the machine, and then sealed the master copy with a flimsy tape which we all signed. There was no way it could be unsealed or interfered without tearing the sealing tape with the signatures on it.

They took us back upstairs, shook hands again, and expressed the hope that my cold would soon be better. That was all there was to it.

Everything was quiet for a few days after that, but on Tuesday 3 November Pat phoned to say he had received another call from Barrie Penrose, followed by a hand-delivered letter, to say that *The Sunday Times* was planning to publish further details about the escape at the weekend, including allegations that Vanessa Redgrave had put up the money to finance it.

We were in an impossible situation. We could not deny the story without first stating explicitly that we had assisted in the Blake escape. We nevertheless prepared a short statement and tried desperately for several days to get hold of Vanessa to read it to her –

without success. The statement we made was probably as good as we could do in the circumstances, but it left us unsatisfied. Here is the full text, as published in the Bradford *Telegraph & Argus*:

> As the two people named by Mr Barrie Penrose in *The Sunday Times* as having assisted in the escape of George Blake, we wish to state categorically that neither in 1966, nor at any other time, did we receive or use money or any other assistance from Ms Redgrave for the kind of activities Mr Penrose describes.[14]

Pat phoned it through to Penrose, but despite this – and despite a categorical denial from Vanessa herself, issued by her solicitors that she was in any way involved – *The Sunday Times* published the story in the issue of 8 November.

It was headed 'Spy escape: did Vanessa Redgrave pay?' and stated that detectives would be interviewing her about the allegation. The source of the story, according to the report, was Seán himself. He had allegedly told a number of people about Vanessa's involvement. These, the report said included Mr John Gore-Grimes, Seán's solicitor; Mr Kevin O'Connor, the Dublin journalist; and Mr Jim Kemmy, the Irish MP. Our denial was briefly quoted, as was the statement from Vanessa which read: 'I had no involvement of any kind, whatsoever, direct or indirect, in connection with the escape from prison of George Blake.' The report, however, went on to hint that a political contribution from her might have been used without her knowledge to buy the van in which Blake was smuggled out of the country.[15]

We can reaffirm that Vanessa Redgrave gave no money for the escape; nor was any contribution of hers used to help finance it. Seán Bourke never knew who gave the money. He wasn't told, and he never expected to be told – any more than did George. We were sufficiently security-conscious to operate a 'need to know' policy. Pat, for example, did not know, and does not know to this day, the name or any details about the doctor who came to Highlever Road to treat George's wrist, and has never asked.

Both Pat and I knew Vanessa, from the Committee of 100. She gave evidence on our behalf at the Official Secrets Act trial in 1962; she also made contributions to a number of projects with which we were involved. We can only surmise that Seán heard us talking about her on a number of occasions and jumped to the conclusion that she had put up some of the money. He then told various friends in Ireland, who in turn repeated it in good faith to *The Sunday Times*.

The Sunday Times returned to the Blake story, and Vanessa Redgrave's alleged involvement one more time on 15 November. It also reported that MI5 officers had re-opened their Blake file to establish the degree to which the Russians played 'a guiding background role' in the affair.

The rumours concerning Vanessa Redgrave's involvement, and the suggestion that the KGB might have masterminded the escape, underlined the inadequacy in the long-term of our *Guardian* statement. As a holding statement it was about as good as we were capable of producing. But it did not enable us to deal with the speculation that must inevitably arise. Thus, within a few weeks of the original allegations, Pat and I had a long discussion about whether we should not issue a second statement acknowledging our role, and saying that we would be writing a book which would set the record straight.

We made no hasty decision. We knew that if we went public we were likely to be prosecuted and perhaps imprisoned, and we had to think carefully about what that would mean for our future and that of our families. Neither Anne nor Pat's wife Sue were happy about what we were proposing, though they acknowledged the strength of the arguments in its favour. But the more we thought about it, the more it seemed to us that we really had no option but to reveal in full what we had done and why we had done it. We had not sought the publicity in the first place, and down the years had done our utmost to prevent our role being made public. But once *The Sunday Times* had named us, the genie was out of the bottle for good.

We had, of course, to think also about the effects of our going public on the peace movement with which we had been associated for so long. But though the publicity that would attend the publication of our book would certainly cause problems for the movement, the damage in the long run could be much worse if we continued to keep our heads down and ignore highly damaging rumours such as the suggestion that we had been agents or dupes of the KGB.

Opinion among friends and colleagues was sharply divided. Some vehemently opposed our going public; others were clear that this was the only possible way to proceed. In the end we had to follow our own judgment.

We eventually decided against making an early public statement about our involvement as we feared we might then be arrested and imprisoned before we had the opportunity to tell the full story and put events in context. Instead we would write a book. In February I started spending my evenings and weekends on the book, while Pat concentrated on research.

Our belief that we were right to go public was strengthened when Blake himself made a dramatic comeback into the news with an interview on a Soviet television chat-show on Saturday 23 April. He spoke, among other things, about his escape from prison, his stay in two safe houses in Britain, and his journey to East Germany hidden in a van. He did not, of course, reveal anything concerning the identity of those who had helped him, but his account did provide for the first time independent and authoritative corroboration of the main elements in Seán's story, including the existence of helpers. The *Daily Express*, reporting the story, said that detectives now believed that Blake had been assisted in his escape 'by two CND members';[16] the *Independent* said Blake told 'how Communist sympathisers helped in his escape.'[17]

As we began working on the book, I cursed myself for having burnt all the material we had amassed after the escape, and in particular my own account written in 1967 which I had destroyed the previous year. However, having skimmed through it at that point, I had refreshed my memory of the events we were describing. I also went systematically through all my papers and photographs and made some unexpected finds, including the photo of the interior of the van showing the hidden compartment, and pictures taken in the Harz mountains near Goslar which had the van in the background. By Easter 1988 we had a first draft of three chapters, and decided it was time to approach a publisher.

Choosing one was no problem. In early November 1987 we had received a letter from Harrap, saying that if we decided to write our memoirs they would be interested in talking to us about publication. At the time we had made no reply, but now I phoned Harrap and set up a meeting. It went smoothly – despite the initial caution on both sides – and soon afterwards we handed over the first draft chapters.

I also talked again to Professor O'Connell and told him what we were planning, repeating my offer to resign if he thought the

241

publication of the book would be a serious embarrassment to the School. He strongly advised against publication, and expressed the hope that I would change my mind.

What we hope will prove to be the final chapter of the story, at least prior to the publication of the present book, began in November 1988 and culminated in a blaze of publicity in early January 1989. The event which triggered it was a phone-call I made during the summer of 1988 to Kevin O'Connor in Dublin inquiring about the location of the tapes Seán had made of his discussions with George when they were planning the escape. As a result of that call Barrie Penrose found out that we were working on a book; he also got to know that Harrap would be publishing it. During the week beginning 6 November he phoned Pat several times and said *The Sunday Times* would be running a story in the next issue. After much discussion, we decided – since the story was going to break in any case – to talk to the *Observer*.

The story appeared in the paper on Sunday 13 November[18] and was picked up by the *Guardian*[19] the following day. In some ways it was a great relief – we were now on record as saying we *had* been involved.

By this time I had come to an agreement with Professor James O'Connell that I should resign my Research Fellowship in Peace Studies with effect from the end of December. I did not want the Department to suffer from the publicity surrounding the publication of the book.

On 19 December there were further developments when BBC's *Today in Parliament* programme reported that the Conservative MP for Colne Valley, Graham Riddick, had demanded that the two peace campaigners who had admitted helping George Blake to escape should be prosecuted.

Two days later, on 21 December, *the Daily Telegraph* reported that I had been 'sacked' by the university. It also quoted a Scotland Yard source to the effect that the matter had been thoroughly investigated and that there had been insufficient evidence to merit further action.[20]

But by now the campaign in the Commons for Pat and me to be prosecuted was gathering momentum – more than 110 Conservative MPs had now signed the Riddick motion.[21] On Tuesday 3 January I learnt that the DPP had ordered Scotland Yard to reopen the investigation into Blake's escape. I also heard that Norris

McWhirter of the Freedom Association had claimed that once again the threat of a private prosecution had pushed the DPP into taking action. I didn't take this seriously – after all, Scotland Yard had re-opened the investigation over a year previously without exciting much attention.

But I soon discovered that the media took an entirely different view. The phone started ringing and never stopped all evening until we took the receiver off the hook at 12.30a.m.

In fact Pat and I did give a couple of interviews acknowledging that we were writing a book, that we had been involved in the Blake escape, and that we were prepared to take the consequences of our actions, including if necessary going to prison. The reasons for our actions, and all the details of what we had done, would be in the book.

Next day the house was again besieged by journalists, photographers and TV cameramen and the phone never stopped ringing. Radio 4 reported the story in its morning news bulletins and the *Today* programme had an interview with someone who had been in prison with Blake and allegedly talked with him about an escape plan. I understand – though neither Pat nor I saw it – that one of the breakfast-time programmes also had an interview with an MP calling for our arrest.

Pat had arranged to come up to Bradford that day (Wednesday), and had now more reason than ever for doing so. As he walked up the street a TV camera crew who had been lying in wait began filming. He thought he would evade them by going round the back, but they followed him round so that by the evening several million viewers could see what a tip the back yard was in! He also told us how at 2a.m. in the morning the whole front of the house was suddenly lit up by floodlights. He had run in alarm to the bedroom window, only to find a BBC crew filming the front of his house. While Pat was up with us, one freelance photographer took pictures of us together sitting on a bench in the park opposite, half frozen to death. These appeared in several papers the next day and at the weekend.

Wednesday, then, was the day the story broke in earnest, some fifteen months after the publication of Hyde's book, and Penrose's article naming us in *The Sunday Times*. At the time of writing, however, neither Pat nor I have been contacted by the police.

If we are arrested and the case goes to trial we intend to plead Not Guilty. This does not mean we will at any point deny that we helped

Blake to escape – the Not Guilty plea would be a pure technicality to allow us to present our case and call witnesses as to the kinds of activities British and Western Intelligence agencies have engaged in during the period after the Second World War.

CHAPTER TEN

The Antigone Choice

Were we right to help George Blake escape from prison? In this final chapter we set forth the reasons for our firm conviction that we were.

The case against us is that Blake was a self-confessed traitor, that he is reported to have been responsible for the death or disappearance of over forty British agents, that he was tried with due process, and sentenced by a member of an independent judiciary. Finally even if we felt that the sentence was cruel and excessive we had no right to 'take the law into our own hands'.

The crux of our reply is this:

- the 42-year sentence was indeed vicious and indefensible, reflecting no credit on British justice but rather the obsessions of the Cold War and the hypocrisy and double standards over espionage activities by 'our' side and 'theirs';
- there were serious anomalies about the trial itself and the circumstances surrounding it;
- the rumour, expanded and distorted down the years, that Blake's 42-year sentence was related to the number of agents he betrayed to imprisonment or death is, in the words of his QC Jeremy (now Lord) Hutchinson, 'absolute rubbish';
- while we do not condone Blake's espionage activities on behalf of the Soviet Union, we find them no more reprehensible, morally or politically, than much of the activity of Western Intelligence agencies – and considerably less reprehensible than some – such as assassination attempts against foreign leaders, and the staging of coups in Third World countries, and including Blake's specific assignment for MI6 to try to subvert members of Soviet forces to betray their position of trust and pass information to the West;
- the practice of exchanging some convicted spies, but not others, for captured Western agents, and of granting some but not others immunity from prosecution in exchange for a confession, contravenes the principle of equal treatment under the law and thus radically undermines the rule of law itself;

● finally, every responsible citizen has the right – indeed the duty – to break the law under certain circumstances. We shall argue that this was one of those circumstances and that a willingness to defy unjust laws or aid the victims of 'cruel, inhuman and degrading' punishment is a vital constraint on State power, as important to the maintenance of a civilized society as the rule of law itself.

Blake – Background and History

Let us begin with Blake the man. His story by any standards is an extraordinary one. He was born George Behar in Rotterdam, Holland, on 11 November 1922, the son of an Egyptian–Jewish father and Dutch mother. His father was a naturalized British subject, but George was brought up in Holland, apart from two and a half years in Cairo from 1936 to 1938 following his father's death.

In 1940, aged seventeen, he survived the German bombing of Rotterdam in which 30,000 people were killed. Soon afterwards he was interned in the Gestapo concentration camp at Alkmaar, from which he escaped to join the Dutch resistance. At the end of the war he was to receive the Cross of the Order of Nassau, the Dutch equivalent of the MBE, for his work there.

In 1942, after being tipped off that the Gestapo were on his trail, he escaped via Belgium and France to Spain. From there, after a further period of internment, he went to Gibraltar and finally to England, where he joined the Royal Navy and volunteered for service in mini-submarines. However, it was discovered that he was unsuitable for this work because he blacked out at certain pressures, and he was transferred to Naval Intelligence. He returned to the Continent with British forces in 1944 and was posted to Hamburg at the end of hostilities, continuing his work there with Naval Intelligence until 1947.

In that year he was recruited by MI6, and after a year studying Russian at Downing College, Cambridge, was attached to the Foreign Office. In 1949 he was posted to Seoul in South Korea as Vice-Consul. According to his own account, it was while he was in Korea and witnessed the cruelty and corruption of the Syngman Rhee regime that he became converted to communism. In June 1950 he and the other members of the British Legation were arrested and interned by invading North Korean forces.

His fellow-internees during this period–including the Consul, Norman Owen, Captain (later Sir) Vyvyan Holt, and the *Observer* correspondent Philip Deane – all spoke highly of his fortitude under extreme hardship. At one point he escaped execution by the North Koreans by a hairsbreadth. This was when he escaped from the Man-po camp near the Yadu river, in an attempt to find the US forces advancing towards the area, and was picked up by a North Korean patrol. He was sentenced to immediate execution by firing squad as a spy. The squad were actually taking aim when he had the inspiration to shout out in Russian: 'I am not a spy. I am a civilian internee, a British diplomat. I went out of the camp at Man-po and lost my way.' The officer in charge of the squad – who had received military training in the Soviet Union – stopped the execution and returned him to custody.[1]

Soon afterwards, Blake and other civilian internees, together with 780 American prisoners of war, were marched across country from the Man-po camp to a camp at Hadjang in temperatures of between 50 and 70 degrees Celsius below zero. Four hundred and sixty of the American POWs died in the march, as well as many civilian detainees. Holt afterwards stated: 'If it were not for George Blake and Philip Deane, I would not have survived even the last lap of the death march. At Hadjang they nursed me and Consul Owen, and they gave us their rations, although they were themselves sick and hungry'.[2]

In 1953 Blake and his companions were finally released and repatriated. Blake is reported to have been considered for an OBE, but this idea apparently was dropped because of his continuing work for MI6; instead he received a personal letter from the Foreign Secretary, Anthony Eden, thanking him for his loyal service and expressing sympathy for his sufferings during his imprisonment.[3]

He was now assigned to the London Headquarters of MI6 – also known as the Secret Intelligence Service (SIS) – in Broadway, Westminster, and later transferred to a branch in Cromwell Road. There, according to his own account, he was appointed Assistant Chief of the bugging department, codenamed Y. Bugging was carried out on an extensive scale, not only in Britain but at foreign legations and trade delegations, and on selected individuals abroad, often in joint operations with the CIA.[4] By now, if the indictment at his trial is correct, he was working actively for the Soviet Union and passing information to them.

In September 1954 Blake married Gillian Allan, the daughter of an Intelligence officer, Colonel Arthur Allan, and in April 1955 he was posted to Berlin. His particular assignment for MI6 was to look out for Soviet officers who might be 'turned'.[5] This is what Knightley and others have claimed and what Blake told us when he was hiding at Pat's flat after the escape. Blake also informed us that his specific task while posted as Vice Consul in Korea was to try to subvert Russian sailors operating from Vladivostok. Instead, because of his political convictions, Blake adopted the role that it was intended he should persuade those on the other side to play, and passed on to his Soviet contacts all the secret information to which he had access. His chief espionage coup was to give the Russians prior notification of the CIA–MI6 project to dig a tunnel from West Berlin under the main Soviet telephone exchange in East Berlin, so that all outcoming and incoming calls could be bugged. Aware of the situation, the Soviet authorities were able to plant misleading information before finally achieving a major propaganda victory in 1956 by disclosing the tunnel's existence.

Some writers on Blake have alleged that he was employed by the West to play the role of a double agent, that he was encouraged to give some information to the Russians so that he could gain some access to more important information to pass on to the West. According to these writers, the plan backfired; the Russians got the big fish and the West the bait, because Blake's loyalty was to the Soviet side.[6] We are sceptical of this theory. However, if it were true it would, in our view, make his 42-year sentence harder than ever to justify. Organizations playing those kind of games – and the states which sanction and finance their activities – are not entitled to cry foul when they discover from time to time that it is they, not the opponent, who have been tricked.

Blake was finally uncovered in 1960 through information supplied by another double-agent, Colonel Michael Goloniewski, vice-Chairman of Polish Military Intelligence, who eventually defected to the West in December 1960. While still in Warsaw, Goloniewski revealed that the KGB had obtained a list compiled by MI6 of twenty-six Polish officials regarded as potential targets for recruitment. Phillip Knightley states that investigations showed that this could only have come from Blake's safe;[7] Chapman Pincher suggests that it was not until after Goloniewski had come to the West and indicated that the leak emanated from the MI6 station in Berlin that Blake came seriously under suspicion. (Chapman Pincher, however, in error in one account puts the date of Goloniewski's defection as December 1959.[8] Confirmation of Blake's role also came from a West German Intelligence agent, Horst

Eitner, who was arrested in September 1960 for passing information to the Russians.[9]

Meanwhile Blake had been recalled from Berlin in April 1960 and posted the following September to Beirut to study Arabic at a school frequented by Western Intelligence Services. In April 1961 he was summoned to London. According to the account by E. H. Cookridge, he arrived back in London on Easter Monday, 3 April, was arrested the following day after signing a confession and remanded in custody that afternoon at a specially convened session at Bow Street Magistrates Court until 22 April.[10]

This conflicts with Blake's account to us of being held incommunicado for several days at a large country house while – according to what his captors told him – a decision was being made whether to charge him or quietly do away with him.

But Cookridge's version of events is incorrect in several respects. First of all the Committal Proceedings took place not on 22 April – which was a Saturday – but on 24 April, as the account in *The Times* for the following day proves.[11] Secondly, Blake could not have been remanded in custody on 4 April for a committal hearing on either 22 April or 24 April since such remands in custody cannot be extended by law for more than eight clear days, and are usually for shorter periods.

We know from a report in *The Times* that Blake was remanded at Bow Street on 18 April, and that he made one – but only one – remand appearance before that date. The evidence for this last statement is the report in *The Times* of the Committal hearing on 24 April which states that Blake was appearing at Bow Street for the *third* time.[12]

Neither *The Times*, nor as far as we have been able to discover, any other newspaper reported the date on which Blake first appeared and was remanded in custody at Bow Street, but we do know that it cannot have been more than eight clear days prior to his second appearance on 18 April. This makes Monday 10 April the earliest possible date he could have first been brought to court. Assuming then that he was apprehended on Tuesday 4 April – as Cookridge, Chapman Pincher and others claim – there was a gap of nearly a week between then and his first court appearance at Bow Street. It was in that period, according to what Blake told us, that he was held in custody in a country house while a decision was made about his fate.

Further circumstantial evidence concerning the date of Blake's first remand appearance comes from the way the news was broken to Blake's wife Gillian in Beirut. According to Hyde, the British Embassy first informed her that her husband had been delayed in London. Then on 12 April a woman from the Embassy broke the news to her that he had been charged with serious offences and was being held in custody.[13] Clearly she could not have done that until Blake had been formally charged, which narrows the possible dates to two – Monday the 10th or Tuesday the 11th April.

The fact that Blake was held for a period incommunicado before being charged does not prove that the option of executing him was seriously contemplated, though Blake informed us that this is what he was told at the time. Moreover, his point that the British authorities were most reluctant to have a trial – because it would mean publicly acknowledging for the first time that Britain had an extensive spy network operating abroad – is plausible.

Blake's trial, held for the most part *in camera*, took place at the Old Bailey on 3 May 1961, amid an extensive press black-out imposed through the D-Notice system. He pleaded guilty on five charges under Section One of the Official Secrets Act to communicating information to another person for a purpose prejudicial to the safety and interests of the State and was sentenced by the Lord Chief Justice, Lord Parker to fourteen years on each count, the first three to run consecutively, the two others concurrently, making forty-two years in all. It was the longest sentence ever imposed in a British court in modern times, and with the exception of the Lonsdale case the previous month, the first time a court had handed down a sentence of more than twenty years since 1887.

The Blake Trial: Time to End the Secrecy

There are a number of gross anomalies about Blake's trial. First that the trial itself and subsequent appeal were held *in camera*. In layman's terms it was a secret trial. This goes against the whole notion of open justice that ought to characterize civilized society.

Second, the trial was accompanied by one of the most extensive press black-outs in peacetime through the operation of the D-Notice system. This provides Ministerial guidelines to the media about material whose publication is regarded as detrimental to national security. Its full title is The Defence, Press and Broadcasting Committee, and it is made up of senior civil servants, representatives from the media and a government-appointed secretary. Its recommendations – the D-Notices – have no force in law, but editors who ignore them lay themselves open to prosecution under the Official Secrets Act.

Third, on the day after the trial – but before the appeal hearing – the then Prime Minister, Harold Macmillan, made a statement in the Commons which included remarks prejudicial to Blake's case. Finally, on the very day of Blake's appeal, when the public were again prevented from hearing evidence, the Secretary of the D-Notice Committee, Admiral George Pirie Thompson, authorized publication of a sensational report about the reasons for the length of Blake's sentence – the validity of which is highly questionable but which could not be challenged by his counsel because of the *in camera* proceedings and the provisions of the Official Secrets Act.

It is argued that a trial *in camera* was necessary to protect national security. We reject that argument. Blake was accused of, and pleaded guilty to, passing information to a foreign power. So the foreign power in question already had those facts and knew all about the activities referred to in the indictment. That cannot have been the aim.

The argument that considerations of national security also necessitated the press clamp-down carries even less weight and is now universally dismissed by those writing about the case. In the House of Commons on 11 May Macmillan hinted darkly that the delay in the publication of details about Blake had been of some importance.[14] According to Chapman Pincher, Macmillan also insisted that Admiral Thompson, Secretary of the D-Notice Committee, should write a confidential letter to all Fleet Street editors stating that the purpose of withholding information about Blake's work for MI6 was to allow more time to withdraw agents who had been put in jeopardy by his disclosures.[15]

But by the time of the trial Blake had already been in custody for about a month, giving MI6 ample time to take precautions to protect its agents. The true reason for the gagging of the Press was, as Pincher and most commentators have concluded, to save MI5 and MI6 (and the Government itself) from acute embarrassment, and to limit the damage to American confidence in British Intelligence, already shaken by the Portland Spy Ring case a month earlier. It is significant that Macmillan wanted a news black-out on all details surrounding the case, including any hint of links between MI6 and the Foreign Office; the ban, moreover, was to apply not for some limited time span but indefinitely. He is later reported to have told Thompson that the statement forced out of him in Parliament that the secret service was run by the Foreign Office was the most damaging admission of his political career.[16]

The chief consequence of this secrecy was that the public was left with no way of judging whether or not justice had been done – at least in respect of the appropriateness of the sentence passed. This would be serious enough if the convicted person were being deprived of liberty for a relatively short period. In a case which saw the handing down of the longest prison sentence in British legal history, it is nothing short of scandalous.

Macmillan's injudicious comments in the House were made on 4 May. Among these were that Blake had been converted 'to what most of this House would regard as an evil faith' and that Blake 'although he no doubt underwent a certain amount of ill treatment' while a prisoner in Korea, had not been brainwashed. It is fair to add that Macmillan also acknowledged that Blake had acted from political motives, not for personal gain.

Sidney Silverman, the lawyer and backbench Labour MP, intervened to argue that statements in the House, while an appeal against sentence 'must be pending', which related 'to the conduct of the accused man and how he may or may not have been influenced to commit offences to which he has confessed, must be directly relevant to any argument that is to be presented by his counsel to the Court of Criminal Appeal in mitigation of sentence and therefore must be *sub-judice* at this stage'.

Mr Grimond, the Liberal leader, also raised objections, stating that it must surely 'be impossible to deal with this case without using all sorts of words which could bear an implication – the word "Communism" or "brainwashing".' Finally, after further interventions the Speaker ruled that as an appeal had not yet formally been lodged the debate could go ahead. Although technically this may have been correct it was wrong in principle, particularly as the Independent Labour MP Emrys Hughes had informed the House that the BBC's one o'clock news that day had reported Blake's intention to appeal.[17]

However, the grossest irregularity was the spreading of the rumour about why Blake had received such an unprecedented sentence. The facts are these. In the Commons debate of 4 May,

Macmillan agreed to meet the Leader of the Opposition, Hugh Gaitskell, and a small group of Labour Privy Counsellors to discuss the Blake case. Among those who attended the meeting was George Brown, Deputy Leader of the Labour Party.[18] The meeting was supposed to have been in confidence, but on 19 June – the very day that Blake's appeal was being heard – Brown had lunch with the *Daily Express* reporter Chapman Pincher and told him, among other things, that Blake had betrayed at least forty British agents, many of whom had disappeared and several of whom had been executed, and that this was the main reason for the severity of the sentence.

Pincher checked with Admiral Thompson if there was any objection to his publishing the story. He had every reason to believe that the request would be turned down, given the restrictions that had previously been in force. Surprisingly Thompson raised no objection.[19]

Meanwhile, at the Court of Criminal Appeal, Blake's counsel, Jeremy Hutchinson QC, pleaded to be allowed to make his points in mitigation in open court. 'What difference', Mr Justice Hilbery, the presiding judge, said, 'does it make to him [Blake] whether it is in public or private?' Hutchinson urged that the court should uphold the principle that justice must be seen to be done as far as possible and pointed out that there had been 'all sorts of speculation as to what Blake had done and what he had not done.' 'We are not concerned', Justice Hilbery retorted, 'with press speculation. We are solely concerned to administer the law. We are not here to scotch some rumour.'[20]

Next day the *Daily Express* published Chapman Pincher's report under the banner headline: '40 Agents Betrayed – and all by this man.' At the top of the page were forty silhouetted figures, a gimmick, Pincher says, which his editor had been seeking to use for some time. Lower down on the same page the paper carried the news that Blake's appeal had been turned down. In common with all the Press, it could give no information about the main proceedings since they had been held *in camera*. However, it and other papers did report part of Jeremy Hutchinson's final plea in mitigation including his comment that the 42-year sentence was 'so inhuman that it is alien to all the principles by which a civilized country will treat its subjects'.[21]

In short, a secret trial and appeal prevented the public from judging the evidence for themselves. But a sensational rumour, stemming from George Brown and ultimately from the Government itself, was published with official blessing on the same day that the national Press reported the rejection of Blake's appeal. Nor could Hutchinson – sworn to secrecy over the proceedings in the closed session – make any public statement about the accuracy or otherwise of Chapman Pincher's allegations.

In our efforts to find out the truth, Pat phoned Chapman Pincher on 5 January 1989 at 12.45p.m., afterwards making detailed notes of the conversation that took place. Pincher said he was not surprised at what George Brown had told him because 'dear old George liked to shock you with his remarks'. When Pat went on to mention that the conversation with Brown had taken place on the same day as Blake's appeal hearing, Pincher claimed that he was completely unaware of that fact, that it could only have been pure coincidence, and that this was the first time anyone had pointed it out to him.

Here Pincher's memory had failed him. The second paragraph of his own *Express* article on 20 June 1961 specifically mentions that Blake's appeal had been turned down the previous day. What is surprising is that in the various accounts Chapman Pincher has given of the story, he never once mentions the fact that his meeting with George Brown took place on the same day as Blake's appeal.

Still more surprising is that, apart from Montgomery Hyde, none of the specialists who have made their reputation writing about espionage in general or Blake in particular have commented on the timing of Brown's meeting with Pincher. Even Hyde, who does note it, makes no comment on its possible significance.[22]

Pat finally asked Pincher: 'Does it now occur to you, in the light of the information I have given you, or has it ever occurred to you down the years, that you were possibly being set up and used to give out disinformation?' Pincher replied: 'No, certainly not. I have verified this story from many sources and believe the man [Blake] to be an absolute bastard.' He then said his lunch was ready and put down the phone.

Chapman Pincher's reading of George Brown's motives in giving him the story is that Brown believed the Government was withholding information to save its face.[23] In other words, his disclosures were an unauthorized and unwelcome breach of confidence as far as the Government was concerned. But whether or not the Government had expected or encouraged Brown to leak the information in the first place, the fact remains that it did nothing to prevent its dissemination once he had spoken to Pincher. Indeed the Government became an accessory to Brown's disclosures once Thompson gave the go-ahead for publication, for it is hardly conceivable that he took such a decision on his own.

A plausible explanation for the sequence of events is this. The Government was clearly embarrassed by the discovery of Blake's activities, and may even have hesitated about bringing him to trial at all. Having decided to do so – though in a closed court – it imposed an extensive press black-out to prevent the disclosure of the fact that he was employed by MI6, was attached to the Foreign Office, or any details about him.

However, the day after the trial one German newspaper reported that Blake was employed by MI6, and by the time of Blake's appeal rumours about his position and the nature of his offences were starting to appear in the British Press and were causing the Government increasing difficulties in Parliament. Once it was clear that there was no longer any possibility of hushing the whole business up, the Government was not averse to the dissemination of an account of his offences which would at least serve to allay any public disquiet about the severity of his sentence. Hence the go-ahead to Chapman Pincher to publish.

We have tried to check the substance of the story about forty betrayed British agents. On 31 January 1989 we had a meeting with one of the few men in a position to speak authoritatively about the issue – namely Lord Hutchinson of Lullington, who as Jeremy Hutchinson QC had represented Blake at his trial and appeal. He explained that he could say nothing about what went on in the court sessions held *in camera*.

However, when we asked him if there could possibly be any truth in the rumour that Blake's 42–year sentence corresponded to evidence produced at the trial about the number of British agents betrayed to imprisonment or death he told us this story was 'absolute rubbish' and authorized us to quote him to this effect.

Further evidence of this is provided by an examination of the comments of the trial judge, Lord Parker, in passing sentence. Had any evidence been adduced in the closed sessions that Blake had sent British agents to their death the judge would surely have made some reference to this when he handed down such an unprecedented sentence. He did not do so. Instead he stressed the point that the information Blake had given a foreign power had 'rendered much of this country's efforts completely useless' – in other words he had sabotaged Britain's own espionage activities against other states. We put this point to Lord Hutchinson who warmly endorsed it and said we could not stress it too strongly.

We are not, of course, arguing that Blake passed on no names of Western agents to the Russians. Nor are we claiming that everything that George Brown told Chapman Pincher was unfounded. Indeed Pincher's claim that information given by Blake to the Russians had made it necessary to withdraw 'almost the entire British Intelligence network in the Middle East', and that he had disclosed the names of agents in British networks elsewhere, is consistent with Lord Parker's comment that Blake had rendered much of the country's efforts completely useless. Moreover in his books Chapman Pincher gives more information about what Brown allegedly told him, including the fact that Blake had disclosed to the Russians details of the tunnel from the American sector to the site of the main telephone exchange in the Soviet sector[24] – a story Blake himself has since confirmed.

But the only way to get at the whole truth would be for the records of Blake's trial and appeal to be released. If the argument at the time that the trial should be held in secret was unconvincing, any suggestion that now, nearly thirty years later, national security would be endangered by the release of the court records is clearly absurd.

Unfortunately, when Pat made enquiries at the Old Bailey Criminal Records office in late 1988 he was informed that the open-court records, in common with all others of that period, had been destroyed. It seems unlikely, however, that the Home Office do not have a copy of the proceedings of an important espionage case that was held *in camera*.

There are further disquieting aspects to the trial and sentence. Blake's uncle, Mijnheer Anthony Bejderwellen, told the writer E. H. Cookridge that Blake had been advised to plead Guilty on all five counts of the indictment on the grounds that he would receive a lighter sentence if he did not contest any of the submissions of the prosecution.[25]

What is particularly disturbing about the Blake case is the evidence that he was induced by the promise of leniency to plead guilty on one count of which he was almost certainly innocent. This was the first count on the indictment which charged him with passing on information in November 1951 while he was still a prisoner in Korea. Montgomery Hyde points out that his Russian interrogator in Korea, Gregory Kuzmitch, later defected to the West and informed the CIA that Blake had revealed very little about his work as Vice-Consul and Intelligence officer in Korea, and had given no information about the training and organization of the British Secret Service which might have been of use to the communists at that time.[26]

Deals of this kind are, of course, common practice in the courts – and though they are normally honoured by the trial judge, this can never be guaranteed. Blake, instead of being treated leniently, found himself being sentenced to *consecutive* terms on three of the five counts against him, including the first count which accused him of spying in 1951 when he was a prisoner in Korea. This was the first time the Official Secrets Act had been used in this way to extend the maximum sentence of fourteen years laid down by Parliament. (The KGB officer Conon Molody, alias Gordon Lonsdale, had been sentenced in March 1961 to twenty-five years, but he and the other members of the 'Portland Ring' had been convicted of *conspiracy* under the Official Secrets Act, and there was at that time no statutory limit to sentences in conspiracy cases.)

Jeremy Hutchinson QC argued in the Court of Criminal Appeal that it was wrong in principle to pass consecutive sentences of fourteen years, thereby evading the limit established in the Act. Blake would be in a better position, he said, if he had been given a life sentence, which in practice usually meant serving ten years; the sentence he had received deprived him of the protection of review by the Home Secretary. He also pointed out that Klaus Fuchs, convicted in 1950 on four counts of passing atom secrets to the Soviet Union, had been sentenced by Lord Goddard to *concurrent* terms of fourteen years on each count.

The Fuchs case is central to the argument about sentencing policy in Official Secrets Act cases. Fuchs provided information to the Russians which aided them in the development of their nuclear weapons; his actions made a material difference to the state of armed balance between East and West, as Blake's did not. This last point was confirmed by Macmillan in his Commons statement of 4 May 1961 when he stated that Blake's disclosures 'will not have done irreparable damage' and that 'he did not have access to secret information on defence, nuclear, or atomic matters'.[27]

True, the official view today is that the existence of nuclear weapons on both sides is what provides the stability of mutual deterrence, and from that standpoint Fuchs did the West as well as the Soviet Union a service. But at that time the disclosure of atom secrets was considered akin to treason; indeed in America Julius and Ethel Rosenberg were executed in 1953 after being convicted of passing atom secrets to the Soviet Union. The trial judge in the Fuchs case was the Lord Chief Justice, Lord Goddard, not a man noted for leniency. Presumably he did not think it proper to pass consecutive sentences in such circumstances. In any case it is absurd that Fuchs should receive a 14-year sentence for passing atom secrets to the Russians, and Blake forty-two years for giving them information about Britain's Intelligence networks and operations.

The Blake case, and the Portland spy ring case, marked the beginning of a period of massive sentences by the courts, not only in espionage cases but in some ordinary criminal cases as well – notably in the case of the Great Train Robbers in 1963. It leads one to ask whether Lord Parker would have imposed these sentences without a guiding nudge from the Macmillan government.

There are some cases where it is reasonable to pass consecutive sentences for separate breaches of the same law – cases of serious assault, for instance. But it is ridiculous to apply this to espionage; after all, once a person makes the decision to act as a spy he or she is going to play that role as and when opportunity permits. If such a person is to be charged separately for every individual document or piece of information communicated, the number of counts could be multiplied almost indefinitely.

Clearly, once Blake had pleaded Guilty to the charges on the indictment the jury had no option but to convict. But justice requires not only sound convictions but appropriate sentences. In the Blake case the sentence was unprecedented and the opportunity to compare the gravity of the offences with the punishment imposed non-existent. There was instead a secret trial, a press black-out, a prejudicial statement in the Commons which avoided breaching the *sub-judice* rule by the merest technicality, and finally the publication with official backing of a sensational report which Blake's legal representatives could not challenge because of the restrictions imposed by the *in camera* proceedings.

Blood on his Hands?

Granted that the rumour that the 42-year sentence on Blake corresponded to the number of British agents he had betrayed to imprisonment or death is a myth, is it nevertheless likely that Blake does have blood on his hands?

The answer has to be yes. But is he any different from colleagues who continued to work faithfully for the British Intelligence Service and ended their careers with OBEs or knighthoods?

Let us be clear first of all what Blake is *not* accused of. He is not accused of planning, or participating in attempts to murder foreign Heads of State. MI6 was so involved in 1956 when Anthony Eden authorized the assassination of President Nasser of Egypt.[28] Peter Wright, the former MI5 agent, states that the original plan was to place canisters of nerve gas in the ventilation system of one of Nasser's headquarters. Later an alternative plan was devised:

> [A]fter the gas canisters plan fell through, MI6 looked at some new weapons. On one occasion I went down to Porton to see a demonstration of a cigarette packet which had been modified by the Explosives Research and Development Establishment to fire a dart tipped with poison. We solemnly put on white coats and were taken out to one of the animal compounds behind Porton by Dr Ladell, the scientist there who handled all MI5 and MI6 work. A sheep on a lead was led into the center of the ring. One flank had been shaved to reveal the coarse pink skin. Ladell's assistant pulled out the cigarette packet and stepped forward. The sheep started, and was restrained by the lead, and I thought perhaps the device had misfired. But then the sheep's knees began to buckle, and it started rolling its eyes and frothing at the mouth. Slowly the animal sank to the ground, life draining away, as the white-coated professionals discussed the advantages of the modern new toxin around the corpse.[29]

The CIA was engaged in similar plots. In 1975 a Senate Sub-Committee investigating alleged assassination plots against foreign leaders concluded that in the autumn of 1960 two CIA agents were asked by officials to assassinate the radical Congolese leader Patrice Lumumba, and that poisons were sent to the Congo to carry this out. It also stated that there had been at least eight CIA plots against the life of Castro in Cuba between 1960 and 1965, some involving underworld gangsters. Much of the report makes chilling reading:

> Although some of the assassination plots did not advance beyond the stage of planning and preparation, one plot, involving the use of underworld figures, reportedly twice progressed to the point of sending poison pills to Cuba and dispatching teams to commit the deed. Another

plot involved furnishing weapons and other assassination devices to a Cuban dissident. The proposed assassination devices ran the whole gamut from high powered rifles to poison pills, poison pens, deadly bacterial powders, and other devices which strain the imagination.[30]

Blake was not involved in attempts to discredit and engineer the downfall of an elected British government. There is now strong evidence that a group of MI5 officers were involved in such an operation in 1974.[31]

He is not accused of organizing coups against an internationally recognized foreign government. MI6 and the CIA have been involved in such operations, sometimes in joint endeavours. Thus in 1953 they co-operated in the coup that toppled Iran's Prime Minister, Mossedeq, after he had nationalized the Anglo-Iranian oilfields. In this instance 'imperialist plot' is no cant phrase but an exact description of what took place. One hundred people are reported to have lost their lives in the coup, and when the Shah returned to power hundreds more were tortured and executed. Mossedeq himself was hanged.[32] And he is not accused of complicity in landing armed insurgents into a country in peacetime in an attempt to overthrow its government. In 1949–50 MI6 and the CIA landed armed insurgents by sea or from the air in Albania, Latvia, the Caucasus, and the Ukraine.[33]

Finally, he is not accused of planning, or participating in, the kind of terrorist bombing the CIA masterminded in Beirut on 8 March 1985. This was a joint CIA–Saudi-Arabian operation, set up by William Casey, head of the CIA. Its aim was to assassinate the leader of the fundamentalist Hizbollah sect in Beirut, Sheikh Fadlallah, who had been involved in attacks on American installations. A car packed with explosives was driven close to Fadlallah's residence and detonated, killing eighty civilians and injuring more than two hundred others. Fadlallah himself escaped unharmed. The person hired by the CIA and the Saudis to carry out the assassination attempt was an Englishman and a former SAS officer.[34]

The CIA-backed operation in Beirut cannot be dismissed as an aberration. In Nicaragua, the American government and the CIA have helped arm, train and finance the Contras in a guerrilla war which has included many acts of terrorism. In October 1984 the *New York Times* revealed details of a CIA training manual advising the Nicaraguan contras to 'neutralize carefully selected and planned targets such as court judges, police and state security officials etc' and to 'kidnap all officials or agents of the Sandinista government'.[35]

Our first point, then, is that no one has suggested that Blake was involved in planning or participating in assassinations, coups, military adventures, or indiscriminate terrorist attacks, though we do know that down the years the major Western Intelligence Agencies – and the KGB – have been involved in such things.

Blake has been accused of providing information to the KGB of the whereabouts of an East German defector, Lieutenant-General Robert Bialek, who was kidnapped in West Berlin in 1956 and subsequently executed. This in our view is the most serious charge levelled against him, for if true it would mean he was an accomplice in an act of kidnapping and judicial killing.

But Blake's activities on behalf of the KGB consisted in the main, according to all accounts, in passing on information about the workings of British Intelligence, presumably including the names of agents in the Soviet bloc and elsewhere. Given the practice of that time we can assume that some of those he named would have been rounded up and imprisoned, some 'turned' and persuaded to act as double-agents, some executed. Blake himself has always denied that he was responsible for any deaths, but having given the names of agents to the KGB he would not even necessarily be aware of what subsequently happened to them.

We emphasize again that we are unequivocally opposed to the acts of espionage and betrayal in which Blake engaged. What we reject is the notion that he bears some special burden of responsibility and guilt. Rupert Allason MP, for instance – who writes on espionage matters under the pen-name of Nigel West – was reported in October 1987 to have compared Blake to the Moors murderer Myra Hindley.[36] Others, without making that explicit comparison, have written about him in that vein.

This is clearly absurd. A major, even a principal, preoccupation of espionage organizations is uncovering the composition and activities of rival – and not infrequently of 'friendly' – networks. It is spies spying on spies in a 'wilderness of mirrors'.

It was not Blake's *role* as a spy that was exceptional, but the strategic position he held; this enabled him to do more damage than most. When highly-placed KGB or other Soviet bloc agents can be induced to act on behalf of the West as he did on behalf of the Soviet Union, this is regarded as a coup and the Soviet spies and double-agents who are arrested as a result of the information they give are seen as receiving their just deserts.

The trial judge in Blake's case, Lord Parker, made much of the fact that Blake had retained his position of trust after becoming convinced of the rightness of the Soviet cause. 'The gravamen of the case against you', he said, 'is that you never resigned, that you retained your employment in positions of trust in order to betray your country.'[37]

Here we agree with the learned judge. Espionage and betrayal have been responsible for immense ill-will and continuing mistrust between East and West – not to speak of terrible personal tragedies. But the argument can hardly have cut much ice with Blake himself, given that his specific assignment in Berlin was to locate officers on the other side who might be persuaded to betray the trust placed in them by their government. Moreover, we can safely assume that Parker would not have addressed his remarks to Colonel Golo-niewski, the Polish Military Intelligence officer whose information led to the exposure of the Portland Spy Ring and of Blake.

At one time it was possible to believe that there were crucial differences between Western and Soviet practice in dealing with exposed spies and double agents – namely that Soviet spies uncovered in the West could expect due process of law, and normally imprisonment rather than execution, whereas there was no such safeguards for agents working for the West in the Soviet bloc. Clearly that is a mistaken view. Detailed evidence of executions by Western Intelligence of defectors from their ranks is obviously hard to come by, but one former CIA agent, John Stockwell, has spoken out with unusual frankness:

> I had an agent I had recruited picked up and shot. No trial, just bang and he was dead. He left behind a wife and six children. When I reviewed his file, there wasn't one report, not one report in five years that we hadn't gotten from some other source elsewhere. There was nothing he had done that had saved the world from anything.[38]

Phillip Knightley gives other examples, not of executions as such but of a callous disregard for human life and feelings on the part of Western agencies. Thus he cites the case of a KGB officer, Nikolai Khokhlov. Sent in 1953 on a mission to assassinate the leader of NTS, a Russian exile movement in West Germany, he had pangs of conscience and warned his victim, intending himself to return to Moscow and report that the mission had failed. But his victim informed American military intelligence who decided that Khokh-lov should be forced into defecting. They therefore called a press conference, announced that he had defected and publicly demanded that his wife and children be allowed to join him. He had no alternative but to remain in the West and never saw or heard from his family again.[39]

Chapman Pincher's account of the betrayed agents also merits more careful scrutiny than it has usually received. First, it is instructive to note how the story has undergone a subtle but vital change in the telling down the years. In his original *Daily Express* piece, Pincher wrote: 'My investigations over the last twelve weeks also reveal that many of these agents have disappeared and *several* are believed to have been executed.' By 1984 Pincher was writing: 'Blake . . . after interrogation confessed to major acts of treachery, including the betrayal of more than forty agents and sub agents, *many* of whom had probably been executed.'[40] (Emphasis added.)

It is interesting too to examine the two specific names mentioned by Pincher and others as having been arrested and/or executed as a result of a tip-off by Blake. Zarb and Swinburn were not working in the Soviet bloc at all but in Cairo in the 1950s, Swinburn (and possibly Zarb too) in the destabilizing campaign against Nasser prior to the Anglo-French-Israeli aggression against Egypt at Suez.[41] Later he mentioned a third man, General Robert Bialek, a former Inspector General of the East German People's Police who had defected to the West and was kidnapped from West Berlin in 1956.[42]

Finally, Nigel West and Montgomery Hyde claim that Blake informed the Russians in 1955 that one of their highly placed officers in the GRU (Soviet Military Intelligence) was passing information to the CIA. Popov was eventually arrested and exe-cuted, according to some accounts by being thrown alive into a furnace in front of his GRU colleagues. The Soviet version is that he was shot. Blake's role in the uncovering of Popov is uncertain; his own carelessness seems to have been a decisive factor. If the story that he was thrown into a furnace is true, this was a piece of sadistic obscenity for which there can be no possible justification.

As far as we are concerned, the imprisonment and execution of spies is a human tragedy whatever their nationality. There is, however, a distinct suggestion in Chapman Pincher's original account, and the accounts of subsequent writers, that the agents allegedly betrayed by Blake were patriotic British lads working for their country behind the Iron Curtain. This is unlikely. The usual Soviet practice when a foreign national is discovered to have been engaged in espionage is to try to extract the maximum propaganda advantage out of the incident by staging a public trial, and then using the prisoner as a bargaining chip in exchange deals. It is when one of their own citizens, and particularly when one of their agents is found to have been passing on information to the West, that the death penalty is likely to be imposed.

This is borne out by the fact that the only two agents named by as having been executed as a result of Blake's actions were in one case a former member of the East German People's Police, and in the other a GRU agent. Bialek had defected to the West; Popov, acting in a way which parallels Blake's, remained within the GRU but passed on information to the CIA.

An account of another incident in Pincher's book *Inside Story* reflects at least as much discredit on the British authorities as on Blake himself. Pincher records that in 1958 Admiral Thompson, Secretary of the D-Notice Committee, told him that the Egyptians had exposed the entire British secret service network throughout the Middle East. Two Britons – Swinburn and Zarb – had been arrested and many more British Intelligence officers working under diplomatic cover were having to be withdrawn. Some three years later is was discovered, according to Pincher and others, that the person who had exposed the network was Blake. However, in 1958 Nasser was threatening to name all the agents on Cairo radio. The British authorities were concerned, not that these agents would face possible imprisonment or even death, but that, to quote Pincher, 'they could never be used again anywhere'.[43]

Thompson's immediate purpose in contacting Pincher was to seek an undertaking that if Nasser carried out his threat, the *Daily Express* would not publish the names; if this was agreed, Thompson would then approach other newspapers. The sole purpose of such an exercise was, as Pincher points out, to save MI6 and the government of the day serious embarrassment. In the event, Nasser did not name the agents.

The activities carried out by MI6 in the Middle East in the 1950s were, in the judgement of two researchers in the field, among the 'most aggressive and cavalier' in its 70-year history.[44] They included the staging, jointly with the CIA, of the 1953 coup against Mossedeq; plots against the life and regime of Nasser in 1956 in the build-up to Suez, and again in 1957; an attempted coup in Syria, codenamed 'Straggle', in October 1956; and intervention in North Yemen and Oman.[45]

Our decision to help Blake was not based on whether or not he had betrayed British agents, but on the fact that the sentence was inhuman and that both East and West were in the business of espionage and betrayal. Our reading of the story of the forty agents is this: Blake did pass on information about the workings of British Intelligence agencies to the KGB, presumably including specific names; no doubt some were imprisoned or killed but the reason for the severe sentence had nothing to do with any evidence brought before the court that he was responsible for the death of British agents but that, in Lord Parker's own words, he had 'rendered much of this country's efforts [i.e. espionage] completely useless.'

And finally, Pincher's account suggests that many of the agents he exposed were working in the Middle East and for the most part were neither imprisoned nor killed but simply withdrawn.

Which Side are we On?

It is sometimes argued that however similar Western and Soviet intelligence methods may be in an operational sense, there is a crucial moral difference between them because the West stands for a free and open society and the Soviet Union threatens it.

We believe passionately in a free society, and consider that the constraints on state power in constitutional democracies are crucial in maintaining this. Even today when there are exciting developments in the Soviet Union and Eastern Europe there is still a major difference as far as the possibilities of free expression and political organization are concerned between the multi-party states in the West and the one-party (or virtually one-party) states of most of the Soviet bloc. Ironically, however, at the very time that moves towards greater openness and democracy in the Eastern bloc are taking place, menacing restrictions are being put on freedom of expression and access to information in Britain.

But though we acknowledge the important differences in the political structures and practices of East and West we do not, firstly, regard this as any justification for the kind of Western intelligence and covert operations described briefly earlier. Second, to represent the East–West conflict simply as one between an aggressive tyranny and a Free World seeking to defend itself is a Cold War distortion.

On the Western side, some of the European colonial powers – notably Britain and France – were concerned in the immediate post-war period to re-establish or strengthen colonial rule, or at least to ensure that power passed upon independence to pro-Western leaders. This was part of a broader effort, involving the United States, to control political and economic developments in the emerging 'Third World'. The British Special Air Service, SAS, was reactivated after the war essentially to suppress unrest in Britain's overseas' territories. By the time of Blake's escape in 1966, the Vietnam war had highlighted these indefensible facets of Western policy. It was no longer possible to dismiss as Soviet propaganda charges of imperialism or neo-imperialism directed against the US and its allies .

On the Soviet side there is no denying the existence or extent of Stalinist repression. The Soviet Union had itself experienced this in the 1930s, and as the Cold War settled in from 1947 onward, Eastern Europe was to experience it to a horrifying degree. Fears of Soviet intentions at that time are in some measure understandable. Nevertheless many historians do now question whether Stalin was bent on achieving the subjection of Western Europe in the late 1940s and early 1950s rather than ruthlessly consolidating control in Eastern Europe.

In the immediate post-war period the hope of maintaining the wartime co-operation between East and West was soon destroyed. Although the reasons for this not happening are many and complex one should not lose sight of the exceedingly negative contribution of Western espionage activities to the souring of relations. Already in October 1944, MI6 had set up an anti-Soviet section.[46] The American OSS (Office of Strategic Services) which had been responsible for intelligence and covert operations against the Axis powers during the war, also saw in the growing strains between Moscow and Washington an opportunity to maintain its position in a post-war world. Early in 1945 it accepted the offer of General Reinhardt Gehlen, commander of a German army intelligence section on the Eastern front, to turn over his files and men and work against the Soviet Union – at that time still an ally in the common struggle to defeat Nazi Germany. Washington approved the plan, and Gehlen was given an office in Frankfurt, later becoming the first head of West German Intelligence.[47]

A further twist of the knife was the project code-named Casey Jones in 1945 in which sixteen squadrons of US and British bombers photo-mapped Central and Western Europe, Scandinavia and North Africa, including all Soviet-occupied Germany, Yugoslavia and Bulgaria. *The Russians became aware of the operation and in the last months of the war and the early peacetime period there were a series of secret air battles between US and British planes on the one side and the Soviet air force on the other.* On one day alone, 2 April 1945, there were six such engagements in which one American Mustang fighter was shot down. And in August 1945, the Soviet Union filed complaints of more than 300 violations of its airspace.[48]

The machinations of the CIA and MI6, and the military incursions of Britain and the USA do not of course begin to justify the reign of terror instituted by Stalin in Eastern Europe in the late 1940s and early 1950s. Nor, after Stalin's death, can the Soviet invasions of Hungary in 1956, and of Czechoslovakia in 1968, and the Soviet pressure on successive Polish governments to close down the independent trade union Solidarity in 1980–81 be defended. We protested vigorously against these Soviet moves, in the case of the invasion of Czechoslovakia helping to organize international teams to carry out simultaneous non-violent protests in Moscow, Budapest, Sofia and Warsaw. We were also outspoken critics of the Soviet invasion of Afghanistan in 1979.

But Soviet interventions in Eastern Europe in the past have been motivated in part by security considerations – principally the fear that without them the Warsaw Pact would begin to break up and leave the USA and NATO in a commanding position in Europe. Today if the West is seriously concerned about the fate of the people of Eastern Europe, it should be willing to respond positively to the disarmament and arms control initiatives from Moscow, and indeed to re-examine the post-war system of security in Europe based on rival military alliances.

Some historians of twentieth-century espionage, notably Phillip Knightley, take the view that its contribution even in wartime has been greatly exaggerated, and that in the period after the Second World War its effect has been almost wholly negative. A major problem is that espionage operates in such a quagmire of deception and double-cross that genuine information is always liable to be dismissed as untrustworthy, while disinformation may be believed. But the much deeper problem is the threat that espionage and counter-espionage organizations, in their current form and with their existing known practices, pose to civil liberties at home, and to détente and arms control in the international arena.

Domestically the establishment and expansion of centralized intelligence services seems invariably to be accompanied by increased restrictions upon civil liberties. In 1911 the Official Secrets Act was introduced; this was in conjunction with the setting up of Britain's first intelligence services independent from the armed forces. The Act remains one of the major obstacles to the open society in Britain today.

At the time of writing the amended Section 2 of the Official Secrets Act is in the final stages of becoming law. It removes much government information from the protection of the criminal law but tightens up the prohibition on disclosures related to defence, international relations and the activities of the security services. The plea that disclosures were in the public interest will no longer be available. This was the argument that the civil servant Clive Ponting put forward in his defence in 1984. He had passed information to the Labour MP Tam Dalyell about the sinking of the Argentine cruiser *General Belgrano* in the Falklands War. Members of the security services will also be bound under the Act to lifelong silence about its activities.

This last restriction follows a number of embarrassing disclosures about the operations of MI5 – notably by one of its former officers Cathy Massiter in 1985, who revealed that telephone tapping and surveillance of trade unionists, CND members and other political activists was widespread, and by Peter Wright in his book *Spycatcher*.

In future not only will persons making such disclosures render themselves liable to prosecution, so too will newspapers or any other media that publishes them.

At the international level, espionage and covert operations in recent times have done incalculable damage not only to East–West relations but to the cause of establishing some kind of equitable relationship between rich and poor nations. We have briefly touched upon these matters earlier, but it is worth adding that nothing except actual military attack confirms more strongly the public image of a sinister enemy than such clandestine operations.

Governments and the opinion-formers working on their behalf are very well aware of this fact. This is why spy-hysteria and war-hysteria so often go hand in hand. Before the First World War, for instance, there were reports and rumours that literally thousands of

German spies were deployed in Britain. Phillip Knightley has concluded that a more accurate estimate would be – none.[49] And the practice of using the diplomatic service as a cover for espionage is now so widespread that governments can create incidents at will by expelling diplomats on the grounds that they have engaged in 'activities incompatible with their status' whether or not there is any substance in the charge.

Finally, espionage work has a deeply corroding influence on the individuals engaged in it. It is no coincidence that the majority of 'traitors' and defectors come not only from the military or other state institutions but from the ranks of the intelligence services.[50]

Obviously it is difficult to take an absolutist line against a state having any kind of Intelligence service for strictly defensive purposes – for instance obtaining information on intended terrorist bomb attacks against civilian targets. In wartime, too, the case for Intelligence operations is much stronger than in peacetime – though this itself is an argument for seeking to develop alternative non-violent approaches for the defence of country and community. What cannot be justified are the nefarious *offensive* operations referred to earlier, in which the major powers and their allies have indulged in the post-war period – and of course long before that.

It is possible to draw a distinction between an Intelligence service whose function is limited to analysing the data available from open sources–plus perhaps that from surveillance satellites–and espionage in the traditional sense of deploying agents abroad and seeking to persuade military, security and civil service personnel from other countries to betray confidential and secret information. There is a case for the first, and indeed the information now provided from that side of Intelligence work tends in the view of some specialists to be far more dependable than that from spies and defectors.

We are particularly concerned about the centralized Intelligence services such as MI6, the CIA and the KGB. States have not always felt it necessary to have such agencies. Prior to the First World War, most major powers – including Germany, Russia, the United States, and until a few years before the outbreak of war, Britain – had *military* intelligence services only. These were geared essentially to wartime operations, and were generally starved of funds in peacetime. In 1909 Britain established the intelligence services which became MI5 and MI6; the USA did not follow its example until 1946 when Truman was persuaded against his better judgment, and in response to rising anti-communist hysteria, to establish the Central Intelligence Group – which became the CIA.

Truman was later to express misgivings about the way the Agency had developed. It had been diverted, he complained, from its original aim and had become 'an operational and at times a policy-making arm of government.'[51] It is the establishment and phenomenal growth of centrally organized intelligence services this century that has led to an explosion of espionage and covert operations unparalleled in any previous epoch. The containment, and finally the abolition, of this sinister industry is an essential step in the building of a more secure world.

We are personally hostile to espionage in the sense defined above and do not think its abolition is a utopian goal. We recognize, however, that it is likely to continue in existence in the near future, and thus that the most immediate task is to bring it under control. This implies not only domestic accountability but the forging of an international consensus about what is and what is not acceptable practice. Peace researchers in recent years have done valuable work in trying to define what a strictly defensive military system might look like and how it could be organized. Similar studies need to be conducted into the possibilities of a genuinely defensive Intelligence system.

Unless stringent curbs are placed on the operations of Intelligence agencies there is a danger that they will succeed in scuttling the whole process of deténte and rapprochement that has marked East–West relations since Gorbachev came to power in the Soviet Union. The superpower intelligence agencies have after all a vested interest, and some experience, in so doing. Already as this book is being completed the CIA and right-wing conservative analysts in the USA are urging President Bush not to base any arms control deals with the Soviet Union on the assumption that Gorbachev will remain in power.[52] In reality, of course, nothing is more likely to undermine Gorbachev's position at home than the refusal of the West to respond to his peace and disarmament initiatives – a fact of which the CIA and its allies are perfectly well aware. Gorbachev in particular needs drastic reductions in military expenditure to release resources for his programme of economic reconstruction at home, but there are limits to the cuts he can make unilaterally without encountering opposition from the Soviet military.

Some of the measures needed to control the security services are self-evident. First, there must be a proper system of accountability.

In Britain the Security Services Bill (in its final stages at the time of writing), establishes for the first time a Security Services Commissioner to oversee the workings of the counter-intelligence agency MI5, and a tribunal to which injured parties can make complaints. But there is no accountability in the true sense of the term, and the Government rejected calls for scrutiny and oversight to be exercised by a Parliamentary Select Committee. Moreover the complaints procedure is rendered farcical by the fact that persons subjected to phone tapping, surveillance or authorized burglary will not normally know this is happening, and anyone within MI5 who informs them that it is will be committing an offence under the amended Section 2 of the Official Secrets Act. Finally MI6 and GCHQ, the electronic intelligence-gathering centre, will remain outside any statutory control. We support the call for accountability to a Parliamentary Select Committee by all the Intelligence agencies. This body, moreover, should in our judgment have a duty to report publicly any criminal activities by security services.

Secondly, the laws governing the conduct of members of Intelligence services, and civil servants – in Britain the Official Secrets Act – must allow for a 'public interest' defence for the disclosure of unauthorized information, and indeed acknowledge a positive duty to report criminal practices. Unfortunately, as we noted, the amended Official Secrets Act provides at present for no such 'public interest' plea, and the legal requirement of lifelong confidentiality it imposes upon members of the security services means that it will be harder than ever in future for the public to learn about abuses, even years after the event.

Third, there is the need to work towards an internationally accepted code of practice. This cannot be expected to take the form of one all-embracing treaty but could develop incrementally, starting with an undertaking to end practices contrary to international law – such as coup attempts, assassinations, and terrorist attacks. Next, since the uncovering of 'traitors' holding positions of trust excites so much concern and animosity in whichever country it occurs, states might agree to forbear trying to suborn military and security personnel, and others with access to confidential information, in each other's countries. A further positive step would be an agreement not to use Embassies and diplomatic missions as bases for espionage activities.

What one should, however, be aiming for at the international level is not simply restraints to be put on espionage but its abolition.

Given the development of satellite surveillance, the provision for international inspection written into new arms-control agreements, and the much greater openness in the Soviet Union, the concluding even at this stage of bilateral agreements between individual Western countries and the Soviet Union to cease espionage activities altogether seems to us an entirely achievable and commendable goal.

Finally, although we feel that espionage is a despicable trade which radically undermines the values on which any kind of tolerable human society must be built, it does not mean that we can have no regard for the individual spy or 'traitor' who may have become caught up in the espionage business, sometimes – as in Blake's case – out of genuine conviction, or that we regard those sentenced to long prison terms, normally by people who fully support the espionage system of their own country, as undeserving of compassion or help.

Criminals or Prisoners of War?

States and governments have a highly ambiguous attitude to spies. On the one hand they treat them as contemptible criminals and provide for the direst penalties for those caught and convicted. On the other hand, they are prepared to do swops and deals, confirming that at another level they do regard them in a different light to ordinary criminals.

The practice of swopping spies, however, completely undermines the notion of equality before the law and leads to curious anomalies and injustices. In the Portland Spy Ring case in 1961, the ringleader Conon Molody, alias Gordon Lonsdale, a KGB agent, was sentenced to twenty-five years in prison. He served only three years, being swopped in April 1964 for the British businessman spy, Greville Wynne. Two of his fellow-conspirators, Helen and Peter Kroger, were sentenced to twenty years apiece but were swopped in July 1969 for Gerald Brooke. But Harry Houghton and Ethel Gee whom the judge had decided deserved lesser sentences – albeit still of fifteen years – had to serve out their time.

Houghton and Gee were British subjects, whereas Molody was Russian and the Krogers – reportedly – US citizens. Standard practice seems to be not to exchange the citizens of one's own state in any spy swop. A distinction is also frequently drawn between spies like Molody and the Krogers, and 'traitors' like Houghton (who worked as a clerk at the Port Auxiliary Repair Unit in Portland, Dorset), or, of course, Blake. The argument is that treachery is more reprehensible than espionage and deserving of harsher punishment.

As a moral argument this would carry more weight if one of the prime tasks of any espionage service were not to seduce, cajole or blackmail people in positions of trust on the other side to betray that trust, and if it were not the case that the whole espionage business would soon grind to a halt if they failed to achieve this.

The argument that 'traitors' like Blake or Houghton should be treated with particular severity by comparison with ordinary spies ignores another practice adopted from time to time by the authorities in spy cases – that of offering immunity from prosecution in exchange for a confession. Blunt is probably the best-known case here. Like Blake, he had been a British Intelligence officer, though he had worked in MI5 – the counter-Intelligence service – rather than MI6, and had left it at the end of the war. He made his confession in 1964. Not only was he granted immunity from prosecution, he was also permitted to retain the highly prestigious post of Keeper of the Queen's Pictures. Only when he was publicly exposed in 1979 was he dismissed from this post and stripped of his knighthood.

Phillip Knightley has suggested that the reason the authorities offered immunity to Blunt was that if he did not confess they would have been unable to proceed against him. But they were in exactly the same position with Blake. Indeed Chapman Pincher claims that he was told by the Attorney General, Manningham-Buller – who led the prosecution in Blake's trial – that even after Blake had signed his confession the case could still have failed if he retracted it and claimed it was obtained under duress, since there were no effective witnesses who could have been brought into court.[53]

The Philby case provides a still closer parallel to Blake's. He occupied a higher position in MI6 than did Blake, and was accused by the British Press at the time of his death in 1988 of being responsible for the death of 'hundreds' of British agents. According to Peter Wright and others, Philby signed a written confession in Beirut in January 1963 in exchange for immunity from prosecution.

One possible explanation for the very different treatment meted out to Blunt and Philby on the one hand and Blake on the other is that the latter was an outsider. He was not part of the English upper-class set who graduated from public schools to Cambridge in the 1930s but a 'foreigner' with an Egyptian–Jewish father and a

Dutch mother who first came to Britain when he was nineteen and had only ever lived in this country for three and a half years at the time of his arrest and trial. But whatever the explanation, the difference in treatment is palpable – and indefensible.

'An Inhuman Sentence'

In 1961 Blake faced the prospect of twenty-eight years in prison, assuming full remission. Perhaps at first he may have hoped for an exchange, but certainly by the time he asked Seán Bourke to help him escape he had abandoned any thought of that. As far as we are aware there is no record of anyone in Blake's position – a British national employed by British Intelligence who gave information about the service to the Soviet Union – being released in an exchange deal.

When we agreed to help free Blake in 1966 it was essentially because of the inhumanity and hypocrisy of the sentence he had received. We did not know many of the details of his case then that we have subsequently learnt, and were less aware also than we are today of the scope of subversion and intervention in 'Third World' by the Western Governments and Intelligence Services.

But we did know Blake had acted out of political conviction; that both East and West were engaged in similar espionage activities; that his nationality ruled out the possibility of an exchange deal which the authorities were quite willing to do in the case of other spies; and that the 42-year sentence was a sentence of slow death. As far as we were concerned he was a prisoner of war in a particularly nasty and underhand war which we could not condone but in which both sides engage.

Because we had been in prison we had some inkling of what a sentence of forty-two years meant for the individual concerned. We have said he faced a 'slow death'; but even a phrase like that fails to convey the unrelenting experience of long-term imprisonment which grinds the life and spirit out of most long-term inmates – as studies have invariably shown. A few fight back in various ways – planning escapes being one of the important survival strategies. But more typical is the 'retreatism' which one lifer in Durham wrote about to the sociologists Stanley Cohen and Laurie Taylor:

> Can you imagine what it is like being a prisoner for life, your dreams turn into nightmares and your castles to ashes, all you think about is

fantasy and in the end you turn your back on reality and live in a contorted world of make-believe, you refuse to accept the rules of fellow mortals and make ones that will fit in with your own little world, there is no daylight in this world of the 'lifer', it is all darkness, and it is in this darkness that we find peace and the ability to live in a world of our own, a world of make-believe.[54]

Blake was better equipped than most to survive, mentally and physically. His intellectual interests, his yoga, his willingness to throw himself into the work of teaching semi-illiterate fellow-prisoners certainly contributed to the extraordinary composure which he maintained, at least on the surface, while he was in prison and which everyone in contact with him noted. So too, no doubt did the hope that he could successfully organize his own escape – a hope which we know from Pat's discussion with him in 1962 he entertained from the earliest days. Had that attempt failed, or had he been moved to a high-security wing like the one at Durham, there is no saying how long he could have held out. The terrible fear of the long-termer, as Cohen and Taylor point out, is 'that one may be overtaken by resignation, by a desire for death, however much one consciously resists.' They cite the words of another long-termer to the writer Victor Serge:

> My intellect . . . has not faltered; but it has grown dim. I have never resigned myself; but resignation has entered me, has bent me to the ground and told me: 'Rest'. To tell the truth, I'm not sure it didn't tell me: 'Die slowly'.[55]

Consequences

What of the consequences of our actions? We must acknowledge that these have been mixed and consider first the problematic ones.

The Blake escape, and the Mountbatten Inquiry which was set up to investigate prison security in its wake, were exploited to reinforce illiberal trends in British penal policy. In our judgment, however, neither were the root cause of these trends.

Mountbatten's recommendations could have been a positive rather than a negative turning point in the administration of British prisons. He insisted for instance on the need for a liberal regime within the prisons which he regarded as a disincentive to attempted escapes. This was to be combined with the stepping up of perimeter security through the use of video cameras, better fences and so forth. The General Secretary of the National Council for Civil Liberties at the time, Tony Smythe, while critical of one particular suggestion – namely that prisoners' conversations during visits should be recorded – welcomed the report as a whole as 'humane'.[56]

Mountbatten proposed the categorization of prisoners according to how likely they were to make a serious escape bid and how great a danger to the public their escape would be. Those in Category A, the highest-risk cases, should be housed in a proposed new 'escape proof' prison on the Isle of Wight.

But the Government rejected the notion of concentrating the high-risk prisoners in a single secure prison and adopted a policy of dispersing them. The result was a huge increase in security through-out the system and the widespread adoption of many of the techniques introduced earlier in the maximum security prison at Durham.[57] Moreover, regimes within prison became less liberal and certainly in some instances educational and leisure activities were cut back, contrary to what Mountbatten had recommended.

It is particularly ironic that the Durham approach to security should have been taken as the model for the system as a whole as Mountbatten himself had condemned the conditions in all the maximum security blocks at the time – at Parkhurst, Leicester and Durham. 'The conditions in these blocks', he wrote, 'are such as no country with a record of civilized behaviour ought to tolerate any longer than is absolutely essential as a stop gap measure.'[58]

The root of the problem was – and remains – the excessively long sentences handed down by the courts, a trend which dates back to the early 1960s with the sentences on Lonsdale, Blake, Vassall, the Train Robbers and others. It is that sentencing policy, and the appalling overcrowding of British prisons, which constitute the main barrier to a sensible and humane penal system. Indeed penologists, prison officers, the Home Office all recognize that men faced with such sentences had nothing to lose by attempting to escape. Thus the first suggestion that special security wings might be created in Britain came not in response to escapes as such but to the massive jail terms imposed on the Great Train Robbers in 1963.

Cohen and Taylor describe the special security arrangements set up for the arrival of three of the train robbers in Durham:

> The environment had been electrified for their arrival. The handles on the doors became 'live' even to finger-tip touch once the electronic robot

controls were switched on at night by prison officers, now nicknamed 'Daleks' because of their new-found automatism. The wing had closed circuit television to aid the monitoring of the prisoners and a specially trained officer sat in a bullet-proof steel and glass cubicle watching over the controls of this and other electronic devices. Subdued light burned all night in the train robbers' cells and at least one of them was forced to sleep with a handkerchief over his eyes. Over the coming years there were numerous permutations in the security arrangements involving dogs, extra electronic devices and the photographing of relatives to prevent impersonation.[59]

Mountbatten himself recognizes the problem of British sentencing policy.

A new factor has been introduced in recent years by the suspension of the death penalty and the unprecedentedly long fixed sentences of imprisonment that have been imposed by the Courts. The whole philosophy of prison administration and treatment has depended on the fact that even a man sentenced to life imprisonment had a reasonable hope that if he mended his ways he would be allowed to return to a free society. Although a man's behaviour under prison conditions is rightly not the only consideration in deciding when to release him, it is certainly relevant, and the hope of release is a powerful disincentive to escape. Similarly, men with long fixed sentences are able to earn remission of which they will lose some or all if they make a successful or unsuccessful attempt at escape. This system of rewards and punishments does not apply to the very long sentences which have been imposed in recent years – or to a sentence which is in fact for life or most of it – and it is certainly unlikely to influence the behaviour of a man making an attempt at escape. *The prison system had no plans for a prisoner like Blake and could not have been adjusted at short notice to provide a place for him* [Emphasis added].[60]

In the last analysis it is absurd if the courts pass massive sentences which everyone (including the prison authorities and the screws) recognize are bound to increase the incidence of attempted escapes and then, when the escapes do occur as predicted, to say that have sabotaged the prospects of prison reform.

The second problematic area is the effect on the peace movement, and specifically on the Campaign for Nuclear Disarmament, CND. As we stated in an earlier chapter we realized from the start that sections of the media would attempt to use the fact of our involvement in anti-nuclear campaigning as a stick with which to beat the movement.

The most damaging accusations, if they could be brought home, would be firstly that the episode was evidence of a pro-Soviet bias within CND, perhaps even that the movement had the ulterior aim of promoting Soviet interests or had links with the Soviet Intelligence service; and secondly, that CND organizational time and money was diverted to the operation. Although the most extreme accusations or insinuations of this kind have not been made in the press handling of the episode since the *Sunday Times* reports of 1987, some stories have stressed an alleged CND connection with the escape.

We hope and believe that this presentation of what happened and why will strengthen rather than weaken the peace movement and that through our book its call for the rejection of the cynical and inhuman practices of the Cold War will reach a wider audience and find a response among a rising generation.

A few of our friends within the movement have been strongly critical of our present decision to go public in writing the present book. They say we should have kept our heads down after the *Sunday Times* allegations rather than inviting media and public scrutiny by openly acknowledging our role.

But once we had been named the story was never going to go away and we would not have been in a position to deal with whatever unfounded rumour was circulated. Espionage stories, whether fact or fiction, hold such a fascination for the British public that it is simplistic to think that in the absence of a clear statement from us there would not have been further articles and books putting forward new theories about our role and motives. Indeed *The Sunday Times* followed up its original article in early October 1987 with others which speculated about the possible involvement of Tom Driberg and the KGB, and of Vanessa Redgrave who was alleged to have put up the money for the escape. In our judgment to have kept silent while such speculation and rumour multiplied would have done far more damage to the movement than our coming out into the open and putting the record straight.

Our book will not put an end to speculation. But though we have had to withhold some details, it will be much harder in future for journalists and writers to weave damaging fictions around the events – or at any rate fictions that will carry much conviction.

The rumours of any involvement, directly or indirectly, by CND as an organization should be easier to scotch. *The Sunday Times* in 1987 stated Pottle and Randle were founder members of CND, and other papers since have repeated this. We were not – indeed neither of us has ever joined CND. Michael was involved in the Direct Action Committee Against Nuclear War and we were both active in the Committee of 100 in the early 1960s. None of the other people who helped us in varying degrees – the two people who put up money for the project, the so-called 'CND doctor' who set Blake's wrist, and the two couples who harboured Blake for a few days each – held any position within CND.

Whatever the wider political and social consequences of our actions, the one incontrovertible effect it had was to give life and hope back to Blake himself. With full remission he would have completed his sentence in 1989, the year this book is being published. Instead he has made a new life for himself in Moscow, is married with a son in his late teens, and works in one of the Moscow Institutes that specializes in international politics and economics. At a human level, we cannot regret that we assisted him to start this new life rather than facing the prospect of decline and despair in a succession of British jails.

The Antigone Choice: Taking the law into our own hands

The final and crucial criticism we have to respond to is that however cruel and unjust the 42-year sentence on Blake was, we had no right to take the law into our own hands. This raises a general issue of profound importance in modern societies where new technology places enormous power in the hands of the centralized state.

We accept that laws, or at least some kind of codes and norms, are necessary in any society in order to ensure that the exercise of freedom by one individual does not deny the basic freedom and rights of others. In the end that is the only justification for placing restrictions on the individual's freedom of action.

In small, egalitarian, communities the rules – and the penalties for infringing them – can be worked out by the community as a whole. These are literally anarchic communities in the sense that there are no separate State institution or law enforcement agencies; responsibility for framing the laws and ensuring that they are enforced rests with every adult member of the society. Some surviving tribal communities are anarchist, or near-anarchist, in this positive sense and have been the subject in recent years of interesting studies.[61]

In the modern state such direct involvement of all members of the society is not deemed possible. We share with many anarchists, libertarians and socialists a belief in the need to work in the long term for the establishment of an egalitarian network of communities under direct democratic control as an alternative to the bureaucratic and centralized State. However, we recognize that representative democracy provides for at least some measure of democratic control by the citizens over how society is run and what decisions are taken in their name.

Britain falls far short of being a model democracy – and indeed there is an ugly and frightening trend towards more authoritarian government.[62] Nevertheless it is not because of the shortcomings of democracy in Britain, or any modern state, that we argue the need on occasions for principled law-breaking. Our case rests, rather, on the proposition that even in a near-perfect democracy it is wrong and dangerous for the citizen to obey the law without question.

Elected governments, like dictatorships, may pursue aggressive, even genocidal policies or introduce laws which are manifestly unjust and deprive individuals or sections of the community of their basic rights. When the Eden government, in collusion with France and Israel, launched a military attack on Egypt in 1956, some people, including servicemen, engaged in acts of civil disobedience to obstruct it. In the United States in the 1950s and 1960s, Martin Luther King and his followers defied manifestly discriminatory laws, not because they were passed by unrepresentative bodies but because the laws themselves were inherently unjust.

During the same period a movement of mass civil disobedience developed in this country with the formation of the Direct Action Committee against Nuclear War and subsequently the Committee of 100 which used the tactics of non-violent obstruction and occupation to oppose the government's preparations for nuclear war. Civil disobedience aimed at preventing nuclear genocide flourished again in this country and across Western Europe in the 1980s during the Euromissile crisis, most dramatically in some of the women's actions at Greenham Common. In these instances the people whose fundamental human rights to life were being threatened lived outside the national frontiers; however, the principle is not different.

The tradition of non-violent direct action extends, of course, far beyond the nuclear disarmament movement in Western Europe and the civil rights campaign in the USA. It was a vital part of the struggle for the recognition of trade union rights throughout the nineteenth and early twentieth centuries, of the campaign for women's suffrage in the early part of this century, and of the independence struggles in the colonies, most notably in India. It was also used in campaigns against the waging of particular unjust wars – France's war in Algeria, for instance, and the US war in Vietnam.

The justification for such action in a Western democracy is that there are two fundamental principles involved in the notion of legitimate democratic government. One is rule by the majority; the other is respect for basic human rights. Where laws, no matter how correctly enacted, or the policies of governments and authorities, deny those rights to some individuals or sections of society, or to the inhabitants of other countries, it is legitimate – indeed sometimes crucial – to disobey the law. This is not to say that individual or collective civil disobedience will always be the best tactic or strategy – sometimes other approaches may be more fruitful; it is to claim that even in a democracy disobedience and non-violent breaches of the law must not be ruled out *in principle*. In this sense the commitment of every responsible citizen to respect the law must be a conditional one.

In the case of the Blake escape, the laws which we contravened – against aiding a prisoner to escape, forging passports, smuggling someone out of the country – are not in themselves unjust or unreasonable. For that matter the laws against obstructing the highway, or railway tracks, or occupying aircraft runways are not unjust in themselves. It may nonetheless be right and necessary to disobey them on occasions to prevent a more serious crime or to put right a flagrant injustice. No one could have complained of an unacceptable breach of the law, for instance, if thousands had sat down in front of the trains taking victims to the concentration camps in Nazi Germany, even though there is nothing inherently unreasonable in a law forbidding people to block railway tracks.

The crucial proviso in all such cases is that the breaches of the law should not cause injury to innocent people. *Unlawful acts* may sometimes be justified; *criminal acts* which harm innocent people cannot be so.

The direst lesson of the consequences of blind obedience to the enactments of constitutionally appointed governments comes from the experience of Germany in the early period of Nazi rule. Hitler was appointed Chancellor in January 1933 by President Hindenburg in accordance with Article 48 of the Weimar Constitution and was able to use emergency decrees and populist agitation to strengthen his position prior to the general election of March 1933 at which the Nazi Party secured 43.9 per cent of the vote. An Enabling Bill consolidating Nazi power was then pushed through both Houses of Parliament, thus maintaining the facade of legal revolution and securing the continued loyalty and obedience of the civil service and judiciary. As one historian of the period has commented: 'It was this apparent legality that inhibited and confused all but the most clear-sighted opponents of the Nazi regime.'[63]

The birth of Nazi Germany is an extreme example in that Hitler's purpose was clearly the destruction at the earliest moment of any semblance of pluralism and democratic rule. He was using the machinery of the democratic state in order to destroy it. However, even in less extreme circumstances where government legislation or policy decisions are not aimed at overthrowing the constitution, it can still be vital to disobey and obstruct them to prevent denials of basic human rights and freedoms.

The rights and liberties of a section of the community were not directly at stake in the 42-year sentence on George Blake. He had broken the law and confessed to it. The crucial point, however, is that the 42-year sentence was indefensible. And, as we argued earlier, the *policy* of imposing what are virtual life sentences removes from a prisoner any real hope of resuming normal existence and has major implications for a country's whole penal policy – and even beyond that for the norms and values society accepts. As John Lilburne, the 17th-century Leveller, put it: 'what is done to anyone, may be done to everyone'.[64]

The clash between individual conscience and state power is as old as recorded history. The classical and still the most powerful treatment of the issue is in the Sophocles *Antigone*. Antigone defies a decree of the newly appointed King of Thebes, King Creon – her uncle – that the body of one of her brothers, Polynices, shall be left unburied while her other dead brother, Eteocles, is given a state funeral. The two brothers, rivals for the throne of Thebes, had died in a battle at the gates of the city, but whereas Eteocles was defending it, Polynices had allied himself with a foreign city, Argos, to attack it.

To Antigone the *punishment* is an outrage – an act of sacrilege that offends the law of the gods as well as human morality. It is this which gives her the right to disobey the law. She says to Creon:

> You are merely a man, mortal
> Like me, and laws that you enact
> Cannot overturn ancient moralities
> Or common human decency.[65]

Creon, no less powerfully puts the argument that without obedience to the laws of the State, society would dissolve in chaos:

> Indiscipline,
> Anarchy, disobedience, what greater scourge
> Than that for humankind. States collapse
> From within, cities are blown to rubble,
> Efficient armies are disorganised,
> And potential victory turned to disaster
> And carnage, and all by disobedience,
> Anarchy, indiscipline. Whereas the well-drilled regiment
> That asks no questions stands firm,
> Knows nothing, and needs to know nothing, and wins,
> Thus saving the lives of millions of honest people.
> Authority is essential in any State,
> And will be upheld in this one, by me.[66]

We do not seek to compare our role in the Blake escape with that of the heroic Antigone who openly defied the law knowing that certain death was to follow. Yet there are certain parallels. To Creon, Polynices is a 'traitor' for whom no punishment can be too harsh, even a punishment which pursues him beyond the grave and prevents his spirit from ever finding rest. Nowhere does Antigone defend her brother's action in joining a foreign power to attack the city – it is simply the punishment that outrages her and moves her to defiance. Creon upholds the necessity of law; Antigone the duty, in some circumstances, of disobedience. In the end Antigone dies; but it is Creon who learns that imposing inhuman punishment even for genuine offences can only destroy his personal and family life and finally undermine his authority as a ruler.

Clearly if there was generalized law-breaking, society would be threatened with chaos; Creon's argument cannot simply be brushed aside. The State, however, has powerful coercive sanctions at its disposal to induce conformity, besides those operating within the social structure itself. The most serious threat today, in our judgment, is not too much disobedience but too little. For if the rule of law is necessary for an orderly society, the willingness to disobey it where basic rights and values are violated is an essential constraint on state power. None of the checks and balances of democratic constitutions will be sufficient to save a society from sliding into barbarism if this constraint is removed.

Although we are convinced we were justified in breaking the law by helping Blake to escape, we do not claim any special rights or privileges and are prepared if necessary to face trial and go to prison for what we did.

Generally, if laws are defied for reasons of principle they should be defied openly so that the issues will be publicly debated and authorities forced to confront them. However, sometimes it is necessary to act clandestinely – for instance in smuggling American army deserters and draft dodgers to Sweden during the Vietnam war. At the present time in the USA, church-based groups have set up escape networks to prevent 'illegal' refugees from the bloody repression in much of Central America being sent back to face imprisonment, torture or death in their countries of origin. This is civil disobedience too but it has perforce to be carried out clandestinely. Openness was equally impossible in planning and executing Blake's escape and his departure from this country.

Clearly by not coming out in the open within a year or two of the event we lost an opportunity to press the case against the kind of sentence Blake received. Perhaps it would have been preferable if we had taken our courage in our hands in, say, 1970 when Bourke's book appeared and had publicly declared our involvement. But we acknowledge that although we were perfectly prepared to run the risk of a long sentence for assisting Blake, we had no wish to invite such a sentence by a public admission unless it seemed to us there were overwhelmingly strong reasons for making it. That did not seem to us to be the case in 1970, especially as our admission then might have led to the arrest of others who helped in the way described in this book. Once we had been publicly named in *The Sunday Times* in 1987 the situation changed completely. Clearly then the 'time to speak' had arrived.

We do not, in retrospect, regret the disclosure of our role. At a personal level the consequences could be severe. Nevertheless it is far better that the revelations should come out now when we are in a position to defend what we did, and indeed to take the argument to the other side, than that all sorts of sinister rumours should have circulated unchallenged after we were dead.

When all is said and done we had a choice. A man we had grown to like and respect was facing the terrible prospect of a lifetime behind bars; we better than most had some idea of what that meant. When he asked us to help him escape, we could either agree and accept the risks involved, or we could plead that concern for our own or our families' safety, or for the reputation of the peace movement, or some other consideration, made this impossible.

George was no dangerous criminal whose confinement was necessary for the safety of the public – the only possible justification there can ever be for restricting a person's liberty. He had betrayed a trust by passing information to the Soviet Union. We have never supported that, but we knew he was employed by this country in a profession whose hallmark is treachery and double dealing, and that he had acted out of genuine conviction. The 42-year sentence was not an act of justice but of revenge.

A man's a man for a' that. All the calculations of the possible political consequences of helping George are in the end a matter of opinion and guesswork. The one thing that was beyond question was that if the escape succeeded George personally would have the chance to start a new life instead of facing the terrifying prospect of twenty or more years in prison. Now that our involvement has been made public we will have to live with whatever consequences that may bring. But we could not have lived with ourselves if we had acted differently. We make no apologies for what we did. We have no regrets.

Chapter Notes

Notes to Chapter 1

1. *Petition & Record, House of Lords Appeal, Terence Norman Chandler & Others versus Director of Public Prosecutions* p.382
2. Ibid, p.385.
3. Ibid, p.385
4. Ibid, p.17.
5. Ibid, p.208.
6. Ibid, p.144.
7. Ibid, p.145–8
8. Ibid, pp.229–30
9. Ibid, pp.235–6.
10. Ibid, pp.276–7.
11. Ibid, p.283.
12. Ibid, p.288

Notes to Chapter 3

1. Zeno, *Life*, Macmillan, 1968, pp.104–106
2. Zeno, *The Cauldron*, Macmillan, 1967.
3. Montgomery Hyde, *George Blake: Superspy*, Constable, 1987, p.63.
4. 'A Death in January', Radio Telefis Eireann programme, 1983 edited and directed by Kevin O'Connor.
5. *The Times*, 4 May 1961.
6. *The Times*, 5 May 1961, p.19; Hansard, Vol 639, 4 May 1961, pp.1613–1614.
7. Norman Cliff, 'The Stinking Net of Espionage', *Peace News*, 28 September 1962 – review of Sanche de Gramont, *The Secret War*, André Deutsch, 1962.
8. Seán Bourke, *The Springing of George Blake*, Cassell 1970, p.335.
9. Zeno, *Life*, p.145.
10. pp. 144–5.
11. Ibid, pp.161–162.
12. *Peace News*, 15 March 1963 'John Balls Column'.

Notes to Chapter 4

1. Seán Bourke, *The Springing of George Blake* (Cassell, London, 1970), p.60.
2. *Report of the Inquiry into Prison Escapes & Security* by Admiral of the Fleet The Earl Mountbatten of Burma, H.M. Stationery Office, Cmnd. 3175, December 1966, paragraph 19, p.5.
3. Mountbatten Report, paragraphs 74 and 75, p.21.
4. Mountbatten Report, para 70, p.20.
5. Mountbatten Report, para 9, pp. 2–3. (to the recommendation of the Security Forces that Blake should be transferred to Birmingham, see para36, p.9.
6. 'The Spies Were Right', *Peace News*, (19 April 1963), p.1.

7. Seán Bourke, *The Springing of George Blake*, Cassell, London 1970, p.36.
8. *Mountbatten Report*, paragraph 42, p.11.
9. Ferdinand Mount, 'Strange . . . George Blake's New Friends'. *Daily Sketch*, 21 July 1968, p.6.
10. *Mountbatten Report*, paragraphs 68 & 69, p.19.
11. H. Montgomery Hyde, *George Blake Super Spy* (Constable, London,1987).
12. Howard Griffen, *Black Like Me* (Panther, 1964).
13. Seán Bourke, op. cit., pp. 110–11.
14. Seán Bourke, op. cit., p.112.
15. Extract published in *News of the World*, 16 February 1969, p.5. For a history of the tapes and how they were returned to Seán in 1968, see Chapter 9.

Notes to Chapter 5

1. Seán Bourke, *The Springing of George Blake*, p.183.
2. *Hansard*, Vol 734, 1966, pp. 650–6.
3. *The Times*, 25 October 1966.
4. *Evening News*, 1 November 1966.
5. Ted Oliver, 'Who Really Sprang Traitor Blake?', *Daily Mirror*, 5 October 1987, p.6.
6. John Le Carré (talking to Julian Holland), 'The Spy Who Went Back into the Cold', *Daily Mail*, 25 October 1966.
7. Zeno, *Life* (Macmillan, 1968), pp. 163–4.
8. Zeno, *Life* pp. 167–8.
9. Seán Bourke, p.190–1.
10. 'Blake's "Escape Car Found" ', *Evening Standard*, 28 October, 1966, p.1; and in the same issue, Peter Fairley, 'Master Spy's Escape Route', p.14.
11. Seán Bourke, p.193.
12. 'Yard Suspects Blake Used Two-Way Radio', *Observer*, 30 October 1966, p.1, and Eric Clarke & Peter Deeley, 'George Blake: An Observer Inquiry', same issue, page 11.
13. Seán Bourke, p.198.
14. *Hansard*, Vol 735, 1966, pp.42–3.

Notes to Chapter 6

1. From the report by Norman Shrapnel, *The Guardian*'s Parliamentary Correspondent, 1 November 1966, p.1.
2. *The Times*, November 1 1966, p.1. The full report of the debate is to be found in *Hansard*, Vol. 735, p.115–66.
3. *Evening Standard*, 21 November, 1966, p.1.

Notes to Chapter 7

1. Seán Bourke, The Springing of George Blake, p.213.
2. *The Times*, 23 December 1966, p.8.
3. E. H. Cookridge, *Shadow of a Spy*, pp.242–4.
4. Seán Bourke, pp.214–5.
5. Seán Bourke, p.214.

6. *Evening Standard*, 13 January 1967, p.12. (The story may well have been on the front page in the early editions.)
7. The *Times*, 14 January 1967, p.1.
8. *Evening Standard*, 20 January 1967, p.1.
9. *The Guardian*, 21 January 1967, p.1.
10. *Daily Mail*, 21 January 1967.

Notes to Chapter 8

1. *Hansard*, Vol 748, 19 June 1967, Written Answers p.196.
2. *The Times*, 22 September 1967, p.1.
3. *The Times*, 23 September 1967.
4. Seán Bourke, p.297.
5. Seán Bourke, p.300–2.
6. *Hansard*, Vol 755, 4 December 1967, Oral Answers, p.946.
7. WRI Statements, 1963–July 1972, pp.24–5.
8. *Izvestia*, 26 September 1968. Cited in WRI pamphlet, *Support Czechoslovakia*, Housmans, London, 1968, p.33. Andrew Papworth, from Britain, and Vicky Rovere from the US, were the two people who demonstrated in Moscow.
9. *The Times*, 15 October 1968, p.2.
10. *The Times*, 23 October 1968, p.1.
11. *The Times*, 24 October 1968, p.10.
12. *The Times*, 5 November 1968, p.2.
13. *The Times*, 21 January 1969, p.2.
14. *The Times*, 24 January 1969, p.3.
15. *The Times*, 4 February 1969, p.3.
16. Ibid.
17. *The Times*, 4 February 1969, p.9.
18. Seán Bourke, pp.58–60.
19. 'Over the Wall and through the Curtain', unsigned review, *Times Literary Supplement*, 11 June 1970, p.365.
20. Phillip Knightley, *The Second Oldest Profession'*, Pan Books, 1986, p.295. See also *The Observer*, 23 November 1986 which published extracts from Knightley's book, including the passage cited.
21. Knightley, pp.294–5.
22. Seán Bourke, p.341.
23. Seán Bourke, p.252.
24. Seán Bourke, pp.262–3.
25. Seán Bourke, p.269.
26. Seán Bourke, p.249.
27. George Blake on the Russian chat show *Before and After Midnight*, 23 April 1988 – as reported in the *Independent*, 25 April 1988, p.1.
28. Post-mortem report, cited in H. Montgomery Hyde, *George Blake: Superspy*, Constable 1987, p.172.

Notes to Chapter 9

1. 'Blake's Triple Bluff', the *Observer* 23 November 1986, pp.25–See also Philip Knightley, *The Second Oldest Profession*. Pan Books 1987, pp.290–5.
2. *Observer*, 30 November 1986, p.19.
3. H. Montgomery Hyde, *George Blake: Superspy*, Constable 1987, p.63.
4. Ibid., p.10.
5. *Guardian*, 13 October 1987.
6. *Guardian*, 29 September 1987.
7. *Irish Independent*, 23 September 1987.
8. *The Sunday Times*, 4 October 1987, p.15.
9. Ted Oliver, 'Who really sprang traitor Blake?', *Daily Mirror*, 5 October 1987, p.6.
10. *Guardian*, 9 October 1987, p.13.
11. *Guardian*, 9 October 1987, p.2.
12. *Guardian*, 13 October 1987.
13. *Sunday Times*, 15 November 1987, p.7.
14. *Telegraph & Argus*, 20 November 1987.
15. *Sunday Times*, 8 November 1987, p.1.
16. *Daily Express*, 25 April 1988, p.4.
17. *Independent*, 25 April 1988, p.1.
18. *Observer*, 13 November 1988, p.2.
19. *Guardian*, 14 November 1988, p.4.
20. *Daily Telegraph*, 21 December 1988.
21. *Observer* 1 January 1989.

Notes to Chapter 10

1. See E. H. Cookridge, *Shadow of a Spy* (Leslie Frewin, London, 1967), pp.100–1. The incident is also recorded in H. Montgomery Hyde, *George Blake: Superspy*, (Constable, London, 1987), pp.37–8.
2. Cookridge, pp.105–6 and Hyde, p.38.
3. Cookridge, p.130; Hyde, p.43.
4. Hyde, p.43.
5. Phillip Knightley, *The Second Oldest Profession*, (Pan Books, London, 1986), p.291.
6. E. H. Cookridge holds this theory, as does Phillip Knightley. See Knightley, above cit, p.293.
7. Knightley, p.291.
8. Chapman Pincher, *Too Secret Too Long* (Sidgwick and Jackson, 1984), pp.258–9.
9. Cookridge, p.188, and Hyde, pp.51–2.
10. Cookridge, p. 190–1. Hyde, p.55, and Chapman Pincher, above cit, p.261, also mistakenly place the date of Blake's Committal Proceedings at Bow Street as 22 April 1961, presumably following the Cookridge account.
11. *The Times*, 25 April 1961, p.8.
12. *The Times*, 25 April 1961, p.8.
13. Hyde, p.55.
14. *Hansard* 640, 11 May 1961, pp.637–38, and *The Times*, 12 May 1961, p.20.

15. Chapman Pincher, above cit note 8, p.261.
16. *Ibid*, p.261.
17. *Hansard*, Vol 639, 4 May 1961, pp.1609–18. *The Times*, 5 May 1961, pp.19–20.
18. Chapman Pincher, *Inside Story*, (Sidgwick and Jackson, 1978), pp.94–5.
19. Hyde, p.19.
20. *The Times*, 20 June 1961, p.15.
21. *Daily Express*, 20 June 1961, p.2; *The Times* 20 June 1961, p.15.
22. Hyde, p.19.
23. Chapman Pincher, *Inside Story*, p.95.
24. *Ibid*, pp.94–5.
25. Cookridge, p.212.
26. Hyde, pp.39–40.
27. *Hansard*, Vol 639, 4 May 1961, p.1614, and *The Times*, 5 May 1961, p.19.
28. See Montgomery Hyde, p.44, and Peter Wright, *Spycatcher*, (Heinemann Australia, 1987), pp.160–2.
29. Peter Wright, *Spycatcher*, pp.161–2.
30. *US Senate Select Committee on Intelligence Activities, 94 Congress, 1st Session – Alleged Assassination Plots involving Foreign Leaders, 1975*, p.71. A summary of the findings on the attempted assassination of Lumumba appears on p.4.
31. Peter Wright, pp.364–72. See also David Leigh, *The Wilson Plot*, (Heinemann, London, 1988).
32. Gregory F. Treverton, *Cover Action: The CIA and American Intervention in the Postwar World*, (I.B. Tauris, 1987), especially pp.44–83.
33. David Leigh, *The Wilson Plot*, pp.11–13. See also Christopher Andrew, *Secret Service: The Making of the British Intelligence Community*, (Heinemann, London, 1985), p.493 on the Albanian landings.
34. Bob Woodward, *Veil: the Secret Wars of the CIA 1981–87* (Headline, 1987), pp. 488–91.
35. *Ibid*, p.479.
36. Rupert Allason as quoted in *The Western Daily News*, October 1987.
37. *The Times*, 4 May 1961, p.17.
38. John Stockwell, former CIA agent in Angola in interviews with Christopher Hird of Diverse Productions for Channel 4 television, September 1985. Cited by Phillip Knightley, p.385.
39. Knightley, p.387–8.
40. Chapman Pincher, *Too Secret Too Long*, p.259.
41. John Bloch and Patrick Fitzgerald, *British Intelligence & Covert Action* (Junction Books, London, 1983), p.122.
42. Chapman Pincher, *Too Secret Too Long*, p. 259; Hyde, pp.47–8.
43. Pincher, *Inside Story*, p.93.
44. Bloch & Fitzgerald, above cit note 41, p.109.
45. For a detailed account see the chapter entitled 'Covert Operations in the Middle East 1950–80' in *Ibid*, pp.109–142.
46. Knightley, p.234.
47. *Ibid*, p.235.
48. *Ibid*, p.237.

49. *Ibid*, p.27.
50. A fact noted by Knightley, p.385.
51. Harry Truman in *Washington Post*, 22 December 1963. Cited by Knightley, p.242.
52. *The Guardian*, 15 February 1989, p.1.
53. Chapman Pincher, *Too Secret Too Long., p.260.*
54. Stanley Cohen & Laurie Taylor, *Psychological Survival*, (Penguin 1981), p.120.
55. Victor Serge, *Men in Prison*, Gollancz 1970, p.170. Cited by Cohen & Taylor, p.121.
56. *The Times*, 23 December 1966, p.6.
57. Paddy Hillyard and Janie Percy-Smith, *The Coercive State*, (Fontana/Collins, 1988), p.307–8.
58. Mountbatten Inquiry into Prison Escapes and Security, HMSO 1966, p.56. paragraph 212.
59. Cohen and Taylor, pp.23–24.
60. Mountbatten Inquiry, p.54, paragraph 205.
61. Michael Taylor, *Community, Anarchy and Liberty*, (Cambridge University Press), 1982.
62. Hillyard & Percy-Smith, especially the chapter entitled 'The State versus the People'.
63. D. G. Williamson, *The Third Reich*, Seminar Studies in History series edited by Roger Lockyer, (Longman, 1988 edition), pp.8–11.
64. Cited by Don Taylor in the Introduction to his translation of *Sophocles: The Theban Plays*, Methuen 1986, p.xlix.
65. From the translation by Don Taylor of *Sophocles: The Theban Plays,* Methuen 1986, p.151.
66. Ibid, pp.160–1.

Select Bibliography

ANDREW, Christopher, *Secret Service: The Making of the British Intelligence Community* (Heinemann, London, 1985).

BLOCH, Jonathan, and FITZGERALD, Patrick, *British Intelligence and Covert Action* (Junction Books, London, 1983).

BOULTON, David, *Voices from the Crowd* (Peter Owen, London, 1964).

BOURKE, Seán, *The Springing of George Blake* (Cassells, 1970).

COOKRIDGE, E. H., *Shadow of a Spy* (Leslie Frewin, London, 1967)

COHEN, Stanley and TAYLOR, Laurie, *Psychological Survival* (Penguin 1981).

GRAMONT, Sanche de, *The Secret War* (André Deutsch, 1962).

GRIFFEN, Howard, *Black Like Me* (Panther, 1964).

HILLYARD, Paddy and PERCY-SMITH, Janie, *The Coercive State* (Fontana, 1988).

HOOPER, David, *Official Secrets* (Coronet Books, 1987).

HYDE, H. Montgomery, *George Blake: Superspy* (Constable, London, 1987).

KNIGHTLEY, Phillip, *The Second Oldest Profession* (Pan Books, London, 1986).

KNIGHTLEY, Phillip and KENNEDY, Caroline, *An Affair of State* (Pan Books, 1988).

LEIGH, David, *The Wilson Plot* (Heinemann, London, 1988).

MOUNTBATTEN of Burma Earl, *Report of the Inquiry into Prison Escapes and Security*, CMND 3175 (HMSO 1966).

PAGE, Bruce, LEITCH, David and KNIGHTLEY, Phillip, *Philby: the Spy who Betrayed a Generation* (Sphere Books, 1977).

PENROSE, Barry & FREEMAN, Simon, *Conspiracy of Silence: the Secret Life of Anthony Blunt* (Grafton Books, 1987).

PINCHER, Chapman, *Inside Story* (Sidgwick and Jackson, 1978).
Their Trade is Treachery (Sidgwick & Jackson, 1981).
Too Secret Too Lonely (Sidgwick and Jackson, 1984).

SERGE, Victor, *Men in Prison* (Gollancz, 1970).

STOCKWELL, John, *In Search of Enemies: A CIA Story* (André Deutsch, 1978.

SUMMERS, Anthony and Dorrill, Stephen, *Honey Trap* (Weidenfeld and Nicolson, 1987 and Coronet, 1988).

TAYLOR, Don, (translator), *Sophocles: The Theban Plays*, (Methuen, 1986).

TAYLOR, Michael, *Community, Anarchy & Liberty* (Cambridge University Press, 1982).

TAYLOR, Richard, and YOUNG Nigel, *Campaigns for Peace* (Manchester University Press, 1987).

TREVERTON, Gregory F., *Cover Action: The CIA and American Intervention in the Postwar World* (I.B. Tauris, 1987).

US Senate Select Committee on Intelligence Activities, 94 Congress, 1st Session – Alleged Assasination Plots involving Foreign Leaders, 1975.

WEST, Nigel, *A Matter of Trust: MI5 1945–72*, Weidenfeld and Nicolson, 1982).

WILLIAMSON, D.G., *The Third Reich*, Seminar Studies in History series edited by Roger Lockyer (Longman, 1988).

WOODWARD, Bob, *Veil: The Secret Wars of the CIA 1981–87* (Headline, London, 1987).

WRIGHT, Peter, *Spycatcher* (Heinemann Australia, 1987).

ZENO, *The Cauldron* (Macmillan, 1967).
Life (Macmillan, 1968).

Index

20.5.03